The Contemporary Poetry Archive

The Contemporary Poetry Archive

Essays and Interventions

Edited by Linda Anderson,
Mark Byers and Ahren Warner

EDINBURGH
University Press

Edinburgh University Press is one of the leading university presses in the UK. We publish academic books and journals in our selected subject areas across the humanities and social sciences, combining cutting-edge scholarship with high editorial and production values to produce academic works of lasting importance. For more information visit our website: edinburghuniversitypress.com

Edinburgh University Press Ltd
The Tun – Holyrood Road
12(2f) Jackson's Entry
Edinburgh EH8 8PJ

Typeset in 10.5/13 Adobe Sabon by
Servis Filmsetting Ltd, Stockport, Cheshire,
and printed and bound in Great Britain.

A CIP record for this book is available from the British Library

ISBN 978 1 4744 3243 6 (hardback)
ISBN 978 1 4744 3246 7 (webready PDF)
ISBN 978 1 4744 3245 0 (epub)

Contents

Acknowledgements

We are grateful to Susan Howe and New Directions Publishing Corp for permission to quote from *Spontaneous Particulars: The Telepathy of Archives*.

Excerpt from *Nox* copyright © 2010 by Anne Carson. Reprinted by permission of New Directions Publishing Corp.

Excerpt from *Paterson* copyright © 1946 by William Carlos Williams. Reprinted by permission of New Directions Publishing Corp and Carcanet Press.

Works by Charles Olson published during his lifetime are held in copyright by the Estate of Charles Olson; previously unpublished works are copyright of the University of Connecticut. Used with permission.

Permission to reproduce draft page from 'Cousin Coat' with permission of Sean O'Brien and Special Collections, Robinson Library, Newcastle University.

Excerpt from *The Book of the Dead*, published by West Virginia University Press, copyright © 2018 by Muriel Rukeyser. Reprinted by permission of ICM Partners.

Archive materials by John H. Updike © John H. Updike in Houghton Library Harvard and New Yorker Records, New York Public Library used by permission of The Wylie Agency (UK) Ltd. Other unpublished materials from the New Yorker Records with permission of Condé Nast Publications, Inc.

We are grateful to Ashley Ashford-Brown, Phyllis Christopher and Kate Sweeney for permission to publish images.

1921 photograph of Constantin Brancusi in his studio with Mina Loy, Tristan Tzara, Berenice Abbott, Jane Heap, Margaret Anderson © Succession Brancusi – All rights reserved (ARS) 2018.

We are grateful to Rachel Hawkes and Graham Robson from Special Collections, The Robinson Library, Newcastle University, and to Theresa Muñoz, Peter Hebden, David Spittle and John Challis of the Newcastle Centre for the Literary Arts for assistance in the preparation of this book.

Notes on Contributors

Jonathan Allison is Chair of the Department of English at the University of Kentucky. His annotated edition of *Letters of Louis MacNeice* (Faber and Faber, 2010) was named a 2010 Book of the Year by the *Times Literary Supplement*.

Linda Anderson is Professor of Modern English and American Poetry at Newcastle University. She is the author of numerous books and essays about autobiography and about modern poetry. She has recently published *Elizabeth Bishop: Lines of Connection* (Edinburgh University Press, 2013), and an essay entitled 'Disturbing the Archive: Repetition and Remembering in Elizabeth Bishop's Poetry' for *Reading Elizabeth Bishop: An Edinburgh Guide*, ed. Jonathan Ellis. She was Principal Investigator on the Arts and Humanities Research Council project 'Poetics of the Archive: Creative and Community Engagement with the Bloodaxe Archive'.

Mark Byers is Lecturer in Contemporary Poetry at Newcastle University. His research interests are primarily in modernist and late modernist poetry, media history and textual studies. His first book is *Charles Olson and American Modernism: The Practice of the Self* (Oxford University Press, 2018).

Suzanne W. Churchill is Professor of English at Davidson College. She is the author of *The Little Magazine Others and the Renovation of Modern American Poetry* and co-editor of *Little Magazines & Modernism: New Approaches*. She has published articles on modernism, the Harlem Renaissance, periodicals, poetry and pedagogy in various journals and collections. Founder and editor of the bibliographic website 'Index of Modernist Magazines', she is currently collaborating on a scholarly website, 'Mina Loy: Navigating the Avant-Garde', which received a 2017 NEH Digital Humanities Advancement Grant.

Carolyn Forché is University Professor at the University of Georgetown, Washington, and former Director of the Lannan Center for Poetry and Social Practice. She is the author of four books of poetry: *Gathering The Tribes*, which received the Yale Younger Poets Award (Yale University Press, 1976), *The Country Between Us* (Harper and Row, 1982), chosen as the Lamont Selection of the Academy of American Poets, *The Angel of History* (HarperCollins and Bloodaxe 1994), which won the *Los Angeles Times* Book Award, and *Blue Hour* (HarperCollins and Bloodaxe, 2003), a finalist for the National Book Critics Circle Award. Her memoir, *What You Have Heard Is True*, is published by Penguin (2019).

Jo Gill is Professor of Twentieth-Century and American Literature and Associate Dean for Education at the University of Exeter. She is the author of *Anne Sexton's Confessional Poetics* (University Press of Florida, 2007), *The Poetics of the American Suburbs* (Palgrave Macmillan, 2013) and numerous other essays on mid-century poetry. She has recently completed work on a new study, *The Harmony of Forms: Modern American Poetry and the Architectural Imagination*.

Amanda Golden is Assistant Professor of English at the New York Institute of Technology. She previously held the Post-Doctoral Fellowship in Poetics at Emory University's Fox Center for Humanistic Inquiry. She edited *This Business of Words: Reassessing Anne Sexton* (University Press of Florida, 2016), and her book *Annotating Modernism: Marginalia and Pedagogy from Virginia Woolf to the Confessional Poets* is under contract with Routledge. She edited a cluster on Feminist Modernist Digital Humanities for *Feminist Modernist Studies* (2018), is Book Review Editor of *Woolf Studies Annual*, and has published in *Modernism/modernity*, *The Ted Hughes Society Journal* and *Woolf Studies Annual*.

Hugh Haughton is Professor of English at the University of York. He is the author of *The Poetry of Derek Mahon* (Oxford University Press, 2007), the first full-scale study of a major contemporary Irish poet, as well as numerous essays on twentieth-century poetry. He is the co-editor of *The Letters of T. S. Eliot* (Faber and Faber, 2009).

Sarah Howe is a British poet, academic and editor. Her first book, *Loop of Jade* (Chatto & Windus, 2015), won the T. S. Eliot Prize and the *Sunday Times*/Peters Fraser + Dunlop Young Writer of the Year Award. She is the founding editor of *Prac Crit*, an online journal of poetry and criticism. She was a Research Fellow at Gonville and

Caius College, Cambridge, before taking up a Leverhulme Early Career Fellowship at University College London. Previous honours include fellowships from Harvard University's Radcliffe Institute and the Civitella Ranieri Foundation. She is a Lecturer in Poetry at King's College London.

Linda Kinnahan is Professor of English at Duquesne University in Pittsburgh. She is the editor of *A History of Twentieth-Century American Women's Poetry* (Cambridge University Press, 2016), and most recently the author of *Mina Loy, Photography, and Contemporary Women Poets* (Routledge, 2017). She has published on modernist and contemporary poetry, including *Poetics of the Feminine: Literary Tradition and Authority in William Carlos Williams, Mina Loy, Denise Levertov, and Kathleen Fraser* (Cambridge University Press, 1994) and *Lyric Interventions: Feminist Experimental Poetry and Contemporary Social Discourse* (Iowa University Press, 2004). She is co-author of the digital humanities project 'Mina Loy: Navigating the Avant-Garde', which recently received an NEH Digital Humanities Advancement Grant, and she has been a lead organizer for international conferences on modernism (MSA, 2014) and on modern and contemporary women's poetry (Lifting Belly, 2008).

Sean O'Brien is Professor of Creative Writing at Newcastle University, and a Fellow of the Royal Society of Literature. He is a poet, critic, translator, playwright, anthologist, broadcaster, novelist and editor. He has published nine collections of poetry to date, including *The Beautiful Librarians* (Picador, 2015) and *Europa* (Picador, 2018). He is a recipient of the T. S. Eliot Prize and Forward Prizes for poetry. His book of essays on contemporary poetry, *The Deregulated Muse* (Bloodaxe), was published in 1998, as was his anthology *The Firebox: Poetry in Britain and Ireland after 1945* (Picador). In 2017, he was Weidenfeld Visiting Professor of Comparative European Literature at St Anne's College, Oxford.

Susan Rosenbaum is Associate Professor of English at the University of Georgia, where she teaches twentieth-century American poetry and American modernism. She is the author of *Professing Sincerity: Modern Lyric Poetry, Commercial Culture, and the Crisis in Reading* (University of Virginia Press, 2007) and has just completed a monograph titled *Imaginary Museums: Surrealism, American Poetry, and the Visual Arts, 1920–1970*. Her recent essays have appeared in *Dada/Surrealism*, *Genre* and *Journal of Modern Literature* and she is collaborating on the scholarly digital platform *Mina Loy: Navigating the Avant-Garde*, funded by a 2017 NEH Digital Humanities Advancement Grant.

George Szirtes is a Hungarian-born British poet. His collections of poetry and literary translations have received awards including the T. S. Eliot Prize, the Bess Hokin Prize and the European Poetry Translation Prize. His *New and Collected Poems* was published by Bloodaxe in 2008 and his latest collection is *Mapping the Delta* (Bloodaxe, 2016), which was a poetry Book Society choice.

Ahren Warner is a poet, critic and literary editor. He is the author of three books of poetry, *Confer* (Bloodaxe, 2011), *Pretty* (Bloodaxe, 2013) and *Hello. Your Promise Has Been Extracted* (Bloodaxe, 2017). He is also Vice-Chancellor's Research Fellow at Loughborough University and was previously Poetry Editor of *Poetry London* from 2013 to 2019.

Preface

One historical-existential trace has been hunted, captured, guarded, and preserved in aversion to waste by an avid collector, then shut carefully away, outside an economy of use, inaccessible to touch. Now it is re-animated, re-collected (recollected) through an encounter with the mind of a curious reader, a researcher, an antiquarian, a bibliomaniac, a sub sub librarian, a poet.

Each collected object or manuscript is a pre-articulate empty theater where a thought may surprise itself at the instant of seeing. Where a thought may hear itself see.

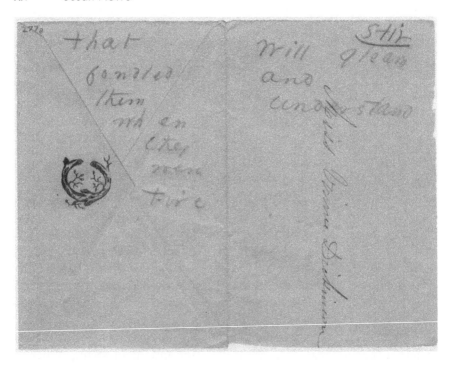

For conversion, there must be a mysterious leap of love. Sometimes, a hidden verso side acts as prior counterpoint. The way improvised children's tales have needlepoint roots in Latin holy words and medieval jargon. What difference does it make if what we see before our mind's eye has already been interpreted? This meanly magnificent 'waste' exists on a scale beyond actual use. It provides us with a literal and mythical sense of life hereafter –

Coming home to poetry – you permit yourself liberties – in the first place – happiness.

> From Susan Howe, *Spontaneous Particulars: The Telepathy of Archives* (New York: Christine Burgin and New Directions, 2014), pp. 24–5

Chapter 1

Introduction:
Poetry, Theory, Archives

Linda Anderson, Mark Byers and Ahren Warner

The aesthetics of collecting

We have taken our preface – and indeed a large part of our inspiration – from Susan Howe's book *Spontaneous Particulars: The Telepathy of Archives*, where she describes her elusive, often rhapsodic, encounters with literary archives, those 'deposits of a future yet to come' that are 'gathered and guarded in the domain of research libraries and special collections'.[1] The future horizon is significant for Howe: objects and texts surprise her in ways which cannot be determined by some prior estimate of their meaning or value. Instead it may be 'so-called insignificant' material details that call forth recognition, whose potential is literally 'seen' by chance and which leap from the page or the archival box to be reanimated by the reader. The process for Howe is intensely personal, akin to poetic inspiration, where new meaning flashes up in a way that is neither planned nor interpretable: 'The inward ardor I feel while working in research libraries is intuitive. It's a sense of self-identification and trust, or the granting of grace in an ordinary room, in secular time.'[2]

The idea of the archive as a room through which one gains entry to an inner world, indeed to interiority itself, depends on it also existing 'outside an economy of use' where 'waste' is never truly wasted, and nothing is extraneous.[3] It is an idea that resonates with Walter Benjamin's reflections on book-collecting in his famous essay 'Unpacking my Library'. Here he describes how the experience of collecting produces its own relationship to objects, one that 'does not emphasize their functional, utilitarian value' but instead locks them within a 'magic circle' where they are fixed and consecrated by 'the thrill of acquisition'.[4] For Jean Baudrillard, this 'culture of collecting', which substitutes possession for function or use in relation to objects, also has the effect of sustaining subjectivity, creating a 'personal microcosm' where objects become abstract, the 'ideal mirror' of their owner. The collection fuels passion, even feelings of sublimity:

> The collection offers us a paradigm of perfection, for this is where the passionate enterprise of possession can achieve its ambitions, within a space where the everyday prose of the object-world modulates into poetry, to institute an unconscious and triumphant discourse.[5]

Jeremy Braddock has argued that a 'collecting aesthetic', such as described by the writers above, seems to have a symbiotic relationship with modernism, shaping its most iconic literary forms and use of literary strategies such as collage and citation. However, for him, it is only in the end by placing modernist art and literature alongside the *practice* of collecting, the varied history of private and public institutions – collections, libraries and archives – that we can arrive at a more complete understanding of their connection.[6] In this view the rise of the modern literary collection or archive in the twentieth century did more than exemplify a set of idealised formal techniques. It also helped to provide interim or provisional spaces, a mode of protection from the exigencies of mass culture and commodification, a way of interacting with, and renegotiating the boundaries between, private patrons, the literary marketplace and the academy. Lawrence Rainey has argued that modernism's 'ambiguous achievement' was less to resist the mass market, as commonly thought, than to prove itself a commodity 'of a special sort', beyond, or 'temporarily exempted' from, consumption.[7] The collection had a role to play, and the transferral in the early twentieth century of private collections into public ownership, the gradual acquisition by libraries and universities of individually accumulated fine books and manuscripts, could be countenanced by the likes of T. S. Eliot because these cultural monuments would thus be preserved, 'accessible to those worthy to examine them'.[8] As Rainey argues, Eliot wanted *The Waste Land* to be 'successful, but not too successful', and its publication history demonstrates Eliot's equivocation about 'placing' his poem in a literary landscape which was rapidly changing, with his decision to publish his poem in a limited edition by Horace Liveright in the USA and the Hogarth Press in the UK perhaps revealing his desire to preserve its status as a collector's item, even as he negotiated publication – and prices – with more widely disseminated magazines and commercial presses.[9] The limited edition also has its own history and, like the collection or archive, was a way of regulating access, and preserving the value of literature as an art form in an interim way, even as it was inexorably assimilated into a mass print economy.

USA versus UK

The story of one private collector, A. S. W Rosenbach (1876–1952), is instructive here. Together with his brother Philip, he ran a fine art dealership in Philadelphia where he took responsibility for rare books and manuscripts, having inherited a passion for books – together with some of the stock – from his maternal uncle, Moses Pollack. Rosenbach later wrote about his boyhood experience of working in his uncle's bookshop:

> At that age I could hardly realize, spellbound as I was, the full quality of mystery and intangible beauty which becomes a part of the atmosphere wherever fine books are brought together . . . Whatever it was, – some glibly speak of it as bibliomania, – it entered my bones then, and has grown out of all proportion since.[10]

Despite the reservations Rosenbach experienced about abandoning academia – where he was building a promising career – for business, he was justified, he believed, by the opportunities he thus had as a researcher 'to unearth unpublished documents and uncover original source-material'.[11] His commercial acumen was also able to furnish him with a fairly lavish lifestyle. Rosenbach occupies a very significant position in terms of bringing together the private devotion of a collector, for whom personal ownership remained a motivation, with entrepreneurial skills and a canny eye for a good investment, and he played a part in building up the collections of some of the most important American libraries, including the Folger, Huntington, Houghton and Widener libraries. One of his most famous purchases reveals his interest in both manuscripts and modernism and his willingness to invest in both. In 1924, two years after the novel was published, he purchased the manuscript of James Joyce's *Ulysses* for $1,975 from John Quinn, to whom Joyce had previously sold it. This was still a risky investment for a relatively unknown work, though Joyce, now realising its value, and angry at its being traded in this way, tried unsuccessfully to purchase it back.[12]

The Rosenbach Museum and Collection, set up in 1954 after Rosenbach's death, has this manuscript as its centrepiece, and it is interesting that such was Rosenbach's 'thrill of acquisition' that he retained the manuscript for his private collection. The Rosenbach also houses a comprehensive Marianne Moore archive, including her manuscripts, papers and personal library, together with – more unusually – the contents of her Greenwich Village living room. The story of the acquisition of Moore's archive provides another fascinating footnote on the complex intersections between private collecting and the institutional accumulation of modern literary manuscripts which, by the mid-century, was gaining pace.[13] In 1958 Moore had been approached by Charles Abbott, Director of Libraries at the University of Buffalo, about contributing to a collection of manuscripts the University was establishing. Moore was sceptical about the value of the project, despite her own penchant for collecting curios and her career as an ardent reviser of her own work.[14] When, towards the end of her life, Moore was choosing where to sell her papers – now the subject of competing offers – she turned to the Rosenbach because she remembered visiting Rosenbach's shop in New York in 1951 and admiring '"the electrically-lighted, suspended magnifying glass", various examples of the art of bookbinding, and a first folio of *Othello* –"*The Moores Tragedy*," she noted with pleasure'.[15] The shop spoke to her own passion for interiors and for collecting – encapsulated in her own densely personalised and old-fashioned living space[16] – and helped to propel the establishment of a modern, and hugely significant, archive.

Charles Abbott had been influenced by Allen Tate, who, as Consultant in Poetry at the Library of Congress 1943–4, wrote to thirty-four colleges in order to assess the state of modern poetry holdings in the USA, including holdings of manuscripts and letters.[17] This mission, a laudable attempt to co-ordinate knowledge and establish a national collection, also reveals a set of underlying difficulties. The first is that holdings are typically acquired piecemeal, with materials to do with particular writers often dispersed to different institutions, as they are variously bought or donated over time. There is also no rule about either the poets themselves or their executors preserving materials, despite an increasing financial incentive, and both carelessness and deliberate censorship have had a part to play in what ends up in archives. Lastly, the question that Marlene Manoff puts of 'who builds the archive and for what purpose' is crucial.[18] She goes on to cite David Greetham's pithy assessment that there is a 'poetics of archival exclusion', referring to his argument that archives, whatever they contain, are also inevitably about what they leave out, and the boundaries they draw around themselves, whether deliberately or not.[19] Allen Tate's well-meaning attempt to build a comprehensive modern poetry archive is a case in point, since it is based on a preliminary selection of sixty poets who, in his opinion, were worthy of inclusion. As Bartholomew Brinkman comments, Tate adopted in relation to libraries a methodology where his own taste predominated, and which thus prevented a more complex picture of library holdings and of poetic modernism from emerging. Though this was also the moment when different materials, including manuscripts, letters and ephemera, were recognised as valuable, there was an emphasis by Tate and others on an authoritative gathering together of archival holdings. Inevitably a hierarchy of poets emerged and the bias towards white male writers and subsequent neglect of gender and ethnic difference were as inevitable as they are depressing. The goal of cultural unity, through a national collection, was perhaps, as Brinkman argues, enacting the same principles as New Criticism at this time, with its belief in the intrinsic value of literature (and the illusory ideal of universality) as opposed to historical or biographical contextualisation.[20] Yet, as an archive of manuscripts, paradoxically, the collection could be said to point in a completely different direction, away from Tate's implicit beliefs in unity, towards the instability and discontinuity of texts, the impossibility of totality in relation to such collections, and a complicating material history in which poetry is embedded.

More than twenty years after Tate had surveyed the fragmented state of the holdings in the Library of Congress and tried to remedy the lack of a national archive, Philip Larkin praised the initiative of the Arts Council in the UK, which, with the support of the British Museum and funding from the Pilgrim Trust, had established something called 'The National Collection of Contemporary Poets', though as Larkin admits, this may also have seemed 'a grandiose title for an assemblage of material which as yet occupies hardly two shelves of a library trolley'. In this preface to the collection catalogue, Larkin registers the importance of the change of perception that had occurred and which had brought about the new initiative:

> Until this century, the acquisition of literary manuscripts by libraries or museums was largely a matter of luck or goodwill, and then largely on the assumption that an author's papers would contain much that was unpublished. As little as thirty years ago there was scant interest in the manuscripts of published works, especially of twentieth century writers, except as a curiosity, and what interest there was came from private collectors.[21]

Larkin is also aware that the UK, as a latecomer to the field, is looking out at a marketplace dominated by American buyers. In the second half of the twentieth century, American libraries and universities had widened their interests, and if the first initiative had been about establishing a representative national collection, latterly it was about accumulating cultural capital more generally which would put particular institutions on the map. This was aided by a culture of philanthropy, a culture relatively unknown in the UK, and the wealth and interests of particular individuals. At Emory University, for example, a former student-cum-businessman, Stuart Rose, had made donations to what is now known as the Rose Library, the world-leading collection of manuscripts, archives and rare books which has purchased the archives of Seamus Heaney, Derek Mahon, Paul Muldoon, Ted Hughes and Carol Ann Duffy, amongst others.[22] The Harry Ransom Center, at the University of Texas at Austin, named after its patron and founder, has similarly become a world-renowned repository for contemporary literary archives and manuscripts, including not just those of leading modernists T. S. Eliot and Ezra Pound, but many later UK poets, including Edith Sitwell, Robert Graves, Stephen Spender and Charles Tomlinson.

Philip Larkin lamented in 1967 a situation where so many UK authors' archives had been sold to the USA, depriving writers and scholars in the UK of important opportunities for study and scholarship. He cited as the reason not just superior institutional buying power, but a lack of government interest and incentive, and a general disregard for contemporary literature.[23] The fact that Andrew Motion in 2006, at a conference entitled 'Manuscripts Matter' held at the British Library, returned to the same theme reveals how slow change has been in the UK, though the Group for Literary Archives and Manuscripts (GLAM), established at that time, has done much since to advocate to government and share information and best practice amongst institutions.[24] While both Emory and the Harry Ransom Center make a case for the success of their 'cultural stewardship' and for the transcending of national boundaries through bringing researchers to their libraries from around the world, the alternative argument, as made by Motion, is that place matters in relation to archives, and that links with national and regional cultures are mutually reinforcing.[25] At the Newcastle Poetry Festival in 2015, Richard Price, then Head of Contemporary British Collections at the British Library, talked about the role the Bloodaxe Archive, now owned by Newcastle University, might have in the regeneration of the region.[26] In this case the collection has international scope in terms of the poets published, but the publisher is regionally based, and its founder-editor, Neil Astley, wished the collection to be located there rather than in the USA. In the case of Cambridge University Library, the Library has a commitment to acquiring the archives of those poets closely associated with the City and the University and known collectively as the 'Cambridge School'. The rationale for gathering the papers of this self-defined group is that through linking them together with each other and through their connections to place, 'a closely-knit nexus of primary resources is preserved' which augments the value of an archive where not all the poets are necessarily nationally prominent.[27]

More recently, the digital revolution and the increasing number of archive-digitisation projects would seem to have removed some of the anxiety about *where* archives are held and helped to democratise access to them. Yet any vision of total accessibility from any place, at any time, is, as Finn Fordham points out, 'far away on the utopian horizon'.[28] In the case of catalogues, many do appear online, and information about collections is more widely available, though rarely is information about the manuscripts as objects – as paper and inscription – included as part of the description. The financial resource required and, in the case of modern and contemporary collections, copyright issues curtail the widespread digitisation of whole collections, but there are examples of partial collections at least: the Marianne Moore Digital Archive, for example, which centres on her beautifully illustrated notebooks; Mina Loy's digitised papers, the subject of one of the chapters in this collection. Arguably, however, digitisation introduces more questions than it answers. Does a digitised archival collection offer the same resource in a different form or a different kind of resource? How is critical and scholarly practice changed by the digital, and how far is technology being reimagined for and by the humanities, rather than humanistic approaches being subsumed into alien conventions and epistemologies?[29] And, perhaps most pertinently for us, how far is this new context inciting us to think again about the representation and transmission of knowledge and the multiple meanings of the archive as both metaphor and critical procedure? In the rest of this introduction, we turn from the history of collecting and the establishment of particular archives to more general questions about reading the archive, the perspectives it engenders on writing as a fluid, elusive process, and the archive as theoretical object or expansive metaphor, which moves between institutional imprisonment and a ghostly revivification, between stasis and the potential of creative reimagining and mediation.

Object or process? Reading contemporary poetry manuscripts

In 1846, in his essay 'The Philosophy of Composition', Edgar Allan Poe criticised a well-worn ideal of literary creation, still prominent in the mid-nineteenth-century, which would see the poet gripped by a 'fine frenzy – an ecstatic intuition'.[30] Foundational to the myths of Romantic authorship, this model of literary production concealed, Poe argued, a decidedly less glamorous reality, one most authors would rather keep from public view:

> Most writers – poets in especial – prefer having it understood that they compose by a species of fine frenzy – an ecstatic intuition – and would positively shudder at letting the public take a peep behind the scenes, at the

elaborate and vacillating crudities of thought – at the true purposes seized only at the last moment – at the innumerable glimpses of idea that arrived not at the maturity of full view – at the fully matured fancies discarded in despair as unmanageable – at the cautious selections and rejections – at the painful erasures and interpolations – in a word, at the wheels and pinions – the tackle for scene-shifting – the step-ladders and demon-traps – the cock's feathers, the red paint and the black patches, which, in ninety-nine cases out of the hundred, constitute the properties of the literary *histrio*.[31]

As the genetic critic Louis Hay has pointed out, Poe was not alone in the nineteenth century in turning attention to the process, as distinct from the product, of literary composition: Novalis, Goethe and Friedrich Schlegel all wondered whether the becoming or evolution of the work was not, in fact, critical to its reception and full appreciation.[32] Why should the literary work in its final, reified form take precedence in criticism over the activity of its gestation?

This particular line of inquiry surfaced only irregularly in the following century.[33] But the acquisition and proliferation of literary archives after the Second World War in the ways we have seen (including archives of contemporary literature) served to reactivate the issue of composition and the possible value of literary genesis for reading and criticism. While editors have traditionally sought out manuscripts and other pre-publication materials for the purposes of establishing copy-texts, by the 1970s increasing attention was being given to the processes of literary composition and revision in their own right. At the forefront of this practice were French scholars associated with the Centre d'Analyse des Manuscrits in Paris, formed after the accession of Heinrich Heine's papers by the Bibliothèque Nationale in 1966.[34] *Critique génétique*, as it came to be known, stresses the 'diachronic' activity of composition over the autonomous and 'synchronic' work of literary critical close reading.[35] However, the emphasis falls not on a recovery of origins (such as authorial intentions), or on the solution of textual problems, but on the processes of writing and rewriting themselves, the manner in which a literary work invents and reinvents itself over time and across material contexts (from rough notebook drafts, for instance, to fair copies and annotated proofs). In recent years, the values and practices of genetic criticism have become more visible in English and American scholarship, for instance in Finn Fordham's *I Do I Undo I Redo: The Textual Genesis of Modernist Selves* and Hannah Sullivan's *The Work of Revision*.[36] Genetic criticism has also been energised by new digital methods; evidenced, for instance, in Dirk Van Hulle and Mark Nixon's Samuel Beckett Digital Manuscript Project <http://www.beckettarchive.org/>, which gathers digital facsimiles of

Beckett's manuscripts with transcriptions and tools for the comparison of multiple versions and witnesses.

Contemporary poetic works are unlikely to be the subject of scholarly editing for a considerable period of time (if, indeed, they ever are). But genetic approaches offer productive and critically revealing ways of reading contemporary poetry (as illustrated by several chapters in this collection), and drawing out the potential of the poetry archive. Crucially, the archive allows us to read the formal and semantic structures of poetic texts against an extended timeframe of experimentation, revision and recreation. In other words, such materials allow us to practise interpretation and close reading *longitudinally*, tracking the changing shape of the poem and its evolving tropes and textures. Moreover, the contemporary archive emphasises the material and technologically mediated nature of these activities. What kinds of (re)writing, for instance, are specific to the small, hardbound notebook or the Microsoft Word document? How do the material and technologically mediated practices of writing and revision bear on the formal, conceptual and thematic content of a work? More broadly, the contemporary literary archive invites us to revisit basic questions regarding the ontology of the literary work itself, particularly its assumed autonomy and unity. Dispersed across notebooks, loose-sheet drafts, annotated page proofs, revised printouts, PDFs and forensically reconstructed Microsoft Word documents, the boundaries of the contemporary literary work may seem to recede as we approach them. Where, then, does the 'poem' proper end, and what status should we give to the materials left on the cutting-room floor? Ultimately, to examine the pre-publication materials of contemporary poetry is not to search for clues that might resolve hermeneutic difficulties, but to investigate the material and imaginative structures in play during a work's making.

The concept of a changeable, unstable and endlessly extensible text may appear counterintuitive. As the American literary historian Albert B. Lord observed:

> We are not accustomed to thinking in terms of fluidity. We find it difficult to grasp something that is multiform. It seems to us necessary to construct an ideal text or to seek an original, and we remain dissatisfied with an ever-changing phenomenon.[37]

Though Lord was discussing the traditional oral epic poem, his judgement refers to a deeply entrenched preference for textual stability. In the field of contemporary poetry and poetics, this fixed and autonomous text is partly the legacy of mid-century New Criticism, which – as we noted above – often wrested the poem from its material entanglements in manuscript and print. At the same time, the modern poem as stable *objet d'art* is also a condition of its success as a commodity; a vendible 'thing' that – unlike the fluid, shapeshifting and alterable texts of traditional song and oral epic – can easily be alienated from its author and sold in the literary marketplace.

However, to move beyond conceptions of the poetic text as self-complete is to open new possibilities for reading and criticism. As Jonathan Culler has argued, contemporary poetry theory and pedagogy generally assume that 'the goal of reading a lyric is to produce a new interpretation' (another legacy of the New Criticism).[38] However, this hermeneutic approach tends to crowd out the questions traditionally posed by poetics, which instead considers 'the conventions that enable [a] work to have the sorts of meanings and effects it does for readers'.[39] For Culler, such questions are primarily answerable within a 'generic tradition' (the historical tradition of the lyric, for instance).[40] But to reframe the poetic work as processive and diachronic, something more than the text immobilised in its published form, is to reactivate the questions of poetics (of structure, of convention, of device) from another – potentially revealing – perspective. That is to say, the materials of the contemporary poetry archive do not lead us away from what is properly poetic but draw us closer to it. Reading the genesis of the poem in manuscript (or even, for that matter, in the post-publication archive of recorded reading and performance) foregrounds structural transformations over time, inviting attention not just to authorial work but to the poetic itself.

This does not mean, however, detaching poetics from the non-literary histories and social lives which a poem leads prior to publication. On the one hand, the poetry archive asks us to think of the text as a social activity, reflecting the labour not only of the author but of editors, publishing assistants, typesetters, designers, marketing gurus and other agents conventionally marginalised by the myth of solitary authorship. Here a genetic approach to the poem supports inquiries into (as Jerome J. McGann puts it) the 'socialization' of the text.[41] Indeed, investigation of the poem's pre-publication life will almost invariably emphasise that, as McGann says, the 'literary work by its very nature sets in motion many kinds of creative intentionalities', not only those of the author.[42] Thus taking 'a peep behind the scenes', as Poe putatively offers in his own essay, is not just to expose the performance of the private *'histrio'* or literary actor but also to foreground their interaction with other protagonists (sometimes antagonists) on the public stage of literary production. In the era of precarious, freelance and obscurely outsourced work (including in publishing and the so-called 'creative industries'), it might seem all the more important to recognise and investigate these 'creative intentionalities' withheld from the public gaze.

For the contemporary poetry archive, another major issue may turn out to be the collision between genre convention and new technology. For instance, how does the computer screen inform approaches to the poetic line, page space or stanzaic form? What are the (formal, semantic) implications of toggling between a digital draft and a Twitter feed? How do analogue and digital writing processes and materials overlap or intersect with one another? With the emergence of 'forensic' textual studies, which treats, as Matthew G. Kirschenbaum puts it, 'electronic texts as artifacts – mechanisms – subject to material and historical forms of understanding', these and similar questions may soon become available to inquiry.[43] In fact, with its combination of analogue and born-digital materials, the contemporary literary archive presents an unusually rich body of evidence for media change, especially the digital transformation of text and textuality.[44]

How, then, should we approach the manuscripts, typescripts, digital drafts, notebooks, proofs and ephemera that would seem to be encompassed in an expanded account of the poetic work? Sally Bushell has argued for 'enlarging our definition of "text" to understand text as process *alongside* the completed text'.[45] Similarly, for John Bryant, 'a literary work is not a conceptual thing or actual set of things or even discrete events, but rather a flow of energy'.[46] On the other hand, as Wim van Mierlo has stressed, the 'process' of composition is never abstract or disembodied: 'Manuscripts . . . are more than texts in creation; they are material objects whose physical features and what they mean for the creative process need to be understood as well.'[47] Keeping in sight both the fluidity of the text and its materiality, its status as an object as well as a process, is a paradox that the contemporary poetry archive seems to invite us to accept. As the chapters in this collection consistently attest, the contemporary poetry archive is a repository of both things and experiences, physical objects and immaterial occasions. For this reason, the analysis of contemporary poetry manuscript material (whether analogue, digital or hybrid) also requires us to theorise the archive in its own right; a task notably undertaken by Jacques Derrida and Michel Foucault, but also – in the work of Howe and others – by contemporary poetics itself.

Memory, fever, law

Language has unmistakably made plain that memory is not an instrument for exploring the past, but rather a medium. It is the medium of that which is experienced, just as the earth is the medium in which ancient cities lie buried.[48]

Written in exile in the early 1930s, Benjamin's archaeological metaphor for the intersections between language, memory and topology might be read as invoking an acute sense of dichotomy. Although rather quixotic, Benjamin's analogy is also extremely challenging for anyone wishing to think about the immaterial occasions of archival space not simply as the repository for textual traces of a literary process, but as a kind of space replete with intellectual, theoretical and properly philosophical considerations. How can the archived word – as statement, as work in progress, or as the fluid process displaced by the publishable object – exist not as mere artefact but as a mediation of experience; not, that is, as the trace of a historical process that might help one interpret the finished poetic product, but as an event at once both alive and profoundly lyrical in itself?

Perhaps the most influential, or at least the most ubiquitous, attempt to approach the archive from a philosophical perspective is Jacques Derrida's *Archive Fever*, a text that also opens by noting the 'privileged topology' of the archive, the archival place, as one in which 'commencement' and 'commandment' intersect, as the site of a profound antagonism between singular events of language and their systematic regulation. As Derrida writes,

> it is thus, in this domiciliation, in this house arrest, that archives take place. The dwelling, this place where they dwell permanently, marks this institutional passage from the private to the public . . . they inhabit this unusual place, this place of election where law and singularity intersect in privilege.[49]

The peculiarity, then, of the *literary* archive might be defined by the way in which it exists both as a highly regulated space, and as the space in which what Alain Badiou calls the 'lawless proposition' of poetic practice must continue to fizz.[50]

It is a not dissimilar friction that Michel Foucault delineates, in the other touchstone of archival philosophy, *The Archaeology of Knowledge*. There, Foucault constructs a reading of the archive as 'first the law of what can be said, the system that governs the appearance of statements as unique events', developing this further:

> The archive is also that which determines that all these things said do not accumulate endlessly in an amorphous mass, nor are they inscribed in an unbroken linearity, nor do they disappear at the mercy of chance external accidents; but they are grouped together in distinct figures, composed together in accordance with multiple relations, maintained or blurred in accordance with specific regularities . . . The archive is not that which, despite its immediate escape, safeguards the event of the statement, and preserves, for future memories, its status as an escapee; it is that which, at the very root of

the statement-event, and in that which embodies it, defines at the outset the system of its enunciability. Nor is the archive that which collects the dust of statements that have become inert once more, and which may make possible the miracle of their resurrection; it is that which defines the mode of occurrence of the statement-thing; it is the system of its functioning.[51]

For Foucault, the space of the archive is not simply an amalgamation of papers resulting from, as we saw earlier, what A. S. W. Rosenbach talked about as a kind of bibliomania, one that leaves the collector 'spellbound' in the presence of fine books (or, perhaps, less charitably, as a figuration of Nietzsche's 'antiquarian man').[52] Rather, precisely because the archive exists as the very possibility of the archival object, it also regulates the way in which such objects can be experienced, the ways such objects can manifest both meaning and affect, and it does so by the very rules and systems that the archive must always necessitate.

It is, fundamentally, this tension between *potential* and *system,* between liveness and stasis, that recurs throughout some of the best thinking around the archive and archival experience. In *Archive Fever,* for example, Derrida points out that

> the archive is made possible by the death, aggression, and destruction drive, that is to say by originary finitude and expropriation. But beyond finitude as limit, there is . . . this properly *in-finite* movement of radical destruction without which no archive desire or fever would happen.[53]

The irony, then, of the literary archive, is that the very act of preservation that appears to be the archivist's *raison d'être* must always be enacted both *because of*, and *as an act of*, radical destruction. The present of literary production must always succumb to its own temporal finitude, to its transition from living present to an archived past. What Derrida points to so wonderfully is that this is not simply a historical process; it is a particularly paradoxical movement of archival care *as* destruction. Just as, as we saw, Greetham points to a 'poetics of archival exclusion' in which the archive is constituted as much by what it excludes, so any epistemology of the archive must recognise that its very conservation of the literary object *as past* functions as a destruction of the possibility of the text as *living present*. The event of archiving as an act of preservation must also be – by the very fact of archiving a past-present as historical object – the qualitative destruction of the archival object as an event that existed – before the archive – as *potential*.

The poet vs the philosopher king

Perhaps one of the greatest opportunities that a collection of essays like this one provides is not simply a chance to gather 'new thinking' about the archive, thinking that will always be performed in the shadow of the philosophers mentioned above. Rather, by virtue of bringing together, as this collection does, scholars and *practitioners* of literature, one can witness properly epistemological concerns regaining a certain liveness by their embodiment within the contingent, lived experience of writers engaged with archives and, perhaps, also with their own archiving.

In Sean O'Brien's chapter, 'I am Already Historical', collected in this volume, one is confronted not only by the same intersecting complexities of topology, destruction, futurity and system that one might also discern in Derrida and Foucault, but even by an explicit – if wry – animosity towards the 'articles of literary-critical faith' that would render 'authorial intention' unavailable to the reader of O'Brien's archival papers, now firmly under 'house arrest' in Newcastle University's Robinson Library.[54] It is a very similar network of tensions to that which is figured by Derrida as a dichotomy between *commencement* and *commandment* that is being performed in O'Brien's chapter. Perusing his early papers, and the early poems among them, the poet concludes that 'the actually existing O'Brien was in a sense nowhere to be found at any stage of this early accumulation. He was a creature *in potentia*, a figment of (largely unexamined) ambition', and then: 'With the handover of the manuscripts to the archive he has ceased to exist even as phantom. Take away intention, and with it the future, and he vanishes like dandruff on a white sheet.'[55]

Here, it is precisely Benjamin's sense of language as 'the medium of that which is experienced' that O'Brien both affirms and – perhaps somewhat ironically – problematises in a way that might be familiar to readers of both *Archive Fever* and, indeed, Derrida's wider corpus.

Reading his own papers, O'Brien asks 'What was I doing back then in the late 1970s', moving beyond coy witticism – 'generally speaking it's hard to say' – towards a passage of near memoir that is both sincere and philosophically intriguing:

> I suppose I was trying to learn to listen, to think, and to discover the coherence of what might have sounded like rather dispersed preoccupations . . . But none of this can be seen as I saw it then, supposing that word doesn't – again – overstate the clarity of what took place. *We lived, as it were, on the inside of an art form* while trying to understand it . . . Here was an escape from self, from mere subjectivity, into a larger dispensation . . . this city

where I'd grown up, these people, these rules and routines and assumptions, were as real as anything else. Poetry made them so.

Whether anyone else would, or could, glean any of this from the sheaves of paper produced in the process seems to me at best uncertain: I'm talking about authorial intention, which the articles of literary-critical faith (the ones I inherited, anyway) suggest is unavailable to the reader.[56]

Here, then, is the writer's recollection of 'commencement', of their own self *in potentia*, of the performance from 'the inside of an art form', and a certain kind of 'commandment', regulation or stasis. Stripped of 'intention' and confronted by the medium of that potential, of that commencement, as an opaque collection of 'sheaves of paper', such words are destined to always-already be experienced as other, as from a position of *exteriority*.

There are plenty of philosophical precedents for this kind of thinking about the problems of epistemology, subjectivity and affect embodied within the archive or the museum. One might turn, for example, to Jean Laplanche, and his critique of the museum in which he maps the problematic movement of the historical object that becomes stripped of 'the love of the object in itself, at once beautiful, bizarre and lucrative', denuded of any 'emotion tied to the exhumed object of the past' and 'set' instead among 'large signboards' *explicating* 'via maps, schemas and diagrams'.[57] Such a movement is not dissimilar to what Derrida sees as the 'institutional passage from the private to the public', to what Foucault writes of as the performance of a 'system of . . . enunciability' and to the movement from private, affective interiority to public exteriority described by O'Brien.

Spectral potencies

Yet there is another way to proceed – philosophically – amongst the archive, and one that Derrida points to in the final pages of *Archive Fever*. It is also one that shares the language of the 'phantom' that O'Brien resorts to, the language of the 'spectral' and of 'haunting', even as such haunting can become the spur to literature itself. Fundamentally, O'Brien's resignation at the sight of an archived younger self, apparently only existing *in potentia*, but stripped of this potential by the very fact of being archived as past, recalls the archive as a place in which, as Derrida writes,

uniqueness does not resist . . . Its price is infinite. But infinite in the immense, incommensurable extent to which it remains unfindable. The possibility of the archiving trace, this simple possibility, can only divide the uniqueness. Separating the impression from the imprint . . . The faithful memory of such singularity can only be given over to the ghost.[58]

However, just as (literary) singularity, which one might also read as *potential*, or even *negativity*, might only be archived as a 'ghost', so too this ghostly haunting, this spectral existence, might be precisely where, as Derrida suggests, 'speculation begins'. Thus, Derrida writes that this is what a certain literature 'attests. So here is a singular testimony, literature itself, an inheritor escaped – or emancipated – from the Scriptures' (those very same metaphysical scriptures, incidentally, that one might call 'authorial intention').[59]

And, indeed, it is precisely the emancipation from a certain kind of *scripture* that one might sense in both some of the best examples of the living writer engaged within the archive – such as Susan Howe, in her *Spontaneous Particulars: The Telepathy of Archives* – and some of the more recent philosophical responses to, and explorations of, archival space, including those of Wolfgang Ernst and Manuel DeLanda. In Susan Howe's *Spontaneous Particulars*, for example, we find the writer ensconced within the archival collections of writers such as Jonathan Edwards, Emily Dickinson and William Carlos Williams. What is astonishing within Howe's work is precisely how the materiality of the archive becomes alchemically fused with the semantic content of, for example, Edwards's papers. So, we read an account of tangential, properly literary speculation as 'the visual and acoustic shock of that first exclamatory "Oh" on paper brown with oxidisation, made me think in a rush of Henry James' great novel, *The Wings of the Dove*', or

> Three of Edwards' manuscript books I particularly love are titled *Efficacious Grace*. Two of them he constructed from discarded semi-circular pieces of silk paper his wife and daughters used for making fans. If you open these small oval volumes and just *look* – without trying to decipher the minister's spidery script, pen strokes begin to resemble textile thread-text. Surface and meaning co-operate to keep alive in one process mastery and service, service in mastery.[60]

It is worth saying that the movement from the archive as a site of informational transmission to it as a site of literary speculation, in which 'surface and meaning co-operate', finds its analogue in recent theoretical thinking about archives. Of particular interest here is the emerging field of media archives, an area of scholarship necessitated by the movement from the book, and the text or image on paper (or other such support), as the primary means of communication and artistic production to a world in which the mediums of communication and production that might be archived have proliferated significantly.

One example, and one of the most thoughtful amongst contemporary thinkers of the archive, is that of Wolfgang Ernst's 'media archaeology', in which the material substrate of the archive becomes the focus of as much attention as the 'information' it contains. In a wonderful analogue to Howe's discussion of Edwards's 'textile thread-text', Ernst writes:

> The broadcast of any football game illustrates the signal-to-noise ratio between plays on the field and amorphous shots of the spectators in the stadium only statistically. The archeology of media searches the depths of hardware for the laws of what can become a program. Has not the character of television shows after the introduction of color sets been determined decisively – indeed down to the clothes of the hosts – by the new standard and what it can do in terms of color and motion? . . . For media archeology, the only message of television is this signal: *no semantics.*[61]

In a certain sense, Ernst's dictum – 'no semantics' – set within the landscape of media archaeology and archival materiality, is simply an object-orientated revision of Derrida's 'impossible trace', of the implications of O'Brien's archivally stunted potential, and of Howe's radical renovation of the limits of the archive as the demarcation of a *new space* for play. It is, perhaps, an analogue for Derrida's revitalisation of the 'spectral' as 'speculation'. It is for this reason that Ernst can write, for example, of a 'phonograph as media artefact' that

> not only carries cultural meanings like words and music but is at the same time an archive of cultural engineering by its very material fabrication . . . The microphysical close reading of sound, where the materiality of the recording medium itself becomes poetical, dissolves any semantically meaningful archival unit into discrete blocks of signals.[62]

What one is approaching here is expressed pithily in Manuel DeLanda's reading of the Foucauldian archive, not as a mausoleum of 'subjective interiority', but as a network, 'an objective exteriority in which human bodies, events and archives interact'.[63] In DeLanda's example, such an 'assemblage' might 'be formed . . . by a set of fingerprints, a murder and the databases of the police', but in our context, might not that set of fingerprints be replaced by O'Brien's 'sheaves of paper' or an '"Oh" on paper brown with oxidation'?

And might not that database be what Derrida calls 'literature itself'? What, elsewhere, Derrida names as that 'interminable network' figured as a structure uncannily redolent of the digital systems used to catalogue archives, or the operating systems within which writers now produce their work: 'an infinite number of booklets enclosing and fitting inside other booklets, which are only able to issue forth by grafting, sampling, quotations, epigraphs, references, etc.'.[64]

But, in that case, what of the murder?

The *murder*, of course, is the literary act itself. Beyond the archive as the destruction of the live, literary moment exists the live, literary moment as the murder of archival silence, as the rebellion against Foucault's 'system of enunciability', wherein the dirty secret of both the archive and philosophy lies: the negative moment as 'productivity' or 'work'.[65] The moment in which a new writing is grafted onto the archive as potential, as destined to be domiciled, and as destined to spur yet more writing.

This process, a kind of eternal return of the past made present again by the intervention of the writer whose own work both *destroys* and *revives* the historical work of literature, might be rather succinctly witnessed in Susan Howe's reworking of both the textual and material artefacts of Jonathan Edwards's archive.[66]

I remember the summer before my sister Jerusha's death, making ... and I was leaning over the south fence and thinking in this manner, that I was never likely to do better and where should I go etc.

Here, Howe works *into* the original text, doubling the traditional relation between *figure* and *ground*, so that Edwards's text is not only the figure laid onto the ground of the white page, but becomes itself a second ground, a second stage for the overlay of another layer of Edwards's text. This second textual layer is broken, but it is also a layer of text that intervenes as *rupture*, as a careful destruction of the original that produces, via delicately murderous means, a new work of literature.

The Contemporary Poetry Archive

In the book that follows, our contributors have approached poetry archives from different angles, as editors, scholars, critics and poets, and in many cases have written about how these roles have merged or collided. Modernism marks the beginning, as it did the beginning of the idea of the collectable archive containing a poet's manuscripts, drafts, letters and ephemera. Hugh Haughton, as distinguished editor of T. S. Eliot's letters, shows us how Eliot's hauteur and wariness about who should have access to his papers were passed on in instructions to his legatees, and in particular his widow, Valerie. Here the archival space, Derrida's domicile or house presided over by the archons or magistrates – an idea that recurs in numerous different guises throughout this book – turns out to be Eliot's study in Kensington, where it is difficult to escape his admonitory, if ghostly, presence. One of the questions posed is, of course, how has our attitude to Eliot changed as volume has followed volume, not just of letters, but unpublished prose and poetry, including early drafts? And is it ever possible for a writer to control their own papers and their publication in perpetuity? This seems to have been Eliot's wish, even as he handed over his early drafts and manuscripts to the literary entrepreneur and dealer John Quinn, making possible, despite himself, the publication of one of the most remarkable literary documents of the twentieth century, the original – and much edited – version of *The Waste Land*. And what is there to learn from an author's papers in any case, as opposed to the published poems? How does the 'voice' of the poems intersect with that of letters? This is the question Jonathan Allison asks as he explores another issue as editor of Louis MacNeice's letters, and travels on both sides of the Atlantic to track down the dispersed and fragmentary archive, with caches of letters stored in many different libraries.

Haughton contrasts the case of Eliot with that of Derek Mahon, one of the many poets who have sold their papers to Emory University during their own lifetime, to support their later careers. Mahon is in the position – as the poets Sean O'Brien and George Szirtes have been, both writing in this collection – of collaborating in and reflecting on the acquisition of his own archive, a vertiginous project where the 'future tense' of the archive can seem strange, even estranging, to the poet. One dimension highlighted in George Szirtes's chapter is how far a digital environment – which includes blogs as well as Facebook and Twitter accounts – has increased the poet's ability to produce not only writing for publication, but an ongoing and prolific public record of the process, which creates inevitable challenges for future archivists. On the other hand, Jo Gill reflects on John Updike's industry in curating and curtailing his own archive, and the disappointment for her, as scholar and critic reading the papers, at how the aleatory or unconsidered seems strangely lacking. This throws up inevitable questions about why we go to archives, what we are looking for and the different answers that might be arrived at by scholar and poet, as Linda Anderson's chapter, reporting on a project which introduced a group of poets and artists to the Bloodaxe Archive, demonstrates. Or is it always the unexpected, the superfluous, the obdurate detail that will captivate, be 're-collected/ recollected', to quote Susan Howe, existing as it does beyond a notion of the archive as simply information space? In this collection we see Ahren Warner patiently trying to tease out the meaning of one detail, a revision in a poem by C. K. Williams, first in both real and imagined conversation with the poet himself, and then through the frames of philosophy and theory, which do not offer, whatever their intellectual rigour, any possibility of a precise answer. How does poetry 'think'? And what is poetry doing in the archive at all? And once there, how can it resist its own capture, maintain its liveness, its potential as 'trace' rather than artefact?

Archives, of course, do not exist autonomously, but are within the force field of institutional, national and world histories, all of which impact in different ways. Mark Byers offers a reading of how modern and contemporary poets have used archival techniques *within* their own poetry, in order to question or evade powerful hegemonic narratives of history. History instead exists for these poets within a textual space, an assemblage of curated documents, which resonate with each other through collage and juxtaposition, and foreground (unlike historical narratives) their own practice and provenance. Suzanne W. Churchill, Linda Kinnahan and Susan Rosenbaum have explored the case of Mina Loy, a writer in the tradition of Surrealism, who experimented both within and across different media, but whose place in the history of that movement is occluded. The digitisation of her papers by Yale University is an exciting prospect, but as these authors point out, availability is not in itself enough. An archive's existence may be a statement about cultural significance, but archives – both paper and digital – are organised and curated, and access to them is never unmediated. The work of feminist revision may also require new narratives and the creation of different contexts, and within a digital environment this may mean new digital platforms.

For many of our authors the question of frames – of who and what is inside or outside the frame of the archive – is crucial. This may be a matter of admitting a dimension of materiality to the archive, or simply admitting different materials to the archive. Amanda Golden, for example, argues that an author's books, and the annotations they contain, should also be a part of the archival record since these 'marginalia' (as is the case with Sylvia Plath) can provide important new insights into individual practices of both reading and writing. The absence of whole archives – and the concomitant absence of cultural recognition – is also, whether consciously or not, a political issue, and Sarah Howe draws attention to the way Derrida's argument about archives and about boundaries and borders has an unexpected resonance with the historical and contemporary policing of national borders, and with the accompanying decisions about who can be admitted and who must be excluded. The discovery of poems written by Chinese and Asian immigrants to the United States on the walls of the barracks of the detention centre on Angel Island becomes both an important archive – the archive as carceral space – and a testament to erasure and loss, something Asian American poets come back to, as Howe says, as 'an intractable problem and a haunting ideal'.

Howe invokes the ghostly quality of archives and the impossibility of creating and preserving a complete record, and asks whether mourning and melancholy are inevitable responses to this loss and absence: 'How do you archive smoke?', she asks. In the final chapter in this volume, Carolyn Forché voices the same question, as the effort to archive smoke – and not just smoke but 'nothingness' or the merest material detritus – becomes central to the 'Museum of Fragments', a concept and collection initiated by her friend, the artist Ashley Ashford-Brown. Even before the destruction of her papers in a flood, Forché was aware of how collecting resonates with absence and loss. Fragments necessarily tell of a totality, of all that is missing, even as they represent poignant 'pressings of attention' and honour a material reality that might be thrown away or categorised as 'waste'. For Forché there is an obvious correspondence with poetry: the collecting of objects also mirrors the note-taking that is part of her practice as a poet. It is perhaps fitting that this collection ends with a poetic evocation of the archive and the archive as poetry, the 'mysterious leap of love' that Susan Howe refers to that turns the archive into a subject and method for poetry itself, and allows us to find in past material, objects and manuscripts, a promise of and for the future.

Notes

1. Howe, Susan, *Spontaneous Particulars: The Telepathy of Archives* (New York: New Directions, 2014), p. 17.
2. Ibid., p. 63.
3. Ibid., p. 24.
4. Benjamin, Walter, 'Unpacking My Library', in *Illuminations*, ed. Hannah Arendt, trans Harry Zohn (1955) (London: Fontana, 1973), p. 60.
5. Baudrillard, Jean, 'The System of Collecting' in *The Cultures of Collecting*, ed. John Elsner and Roger Cardinal (London: Reaktion Books, 1994), pp. 7–9.
6. Braddock, Jeremy, *Collecting as Modernist Practice* (Baltimore: Johns Hopkins University Press, 2012), pp. 2–3.

7. Rainey, Lawrence, *Institutions of Modernism: Literary Elites and Public Culture* (New Haven and London: Yale University Press, 1998), p. 3.

8. Eliot T. S., 'Address to Members of the London Library', quoted in Bartholomew Brinkman, *Poetic Modernism in the Culture of Mass Print* (Baltimore: Johns Hopkins University Press, 2017), p. 4.

9. Rainey, *Institutions of Modernism*, pp. 104–5.

10. Rosenbach, A. S. W., *Books and Bidders: The Adventures of a Bibliophile* (Boston: Little, Brown, 1927), quoted in Bodmer, George R., 'A. S. W. Rosenbach: Dealer and Collector', *The Lion and the Unicorn*, 22 (1998), 1–16 (p. 4).

11. Rosenbach, *Books and Bidders*, quoted in Bodmer, 'A. S. W. Rosenbach', p. 3.

12. <https://www.nytimes.com/1997/06/30/opinion/l-poet-s-ire-at-a-sale-89 6888.html> (accessed 16 August 2018).

13. Rota, Anthony, 'The Collecting of Twentieth-Century Literary Manuscripts', *Rare Books & Manuscripts Librarianship* 1(1986), 39–53 (p. 39).

14. Brinkman, Bartholomew, *Poetic Modernism in the Culture of Mass Print* (Baltimore: Johns Hopkins University Press, 2017), p. 186.

15. Leavell, Linda, *Holding On Upside Down: The Life and Work of Marianne Moore* (New York: Farrar, Straus and Giroux, 2013), p. 383.

16. Elizabeth Bishop talks about the Moore's apartment in Brooklyn as 'old-fashioned' and belonging to a 'different world'. See 'Efforts of Affection: A Memoir of Marianne Moore', in *Elizabeth Bishop: Prose,* ed. Lloyd Schwartz (London: Chatto and Windus, 2011), p. 127.

17. See Brinkman, *Poetic Modernism*, pp. 178–9.

18. Manoff, Marlene, 'Theories of the Archive from Across the Disciplines', *portal: Libraries and the Academy*, 4 (2004), 9–25 (pp. 19–20).

19. Greetham, David, 'Who's In, Who's Out: The Cultural Politics of Archival Exclusion', *Studies in the Literary Imagination* 32/1 (1999), 1–28 (p. 9).

20. Brinkman, *Poetic Modernism*, p. 198.

21. Larkin, Philip, 'Operation Manuscript', in *Poetry in the Making: Catalogue of an Exhibition of Poetry Manuscripts in the British Museum April–June 1967* (London: Turret Books, 1967), p. 15.

22. <http://news.emory.edu/stories/2015/09/upress_rose_library_naming/ind ex.html> (accessed 18 August 2018).

23. Larkin, 'Operation Manuscript', p. 16.

24. <http://www.bl.uk/onlinegallery/pdf/manuscriptsmatter.pdf> (accessed 18 August 2018).

25. <https://www.finebooksmagazine.com/press/2015/09/emory-names-man-uscript-archives-and-rare-book-library-for-alumnus-stuart-rose.phtml> (accessed 18 August 2018)

26. Prescott, Andrew, 'Being Local and Connected', in *Crafting Our Digital Futures*, ed. Irini Papadimitriou, Andrew Prescott and Jon Rogers (London: Uniform Communications, 2015), n.p.

27. Wells, John, 'Collecting the "Cambridge School"', paper presented at 'Archival Afterlives: Postwar Poetry in English', John Rylands Research Institute, University of Manchester, 28 June 2017.

28. Fordham, Finn, 'The Modernist Archive', in *The Oxford Handbook of*

Modernisms, ed. Peter Brooker, Andrzej Gasiorek, Deborah Longworth and Andrew Thacker (Oxford: Oxford University Press, 2010), p. 48.

29. This is the question addressed particularly by Johanna Drucker. See 'Graphical Approaches to the Digital Humanities', in *A New Companion to the Digital Humanities*, ed. Susan Schreibman, Ray Siemens and John Unsworth (Chichester: John Wiley & Sons, 2016).

30. Poe, Edgar Allan, 'The Philosophy of Composition', in *Essays and Reviews*, ed. G. R. Thompson (New York: Library of America, 1984), p. 14.

31. Ibid.

32. Hay, Louis, 'Genetic Criticism: Origins and Perspectives', in *Genetic Criticism: Texts and Avant-Textes*, ed. Jed Deppman, Daniel Ferrer and Michael Groden (Philadelphia: University of Pennsylvania Press, 2004), p. 18.

33. Ibid., pp. 18–19.

34. See the editors' introduction to Hay's essay, p. 17.

35. These terms are used by Pierre-Marc de Biasi in 'Toward a Science of Literature: Manuscript Analysis and the Genesis of the Work', in *Genetic Criticism: Texts and Avant-Textes*, ed. Jed Deppman, Daniel Ferrer and Michael Groden (Philadelphia: University of Pennsylvania Press, 2004), p. 41.

36. Fordham, Finn, *I Do I Undo I Redo: The Textual Genesis of Modernist Selves* (Oxford: Oxford University Press, 2010); Sullivan, Hannah, *The Work of Revision* (Cambridge, MA: Harvard University Press, 2013).

37. Lord, Albert B., *The Singer of Tales*, 2nd edn, ed. Stephen Mitchell and Gregory Nagy (Cambridge, MA: Harvard University Press, 2003), p. 100.

38. Culler, Jonathan, *Theory of the Lyric* (Cambridge, MA: Harvard University Press, 2015), p. 5.

39. Ibid., p. 6.

40. Ibid.

41. McGann, Jerome J., *The Textual Condition* (Princeton: Princeton University Press, 1991), p. 75.

42. Ibid.

43. See Kirschenbaum, Matthew G., *Mechanisms: New Media and the Forensic Imagination* (Cambridge, MA: MIT Press, 2008), p. 17.

44. See also Kirschenbaum, Matthew G., *Track Changes: A Literary History of Word Processing* (Cambridge, MA: Belknap Press of Harvard University Press, 2016).

45. Bushell, Sally, *Text as Process: Creative Composition in Wordsworth, Tennyson, and Dickinson* (Charlottesville: University of Virginia Press, 2009), p. 1.

46. Bryant, John, *The Fluid Text: A Theory of Revision and Editing for Book and Screen* (Ann Arbor: University of Michigan Press, 2002), p. 61.

47. Van Mierlo, Wim, 'The Archaeology of the Manuscript: Towards Modern Palaeography', in *The Boundaries of the Literary Archive: Reclamation and Representation*, ed. Carrie Smith and Lisa Stead (Farnham: Ashgate, 2013), p. 27.

48. Benjamin, Walter, 'Excavation and Memory', in *Selected Writings, Vol. 2, Part 2 (1931–1934)*, ed. Marcus Paul Bullock, Michael Williams Jennings,

Howard Eiland, Gary Smith and Rodney Livingstone (Cambridge, MA: Harvard University Press, 2005), p. 576.

49. Derrida, Jacques, *Archive Fever*, trans. Eric Prenowitz (Chicago: University of Chicago Press, 2017), pp. 1, 3.

50. Badiou, Alain, *Handbook of Inaesthetics*, trans. Alberto Toscado (Stanford: Stanford University Press, 2005), p. 17.

51. Foucault, Michel, *The Archaeology of Knowledge,* trans. A. M. Sheridan Smith (New York: Pantheon Books, 1972), p. 129.

52. For Nietzsche, the 'antiquarian man' is the person whose relation to the past is defined by both piety and veneration, but also the person whose own veneration for the past limits them to an 'extremely restricted field of vision' (Nietzsche, Friedrich, *Untimely Meditations*, ed. Daniel Breazeale (Cambridge: Cambridge University Press, 1997), p. 74).

53. Derrida, *Archive Fever*, p. 94.

54. See p. 164 below.

55. See p. 162 below.

56. See pp. 162–3 below.

57. Laplanche, Jean, 'L'interprétation entre déterminisme et herméneutique: Une nouvelle position de la question', in *La révolution copernicienne inachevée: Travaux 1967–1992* (Paris: Aubier, 1992), p. 410. For an excellent essay both indebted to, and developing, Laplanche's critique, see Dean, Tim, 'Art as Symptom: Žižek and the Ethics of Psychoanalytic Criticism', *Diacritics*, 32/2 (2002), 20–41.

58. Derrida, *Archive Fever*, p. 100

59. Ibid., p. 63.

60. Howe, *Spontaneous Particulars*, p. 52.

61. Ernst, Wolfgang, 'Between Real Time and Memory on Demand', in *Digital Memory and the Archive*, ed. Jussi Parrika (Minneapolis: University of Minnesota Press, 2013), p. 104.

62. Ernst, Wolfgang, 'Media Archaeography: Method and Machine Versus the History and Narrative of Media', in *Digital Memory and the Archive*, ed. Jussi Parrika (Minneapolis: University of Minnesota Press, 2013), p. 60.

63. DeLanda, Manuel, 'The Archive Before and After Foucault', in *Information is Alive: Art and Theory on Archiving and Retrieving Data*, ed. Joke Brouwer and Arjen Mulder (Rotterdam: NAI, 2003), p. 11.

64. Derrida, Jacques, *Dissemination*, trans. Barbara Johnson (London: Continuum, 2004), p. 223.

65. For a philosophical exploration of 'creative destruction' in the shadow of the Hegelian concept of negativity, see Malabou, Catherine, *The Future of Hegel: Plasticity, Temporality, and Dialectic*, trans. Lisabeth During (London: Routledge, 2005).

66. Howe, *Spontaneous Particulars*, p. 44.

Chapter 2

T. S. Eliot and Derek Mahon: A Tale of Two Archives

Hugh Haughton

'One would think you expected to find in them the answer to the riddle of the universe', she said; and I denied the impeachment only by replying that if I had to choose between that precious solution and a bundle of Jeffrey Aspern's letters I knew indeed which would appear to me the greater boon.

Henry James, *The Aspern Papers*[1]

The Aspern syndrome

Auden, in 'In Memory of W. B. Yeats', said 'The death of the poet was kept from his poems.' Mourning Yeats, Auden affirmed that the poetry 'survives / In the valley of its making where executives / Would never want to tamper'.[2] Whatever Auden claims about the valley of making, the archive is different. Executives might not want to tamper, but executors do. When the archives are made available after a poet's death to be mined industriously – and often industrially – by editors and biographers, the valley of the poem's making is revealed to be part of a much larger, multi-dimensional landscape. The poet's carefully curated oeuvre becomes the tip of a textual iceberg.

Poets have very different relations to their archives. Some embrace them, some dread them and almost everyone wants to control them. The relationship between a poet's published oeuvre and his or her posthumous *Nachlässe* is also different in every case, offering radically individual relationships between their poetic canon and the promiscuous stash of letters, diaries, notes, manuscript materials and drafts, circulated in correspondence or deposited in libraries. Such archives hold a wealth of textual and documentary material which can illuminate the published texts. Equally, each archive erodes the distinction between primary and secondary texts, and between published and unpublished or finished and unfinished material. It threatens the shaky distinction between literature and its biographical or historical contexts, and it also always raises vexed editorial issues which change the relationship between the valley of the poem and the larger landscape of which it is part.

The issue became visible to me when I was working at different times on the archives of two poets with contrasting attitudes towards the archive: T. S. Eliot and Derek Mahon. My attitude was different in each case too. In the case of T. S. Eliot I had been brought in by the Eliot estate to work with his widow Valerie on the first two volumes of his letters, whereas in the case of Derek Mahon I was working on a biographically orientated critical study of his poetry, with my eyes focused on the archive mainly as a source of information about the oeuvre itself. The archive functions quite differently for the critic and the editor, or rather the critic and editor – and indeed biographer – perform completely different functions in relation to it. Working on Eliot's letters in 2007 at the poet's desk in his study (in the flat he had shared with Valerie Eliot in Kensington) provided a unique experience of this particular archive, and the ambiguous threshold between private and public – and between the critical and editorial – in terms of working on a poet's personal papers. Digging out incoming letters and photocopies of the poet's correspondence in the filing cabinets around the walls of Mrs Eliot's study, I felt as if I had stumbled into the world of Henry James's *The Aspern Papers* (1888), knowing as I did the poet's misgivings towards his archive, his decision to entrust the editing of his correspondence to his widow, and her own frail health. Much of Eliot's archive is housed in libraries across the USA and the UK or at Faber and Faber, but working in his one-time flat, often alongside Ron Schuchard working on his edition of Eliot's prose, I sometimes found myself identifying with the invasive protagonist of the *Aspern Papers*, a trespasser on the scene of the crime or at the primal scene of archivisation. Around the walls were filed original letters from Virginia Woolf, Ezra Pound, James Joyce and a thousand others, often cheek by jowl with originals and photocopies of Eliot's own letters his widow had bought or had copied from libraries across the world, as part of her lifelong task of editing her husband's vast correspondence.

I had had a variant of the same sensation a few years earlier in the library at Emory University in Atlanta, where I had gone to work on a critical study of Derek Mahon and was sifting through the mass of his catalogued and still-to-be-catalogued papers, including letters, drafts, postcards, newspaper cuttings and photos. While going through a still-unsorted box of materials relating to his 1990s sequence *The Yellow Book*, I found a notebook headed 'Scrapbook 1996–7', where some twenty pages in I read the heading 'The Yellow Book; or the Decadence' and found not only jotted-down headings, quotations and ideas for the sequence but a scribbled note in Mahon's hand which said: 'The Aspern Papers: the Emory archive?'[3] In this case the poet himself was thinking about James's grisly Venetian Gothic fable and questioning its relation to his own papers. As a biographically minded reader of Mahon, I realised I was caught up in Mahon's self-conscious allusion to – and embodiment of – James's fable. Here was a poet collaborating in and reflecting on the formation of his own archive and recording this in a document destined for it. If this captures a different attitude of a particular writer to the archive, it also epitomises later developments in the history of the twentieth- and twenty-first-century archive itself.

The Aspern Papers, with its story of a literary scholar's ruthless attempts to gain access to the private letters of the fictitious Romantic poet Jeffrey Aspern, is haunting for anyone working in a recent poet's archive. It reminds us of what is at stake in the relationship between a poet's legacy as a person and as a writer, between their oeuvre and their archive, or between what T. S. Eliot called 'the man who suffers and the mind which creates'.[4] The many complex questions the editor, critic or biographer have to ask include the following. How can archival material enhance our understanding of the author or our reading of the oeuvre? Should the poetry guide our approach to the archive and/or vice versa? How does the archive affect our understanding of the vexed relationship between text and context, poem and associated documentation? And, in the case of editing, how should we present the mass of archival raw material in relation to the authorially cooked output of poems?

I want to reflect on these questions primarily in relationship to T. S. Eliot, since we are currently in the middle of the long-delayed process of the posthumous translation of his massive archive into new editions of his correspondence, collected prose and poetry. I will touch briefly, however, on the contrasted case of the Mahon archive, since the tale of the two archives taken together is instructive. In the case of Mahon, who is very much alive and publishing, scholars can access the hoard of his papers acquired by Emory and use it for critical or biographical ends, but they are in no position to 'tamper' with his oeuvre itself in the form of new editions of the poetry or prose. As Mahon said of the poetry of Louis MacNeice in his elegy 'In Carrowdore Churchyard', his archive is still consecrated 'To what lies in the future tense'.[5]

The prosaic Eliot: terror and biography

There are few more dramatic indices of the impact of a posthumous archive on an oeuvre than the difference between Eliot's final slim volume of *Collected Poems 1909–1962* (1963) – about 240 pages long – and the monumental annotated edition of *The Poems of T. S. Eliot* in two volumes, published in 2015 under the editorship of Christopher Ricks and Jim McCue, which weighs in at almost 2,000 pages. For forty years or so the Eliot estate had been a byword for protectiveness towards his archival legacy, but in the 2010s all was changed, and an editorial equivalent of Yeats's 'terrible beauty' has been born.

When Eliot died in 1965 his published canon of poetry and prose was relatively small. The *Collected Poems 1909–1962* was complemented by a handful of volumes of critical essays, including *Selected Essays* (1932), *The Use of Poetry and Use of Criticism* (1933) and *On Poetry and Poets* (1957). These were supplemented by two influential volumes of cultural criticism, *The Idea of a Christian Society* (1939) and *Notes Towards the Definition of Culture* (1948); the plays, mainly written in the latter half of his career; and his early projected doctoral thesis, *Knowledge and Experience in the Philosophy of F. H. Bradley* (1964). All had been published by Faber and Faber, the firm in which Eliot worked as editor and director from 1925 to his death. The critical canon was enlarged subsequently with the posthumous publication of *To Criticize the Critic* in 1965, and the poetic canon by a reprint of *Poems Written in Early Youth* (1967), but, with a few exceptions, the Eliot canon then remained frozen for almost three decades after his death, despite intense critical and biographical interest.

With good reason, it might be said. Eliot stipulated that his correspondence could only be published under the editorship of his widow and added a memorandum to his will that 'I do not wish my executors to facilitate or countenance the writing of a biography of me.' As a result, the archives were off limits for decades, and a Chinese wall set around it, guarded by his widow, Faber and Faber, and the Eliot estate. Meanwhile, Valerie Eliot, as his literary executor, was working on the immense task of assembling and editing the letters. Scholars and would-be biographers could have access to the correspondence and manuscripts held in Yale, Texas, the Houghton Library and other archives, but were prevented from using them in a sustained way in print. In his pioneering 1984 life of Eliot, for example, Peter Ackroyd wrote: 'I am forbidden by the Eliot estate to quote from Eliot's published work, except for purposes of fair comment in a critical context, or to quote from Eliot's unpublished work or correspondence.'[6] In his 1992 study of literary estates, *Keepers of the Flame*, Ian Hamilton observed that 'if Mrs Eliot holds to the no-biography ruling, critics will have trouble reading the Eliot life into the work, and vice versa'.[7]

Eliot's own attitude towards the publication of letters is dramatised in his play *An Elder Statesman*, written when he was a Nobel Prize-winning elder statesman. In it, the distinguished politician Claverton is confronted, to his consternation, by Mrs Carghill, a former actress who has copies of his early romantic correspondence to her and tells him 'I read your letters every night.' In the subsequent confrontation, Eliot dwells on the letters' saleability ('They'll be worth a fortune to you, Maisie'), their reproduction, and their possible uses in court as evidence of indiscretions in his earlier life:

> Mrs Carghill . . . They would have figured at the trial, I suppose,
>   If there had been a trial. Don't you remember them?
> Lord Claverton: Vaguely. Were they very passionate?
> Mrs Carghill: They were very loving. Would you like to read them?
>   I'm afraid I can't show you the originals;
>   They're in my lawyer's safe. But I have photostats
>   Which are quite as good, I'm told. And I like to read them
>   In your own handwriting.[8]

The play dramatises Eliot's self-consciousness about the materiality of letters, their different kinds of value and their uses in biography, blackmail and court of law. It seems to have been triggered by his being 'disagreeably surprised' by Emily Hale's gift to Princeton of the archive of the intimate letters he wrote to her over a period of fifty years. Valerie Eliot records that the poet wrote that: 'her disposing of the letters in that way at that time threw some light upon the kind of interest which she took, or had come to take, in these letters. *The Aspern Papers* in reverse.'[9] As it happens, the Eliot–Hale letters also became the subject of Martha Cooley's *The Archivist* (1998), a fictional thriller in the tradition of *The Aspern Papers*, exploring the politics of the archive in a story involving a librarian, a young woman with a psychiatric history (like Eliot's first wife, Vivien), and Jewish scholars troubled by the poet's anti-Semitism. It tells how the archivist of an unnamed library which holds these Eliot letters turns out to have saved the envelopes but secretly burned the actual letters in obedience to what he took to be the poet's wishes.

Eliot's distrust of both letters and biography developed long before he became an elder statesman. In May 1930, having retrieved his youthful letters to his mother after her death, he reported just such an epistolary holocaust to his brother Henry:

> And I am glad to have the letters to make ashes of. I should never have wanted to read them again, with all the folly and selfishness; and I don't want anyone else ever to read them and possibly print them; and if I could destroy every letter I have ever written in my life I would do so before I die. I should like to leave as little biography as possible. So that's done and done with.[10]

The burning of these early letters destroyed a priceless record of his youthful correspondence, his early life in America and his intellectual development during the formative years in Harvard and Paris. The reasons for Eliot's hostility to biography are multiple, no doubt, but are clearly related to the domestic horror story of his first marriage. This is suggested by his comments to his brother Henry on 29 July 1927 that 'Unitarianism is a bad preparation for brass tacks like birth, copulation, death, hell, heaven and insanity', and that 'it often seems to me very bizarre that a person of my antecedents should have had a life like a bad Russian novel'.[11]

Eliot remained hostile to the publication of his correspondence until almost the end of his life. In the introduction to her edition of the first volume of letters in 1988, Valerie Eliot wrote that 'at the time of our marriage in 1957 I was dismayed to learn that my husband had forbidden future publication of his correspondence, because I appreciated its importance and fascination'.[12] The poet relented, she says, 'on condition that I did the selecting and editing'. The result was her landmark edition of *The Letters of T. S. Eliot* (1988), which opened the archive. A second volume was promised the following year, but the publication of the poet's correspondence then stalled, and later volumes failed to materialise. This caused not only frustration to Eliot scholars but a generalised suspicion towards the Eliot estate for guarding the gate of the archives and preventing access to biographers such as Lyndall Gordon, who in her two-volume life of the poet was unable to quote off-limits correspondence and manuscripts. The second volume of Gordon's biography, *Eliot's New Life*, appeared in the same year as Valerie Eliot's edition of the letters, and in her revised edition Gordon noted that the publication of that edition changed her impression that the poet was only 'adept at the distant letter' and that 'the letter was Eliot's least distinctive mode'.[13] In an early letter to Conrad Aiken from Oxford in 1914, for example, Eliot said 'I think one's letters ought to be about oneself ... Letters should be indiscretions – otherwise they are simply official bulletins.'[14] As epigraph to her 1988 edition, Mrs Eliot used a fragment from her husband's 1933 lecture on 'English Poets as Letter Writers':

> The desire to write a letter, to put down what you don't want anybody else to see but the person you are writing to ... is ineradicable. We want to confess ourselves in writing to a few friends, and we do not always feel that no one but those friends will ever read what we have written.[15]

Thanks to Valerie Eliot, we can now read his letters, including bulletins, indiscretions and (more rarely) confessions.

It was not until nearly thirty years after Volume One, however, that, as a result of a major change of policy by the Eliot estate, other scholars were invited to collaborate on the edition of the correspondence alongside new editions of the poetry and prose. I was drafted in to revise Volume One and produce a new Volume Two until John Haffenden took over as co-editor to carry through a full-scale edition. In his retrospective appreciation of Mrs Eliot's decades of work amassing and transcribing the correspondence, Haffenden notes that the result is 'a culturally priceless trove of tens of thousands of letters', which 'owes everything to Valerie Eliot'.[16] Unlike in *The Aspern Papers*, it was the keeper of the flame herself, as Haffenden records, who showed the necessarily ruthless dedication to acquiring the poet's papers, tracking down material, chasing correspondents, negotiating with libraries and overseeing the edition. Haffenden offers a nuanced account of her contradictory role as archivist of the correspondence on the one hand and person responsible for closing the door on biographers on the other. 'As the sole literary executor', she told *Time-Life* on 3 March 1970, 'I must carry out his instructions, and refuse any would-be biographer access to private papers and unpublished material.'[17] On the other hand, as she told Robert Giroux in 1966, she was always convinced that 'the letters will make a most marvellous autobiography and be a quarry for biographers 50 years hence!'[18]

More than fifty years hence, and since the relaunch of the edition with the first two volumes in 2009, another six equally massive volumes have appeared, taking his correspondence up to the mid-1930s. Despite the comic idea of leaving 'as little biography as possible', Eliot has left an epic 'quarry for biographers'. The bulk of it consists of 'official bulletins' about his professional life as writer, editor and publisher, which are of immense value to editors of his poetry and prose in tracing the composition of poems, articles and his responses to the work of other writers. The publication of the letters has given Eliot scholarship a new archival turn, comparable to that in Beckett studies, giving unequalled access to information about his stressful marriage, his cult of Charles Maurras and L'Action Française, his religious conversion, the daily grind of his editorial work at Faber and for *The Criterion*, his professional life as a man of letters (in many senses), and his friendship and correspondence with other intellectuals in England, Europe and America. It documents, often in excruciating detail, Eliot's punitive sense of public duty as critic, editor and publisher, but also his neurotic, vulnerable and passionate personal life and his many long-term friendships.

There are some unbearably 'private' ones, like the scrawled confessional letter to his intellectual sparring partner John Middleton Murry of April 1925, lifting the lid on the horror story of his first marriage:

> In the last ten years – gradually, but deliberately – I have made myself into
> a *machine*. I have done it deliberately – in order to endure, in order not to
> feel – *but it has killed V.* In leaving the bank I hope to become less a machine
> – but yet I am frightened – because I don't know what it will do to me – and
> to V. – should I come alive again. I have deliberately killed my senses – I have
> deliberately died – in order to go on with the outward form of living – This I
> did in 1915. What will happen if I live again?[19]

Such words cast an X-ray-like light on the psychological world of *The
Waste Land*. Indeed, the poem's 'I shall show you fear in a handful of
dust' is echoed in another letter to Murry where he says: 'I know that the
spring is Fear – a fear which I cannot account for. And I know that I have
killed *her*. And this terrible sense of the most subtle form of *guilt* is itself
paralysing and deadening.'[20] A genial letter of late 1927 to Geoffrey
Faber is revealing in a different way. There Eliot writes that, 'I have
found my own love of a woman enhanced, intensified and purified by
meditation on the Virgin', but then, less piously, recalls the 'minor pleasures of drunkenness and adultery', memories of a particular *canard aux
oranges* and 'a certain wine in Fontrevault'. He winds up by declaring:
'I take pleasure in Adam of St. Victor and in Paul Whiteman; in High
Mass at the Madeleine and in the Café des Ambassadeurs. Will you still
say that I am a Puritan ascetic?'[21] In a different vein, letters to friends
show the poet as comedian – from the early spoof cinematic letters to his
cousin Eleanor Hinkley on first arriving in Europe in 1914, to the bawdy
cod-anthropological ones to Bonamy Dobrée (or 'Bungamee') before
and after his conversion, and the *Uncle Remus* vaudeville-style letters to
Pound under the name of Possum. Like Prufrock, Eliot in Possum mode
was more than happy to be 'even at times, the Fool'.[22] Taken together,
the vast output of letters provides a complex, multi-dimensional portrait
of the man Virginia Woolf thought of as wearing a 'a four-piece suit',
and the poet himself thought 'How Unpleasant' to meet.[23] They offer
innumerable glimpses across the gulf between 'the man who suffers and
the mind which creates'.

The new online publication of Eliot's prose in eight volumes curated by
Ron Schuchard represents a parallel opening of the archival floodgates.
Six richly annotated volumes are now available, giving unparalleled
access to the full range of critical prose and cultural commentary by the
most influential literary critic of the twentieth century. As it announces,
'this eight-volume critical edition dramatically expands access to material that has been restricted or inaccessible in private and institutional
collections for almost fifty years'. Currently only available online, it
includes, we are told:

all of Eliot's collected essays, reviews, lectures, commentaries from *The Criterion*, and letters to editors, including more than 700 uncollected and 150 unpublished pieces from 1905 to 1965. Other highlights include essays from his student years at Smith Academy and Harvard and his graduate work at Harvard and Oxford, including his doctoral dissertation; unsigned, unidentified essays published in the *New Statesman* and the *Monist*; essays and reviews published in the *Egoist*, *Athenaeum*, *TLS*, *Dial*, *Art and Letters*; his Clark and Turnbull lectures on metaphysical poetry, Norton Lectures, Page-Barbour Lectures, Boutwood Lectures; unpublished essays, lectures, addresses from various archives; and transcripts of broadcasts, speeches, endorsements, and memorial tributes.[24]

Though Eliot might be horrified to find his Harvard student notes and later speeches for school, literary and ecclesiastical functions reprinted, this new, comprehensive record of his critical, philosophical and religious thinking is a unique record of his role as twentieth-century critical and cultural guru. It restores to the light of day many texts that Eliot chose not to republish – including reviews of contemporaries like Joyce, Stein and Pound, and a fascinating essay in French for *NRF* on the contemporary English novel, where he argues that 'nearly every contemporary novel' known to him is 'affected by psycho-analysis' or inspired by a desire to 'escape from psycho-analysis', and argues that Virginia Woolf reminds him of Conrad, 'having performed at Kew and at seaside watering places what Conrad performed in the tropics and south seas'.[25]

More importantly, perhaps, the *Complete Prose* enables us to trace in chronological order his development from novice reviewer, maverick literary theorist and political young fogey to the most influential Anglophone literary critic of his time, who in his Preface to *For Launcelot Andrewes* announced his position as being 'classicist in literature, royalist in politics, and anglo-catholic in religion'.[26] It reveals how selective and in many ways misleading Eliot's *Selected Essays* and other collections of critical prose are, and how much more various, unpredictable and wide-ranging he was as critic and commentator. Canonical essays like 'Tradition and the Individual Talent' and 'The Metaphysical Poets' now look different alongside lesser-known essays and reviews.

The first volume alone, covering the period 1905–18, contains twenty-six previously unpublished essays and nearly one hundred periodical pieces that have never been reprinted. It documents Eliot's thinking as a young philosopher in Harvard and Oxford, partly mitigating the absence of his early letters, as well as fleshing out his years as a greenhorn reviewer of philosophy and apprentice literary critic after arriving in England in 1914. The second volume, covering the period 1919–26, contains his most famous literary critical essays – 'Tradition and the Individual Talent', 'Hamlet', 'The Metaphysical Poets' and others –

but sets them in the unfolding, multifarious context of the 130 essays, reviews and letters to periodicals that he wrote in these astonishingly fertile years. Across the six volumes published so far, Eliot grows in cultural authority, with an increasingly reactionary agenda but also a surprising range of sympathies. The fascinating 'Letters from London', published in *The Dial* during the period when he was working on *The Waste Land*, provide an essential backdrop to the parallel representations of the 'Unreal City' of London in the poem, and ground the pseudo-Aristotelian hauteur of the critic of 'The Metaphysical Poets' in the material culture of the moment. Across the board, he shows himself to be a consistently intelligent, forensically focused and provocative critic, whether speaking of detective fiction or Jacobean plays, on contemporary literature or Anglican theology (though his polemical political editorialising is often inexplicably blinkered and dull).

The *Prose* documents Eliot in his other public roles as editor and lecturer (or broadcaster). The lecture is one of the less-recognised modernist genres, but practised to crucial effect by Pound, Marinetti, T. E. Hulme, Gertrude Stein, Wallace Stevens, Virginia Woolf, Paul Valéry and Joyce's Stephen Dedalus. Eliot did publish his Norton lectures at Harvard as *The Use of Poetry and the Use of Criticism* as well as publishing (but not reprinting) the politically controversial *After Strange Gods* (1934), but not his Clark lectures at Cambridge of 1926, *The Varieties of Metaphysical Poetry*, which are a crucial document of his thinking about poetry, philosophy and religion, bringing together his interest in the English Metaphysicals, Dante and the French Symbolists during the moment of his self-reinvention after *The Waste Land* and on the verge of his conversion. Ron Schuchard gave us a useful earlier edition of the lectures in *Varieties of Metaphysical Poetry* (1993) but it is valuable to have access to all of Eliot's lectures in the new edition. These include the lecture series listed above, as well as many unpublished lectures, including the fascinating ones on Shakespeare given in Edinburgh in 1937, as well as transcripts of Eliot's numerous occasional speeches and broadcasts, including school addresses and speeches to Anglican conferences. We see Eliot taking up the mantle of public intellectual adopted by so many of his New England family predecessors, always dutifully but sometimes in reactionary English Anglican guise, and occasionally at his most questionable, as in the long-banished *After Strange Gods*, his 'Primer of Modern Heresy'. There he argues oppressively that 'a right tradition for us must also be a Christian tradition', as well as claiming notoriously that 'reasons of race and religion combine to make any large number of free-thinking Jews undesirable'.[27]

Most of the ephemeral lectures and essays are familiar to Eliot scholars but have not been widely available, and they are given new life by way of nuanced contextualisation and annotation. Many, however, have never been identified or circulated before, having emerged as a result of detective work by Ron Schuchard and his collaborators. They include a long-lost lecture on 'A Neglected Aspect of Chapman', delivered at Cambridge in 1924, which argued that, in Chapman's plays, 'the personages are acting and accepting, inevitable roles in *this* world, and the real centre of the action is in another Kingdom'. The claim casts a light on the poems of 'The Hollow Men' (with its 'death's dream kingdom') that he was working on at the time. It also casts a light on Eliot's own sense of playing different intellectual and worldly roles, with another reality in the background – and about to come into the foreground: by his brave new life as an Anglican churchman and eventual doyen of Lambeth. We tend to associate Eliot with modernism, but, as he says in a 'Commentary' in *The Criterion*, he saw theological 'Modernism' as a 'mental blight which can afflict the whole of the intelligence of the time, whether within or without the Church', and for much of his later career he writes – often brilliantly – as a theological Eliot Agonistes, setting himself against the spirit of the age.

Eliot's huge prose archive documents the sheer scale and intensity of his Arnoldian mission. It also invites us to reconsider the relationship between the relatively small body of poetry and prose he collected in his lifetime, on the one hand, and his writing life as critic, social commentator, churchman and editor of *The Criterion* and at Faber and Faber, on the other. There can be little doubt that Eliot himself, though he preserved much of his correspondence, would have deplored the scale and nature of the biographical record that has emerged as well as its invitation to biographies such as Robert Crawford's *Young Eliot* (2015).

In a newly reprinted review about Shakespeare's sonnets, Eliot commends J. M. Robertson for leaving Shakespeare 'with the dignity of his mystery and his privacy'. Observing that 'nowhere is the public, in general, more at fault than in its decipherings of the meanings of poems according to some "experience"', he says 'I do not say that poetry is not "autobiographical": but this autobiography is written by a foreign man in a foreign tongue, which can never be translated.'[28] Making available the complete prose and letters may not resolve this, but it certainly makes the exercise of translation a lot more viable.

Eliot's poetry: the canon and the bureau drawer

The 'foreign tongue' of Eliot's poetic canon has also been transformed by the explosion of archival material erupting into print. In 1919, soon after the publication of *Prufrock and Other Observations* (1917), Eliot told J. H. Woods in a letter that, 'My reputation in London is built upon one small volume of verse, and is kept up by printing two or three more poems in a year. The only thing that matters is that these should be perfect in their kind.'[29] To a large extent *Collected Poems 1909–1962* (1963) was conceived with comparable values in mind, condensing the work of fifty years into about 240 pages, with the poems of each volume or work grouped together and others gathered as 'Unfinished Poems', 'Minor Poems' and 'Occasional Verses'. In the immediate wake of Eliot's death, Valerie Eliot republished *Poems Written in Early Youth* (1967), originally collected and privately printed by John Hayward in 1950, documenting Eliot's poetic beginnings in the Harvard years. However, it was with her publication of *The Waste Land: A Facsimile and Transcript of the Original Drafts, Including the Comments of Ezra Pound* in 1971 that the impact of the archive first impinged on public understanding of Eliot's career.

The facsimile was made possible by the revelation that the New York Public Library was in possession of the early manuscripts Eliot gave to John Quinn in 1922, an archive that Eliot himself valued for its documentation of Pound's seminal role in shaping the mass of unstable, polyphonic, protean material he had been writing in the period culminating in his breakdown of 1921 and recovery in Lausanne, though he said 'naturally I hope the portions which I have suppressed will never appear in print'.[30] Valerie Eliot's authoritatively edited facsimile cast unprecedented light on the genesis of this landmark of poetic modernism, with its new forms of order and disorder, fragmentation and assemblage, setting it in the context of his 'aboulie and emotional derangement' and treatment in Lausanne. Indeed, the drafts themselves soon began to acquire the status of primary texts in their own right (rather as the 1799 *Prelude* of Wordsworth and Goethe's *Ur-Faust* have done). It also provides evidence for some of the more unsavoury aspects of Eliot's sensibility, in particular his anti-Semitism ('Full fathom five your Bleistein lie / Under the flatfish and the squids. / Graves's Disease in a dead jew's eyes / Where the crabs have eat the lids'), material which had been largely 'edited out' in the text published in *The Criterion* and *The Dial* in 1922.[31] Its publication might be said to have done for the modern poetic archive what the poem did for 'modernist poetry' in the 1920s.

Eliot gave *The Waste Land* drafts to John Quinn in 1922 at the same time as he sold Quinn the notebook in which he had written his earlier poems, dating back to the Harvard and Paris years. He described it in a letter to Quinn of 21 September 1922:

> The leather-bound notebook is one which I started in 1909 and in which I entered all my work of that time as I wrote it, so that it is the only original manuscript barring of course rough scraps and notes which were destroyed at the time, in existence. You will find a great many sets of verse which have never been printed and which I am sure you will agree never ought to be printed, and in putting them into your hands, I beg you fervently to keep them to yourself and see that they never are printed.[32]

Despite Eliot's fervent plea, these poems were published in 1996 as *Inventions of the March Hare: Poems 1909–1917*, edited by Christopher Ricks, accompanied with an elaborate editorial apparatus and notes. This contained early drafts of all but five of the poems published in *Prufrock and Other Observations* (1917) and another twenty-seven unpublished poems post-dating *The Harvard Advocate* poems published in *Poems Written in Early Youth*, as well as a further seventeen poems 'from loose papers in the Notebook' and 'bawdy verses which survive on leaves (now at Yale)'. The result was a 400–page book with nearly fifty new poems, a couple in French, recording Eliot's apprenticeship in Boston and Paris in which he 'modernised himself' (in Pound's words) in such Frenchified experiments as 'Embarquement pour Cythère', 'Petit Epître' and such post-Laforguian exercises in metropolitan psychic dissonance as 'Interlude in London' and 'Suite Clownesque'. In one ironic reflection on how 'The Absolute sits waiting, till we get / All tangled up and end ourselves inside her', Eliot writes: 'He said I am put together with a pot and scissors / Out of old clippings / No one took the trouble to make an article.'[33] This could be read as a prophetic comment on *Inventions of the March Hare* itself, but that volume's publication transformed our understanding of Eliot's development as a new kind of Anglophone poet.

However, with the publication in 2015 of *The Poems of T. S. Eliot* in two volumes and over 2,000 pages edited by Christopher Ricks and Jim McCue, the poetic canon has been transformed. Prufrock famously asked 'Do I dare / Disturb the universe?', and Ricks and McCue certainly dared to disturb the Eliot universe with their massive editorial intervention. With this edition, material from the archives exponentially expands the canon of Eliot's work with hundreds of pages of minor, occasional and throwaway verse from letters and private papers, and an editorial construction of the urtext of *The Waste Land* described as 'A Composite'. The edition has an epic ratio of editorial commentary to actual poetic text. In Volume One, 350 pages of poems are followed by 850 pages of notes and commentary, supplemented by another 680 pages of textual history in Volume Two. The 'Notes' to *The Waste Land*, once thought of as the height of modernist obscurantism, fade into insignificance beside the 160 pages of critical commentary and 50 pages of textual notes in the new edition.

Meticulously edited, documented and annotated, the new edition not only draws on manuscripts and typescripts of letters and poems and drafts from the archive but is now an indispensable archival resource in itself. It brings unpredictably informative material of every kind to bear on the major poems such as *Ash Wednesday* and *Four Quartets*, as well as *Old Possum's Book of Practical Cats*. These are now inserted amidst huge amounts of playful, parodic and obscene verse in Eliot's comic Possum persona – indeed it might be described as an Opus Possumus – as well as a labyrinth of other new material from the archive. Eliot is revealed as a fluent and prolific entertainer able to conjure up light verse, literary pastiche, satire and nonsense for his coterie of friends and children of friends – a follower of Edward Lear, who is also an agile practitioner of Clerihews, spoof Scots ballads and grotesque satirical bawdy. Readers of Eliot's letters know many of his obscene and cartoon-like Bolo verses, but Ricks and McCue have created an extended editorial composite entitled *The Columbiad*, forty-nine stanzas long. At 432 lines this extravagantly scatological and pornographic fantasia weighs in at almost exactly the same size as *The Waste Land*. The stanzas it includes are drawn from a notebook dating from 1915 and extracts included in letters between 1927 and 1932, with extra material later copied by Eliot in *Valerie's Own Book of Poems by T. S. Eliot* (two exercise books into which, according to Ricks and McCue, the poet copied out 'a wide range of his poetry, in blue ink, on rectos only . . . perhaps in the late 1950s'.[34] The editorial construction of *The Columbiad* attempts to recreate the contents of an apparently lost small black notebook in the Beinecke, which David Moody reported contained 'a fair copy of the full King Bolo or Colombo epic, written in a very small neat hand'. This certainly suggests Eliot had an investment in it as a complete poem, but he might have baulked at its occupying as much space as *The Waste Land*.

The expanded archival Eliot shows him as the kind of poet he invoked at the end of *The Use of Poetry and the Use of Criticism*: 'He would like to be something like a popular entertainer, and be able to think his own thoughts behind a tragic or a comic mask.'[35] The new edition enables us to gauge the creative continuum between Eliot as Possum-style entertainer or Bolovian bard and the poet of 'The Love-Song of J. Alfred Prufrock', 'Sweeney Agonistes' and *The Waste Land*, with their combination of polyphony and allusiveness, tragi-comedy and ironic dissonance. Nevertheless, the sheer scale of the comic and occasional verse drawn from the archives highlights the discrepancy between the prolific, light-versifying entertainer and the intransigent oeuvre Eliot himself curated, which was represented by the formally ambitious, intellectually demanding poems of *Prufrock and Other Observations*, *Poems* (1920), *The Waste Land*, *Ash Wednesday* and *Four Quartets*. One of the early poems from the *Inventions of the March Hare* notebook, the third section of 'Goldfish (Essence of Summer Magazines)', lists the 'the débris of the year / Of which the autumn takes its toll', enumerating 'Old letters, programmes, unpaid bills / Photographs, tennis shoes and more, / Ties, postal cards, the mass that fills / The limbo of a bureau drawer'.[36] The Eliot archive, long left in the 'limbo' of the Kensington flat and great libraries, has now fed its vast debris into the monumental volumes of Eliot's correspondence and the two volumes of the *Poems*, offering an enormously more comprehensive poetic and epistolary literary repertoire than we or he could have imagined.

The result is a hugely expanded poetic oeuvre surrounded by a labyrinth of editorial, contextual, biographical and bibliographical information. It offers readers an immensely more informed access to Eliot's poetry, including the good, the bad and the ugly. There are times, though, when the reader will scratch their head and wonder where this leaves the small body of superlative poems Eliot saw as his legacy. He defined a major poet as 'one the whole of whose work we ought to read, in order fully to appreciate any part of it', but the relation of part to 'the whole' in his own work looks very different after this *Poems*.[37] Is the uncanny self-reflective music of the 'major' poems in danger of being buried under the fabulous avalanche from the archives?

Where are the eagles and the trumpets?
Buried beneath some snow-deep Alps.[38]

Derek Mahon: raw material and the rage for order

The case of Mahon is different, since the poet himself, like many of his contemporary Irish poets, came to an arrangement – or possibly a Faustian pact – to sell his papers. Mahon was the beneficiary of the fact that, as Stephen Ennis reports, 'Linda Matthews and Ron Schuchard had established the Mahon archive at Emory University.'[39] Since an agreement signed in 1991, when he was characteristically in debt and crisis, Mahon has regularly submitted his archive in instalments to the Library, including drafts of poems, letters, documents, notes and fragments, and in some cases the ties, postcards and newspaper clippings mentioned in Eliot's poem. This provided Mahon with a much-needed income. The archive includes not only important correspondence but also detailed evidence about the process of composition of his later poems, like Yeats's archive in the National Library in Dublin or Elizabeth Bishop's in Vassar, or Proust's in Paris. It also, however, like Marianne Moore's notebooks at the Rosenbach, documents the raw material used in poems, such as an article about birds escaped from the Bronx Zoo used for a section of *The Hudson Letter*, and period views of Cobh that an Irish emigrant might have seen, or, among the material for *The Yellow Book*, a photocopy of definitions of 'yellow' and 'gold' plus a printout of 216 entries for titles with the word 'Yellow' in it, and a piece from *The Irish Times* about 'Howth Head to be the last "manned" Irish lighthouse' (which contributes to 'Section XIX On the Automation of the Irish Lights'). There is also a scrap of paper advertising a 'Symposium on Clutter' which talks about 'a poetics of clutter' and about 'rethinking the recognised forms of our relations to objects' in relation to 'litter, waste, junk, ephemera collecting, recycling, antiquarianism fetishism, museums, the home, memorabilia, memory, mess, disorder, space and freedom'.[40] All this bears on the form and preoccupations of the sequence on the legacy of the 1890s, which is built out of and conceptually projects bits and pieces of recycled material.

As I noted in my study of his poetry, when in *The Yellow Book* Mahon speaks of night-writing 'blind' in a 'bedside notebook', this could refer to the A4 notebook headed 'Scrapbook 1996–7' in the Emory archives.[41] It certainly contains early drafts of lines with plans and ideas for *The Yellow Book,* while in its early pages we also find a reference to '"materials" scholarship' – thus anticipating one of its major concerns. I suggested the archivally conceived, palimpsest-like *The Yellow Book* itself could be seen, on the model of Walter Benjamin's *Arcades Project*, as a reflection of 'materials scholarship' as a 'vertiginous mirror of modernity'. It also offers a vantage point for looking at the fetishism of the archive itself in all its clutter, and documents the emergence of 'style' from its raw materials.

The drafts in the archive of *The Hudson Letter* and *The Yellow Book* – or *New York Time* and *The Decadence* as they are now called – and of Mahon's subsequent volumes document the slow process of poetic composition and publication of the two long sequences from the 1990s, from notes and multiple drafts to published texts and their revisions, as well as comparably multiple drafts of the self-contained lyrics of *Harbour Lights* and afterwards. Eliot sold the MS notebook of

Inventions of the March Hare to John Quinn and gave him the MSS to *The Waste Land*, but he did not expect these to be made available within his lifetime, and the drafts were published only after his death and under the editorship of his wife. In the case of modern poets like Mahon and his Irish contemporaries, the sale, acquisition, cataloguing and accessing of their archive have become an integral part of the rhythm of production as well as a crucial source of economic income. Well-heeled patrons of the past like John Quinn have largely been replaced or displaced by the well-financed libraries, keen to invest in the soft power of the literary archive, conserved, as Derrida insists, in the name of the future.[41] This has meant a new kind of access in the present to the workshop of living poets – the workshop, but also, potentially, the personal and professional correspondence, diaries (though Mahon's diaries in the archive have the entries for each day totally blacked out after it has passed) and personal documents; ranging from family birthday cards to letters such as the long, reflective and often playfully comic but also uniquely revealing ones from the USA and Canada that Mahon sent to his friends Michael and Edna Longley back in Ireland. His first extended Letters from America became studies in place and displacement that are in many ways a model for his many later letter poems, from 'Beyond Howth Head' to *The Hudson Letter* from New York, and 'Resistance Days' from Paris (which, again, the archives document, as the poem was patiently elaborated to mimic a time-and-place bound letter).

In Mahon's case, the archive opens up the poet's relationship to what the notebook calls 'materials scholarship', his plundering of other texts, the relationship between criticism and creation, and his principle of composition by way of *bricolage* and revision. Like Beethoven's Notebooks, or Leonardo's, the archive offers us an unparalleled point of entry to the poet's creative process – the work of selection, fine tuning and rejection, the route to the roads taken, as well as evidence of the roads not taken – the sections on 'Nostradamus' and 'Dracula' (or 'Nosferatu') in *The Yellow Book*, for example. Among the materials for *The Hudson Letter*, for example, there is a five-line draft or plan of Section II ('Out There') headed 'Last night', which reads 'madwoman / barking dog (full moon) / furniture mover / car symphonist; Gershwin hand: NY Symphony / Harley Davidson', anticipating the trajectory fully orchestrated in the final poem. In a draft for 'Bangor Requiem' in *The Yellow Book*, an elegiac response to his mother Maisie's death, we likewise get a one-sentence note on 'Mum's rage for order', which, with its allusion to his own early poem with that Stevensian title, anticipates his line in *The Yellow Book* 'You too were an artist, a rage-for-order freak / setting against a man's aesthetic of cars and golf / your ornaments and other breakable stuff'. It also, in a sense, captures something of the shaping force within the sequence, with its combination of witty aestheticism and chaotic, miscellaneously amassed journalistic detail, and suggesting a biographical dimension to the poet's fanatical commitment to it.[43]

The publication of *The Waste Land: A Facsimile and Transcript of the Original Drafts* was a landmark in the genetic documentation of modern poetry, and it may be that in the years to come, there will be digitised versions of the Mahon archive, or the comparably rich, multiple notebooks and drafts of W. S. Graham, offering us searchable public incarnations of the messy business of transforming notes into poems that is recorded in the archives but that could never be reduced to book-form like *The Waste Land* (as in Ricks and McCue's 'Composite text'). For the moment, the archive records the work in the workshop, a triumph of 'materials scholarship', documenting the struggle to produce order out of the raw materials for the poems, whether these are personal experiences or other texts, jotted notes, newspaper clippings, research printouts or existing works of art.

Robert Stilling, in a chapter on *The Yellow Book*, notes how self-consciously Mahon participated in the archivisation of his own work, as well as suggesting that *The Yellow Book* is not only supremely conscious of archives in relation to *The Aspern Papers*, but was to some degree written for, and in response to, the poet's archive in Emory. Stilling writes:

> It is also clear from correspondence in the collection that during his 1996 visit to Emory, Mahon met with the curators of the Manuscript and Rare Book Library and consulted with them on improving their bibliographic database of his papers ... Several photos in the archive show Mahon presumably examining his own papers in the tenth-floor reading room as the librarians proudly look on. Just two months after Mahon's visit, one of the manuscript librarians wrote to find out if Mahon would be willing to grant them permission to digitise two manuscript drafts and mount them on their web site. The librarian also asks whether Mahon would be willing to have a recording of himself reading one of his poems posted to the library web site. A later letter confirms that this was done, while other letters indicate that Mahon offered advice regarding Emory's holdings of work by other Northern Irish poets.[44]

In a sense, nothing could be less like Eliot's hostile relationship with his prospective archive, or less like Valerie Eliot's flat in Kensington with its vast, personally curated archive of her husband's work.

Ironically, the first biography of the Northern Irish poet was undertaken by Stephen Ennis, who, as Director of Emory University's Manuscript, Archives and Rare Book Library, was responsible for handling the Mahon papers for some time. In his Preface, Ennis notes that previous commentators on Mahon such as Edna Longley and myself 'have been complicit in separating the poems from the life'.[45] Drawing on the archives as well as interviews with the poet and various friends, Ennis seeks to undo that critical separation between poems and life, arguing that Mahon was writing 'an autobiography from the very beginning, and his poems, prose and dramatic writing offer the most intimate glimpse of a soul in the making'.[46] Strangely, however, he offers remarkably few glimpses into the process of the poems in the making by drawing on the drafts in the archive. He prefers to foreground a narrative of biographical trauma, focused on a possible car accident, a near-drowning in the Liffey, and the high price paid by the poet in the fallout from his chronic alcoholism and broken marriage. There are certainly times when Mahon's life, like Eliot's, is 'like a bad Russian novel', but if the archives offer plenty of evidence documenting this, they also document the combination of inspiration and hard work that transformed this raw material into an astonishing body of poetry intensely aware of a larger cultural, geographical and ecological universe beyond the autobiographical. As Mahon wrote in one of his poems about visual artists, 'Wave Shadow': 'A gleaming boardwalk bridges the divide / from raw experience to the other side.'[47] Towards the end of his biography, Stephen Ennis records that Mahon was becoming 'increasingly anxious about the story it would tell', wanted to read the manuscript and was unhappy when he could not. As a result, he says, the poet and his archivist biographer decided to 'go our separate ways'.[48] The admission gives a new resonance to Mahon's queried jotting in his notebook: 'The Aspern Papers: the Emory archive?'

Notes

1. James, Henry, *The Aspern Papers*, in *The Complete Stories 1884–1891* (New York: Library of America, 2013), p. 229.
2. Auden, W. H., *Selected Poems*, ed. Edward Mendelson (London: Faber and Faber, 1979), p. 82.
3. Mahon Papers, Emory University, 'Scrapbook, 1996–1997'. MS 689.
4. Eliot, T. S., 'Tradition and the Individual Talent', in *Selected Essays* (London: Faber and Faber, 1932), p. 18.
5. Mahon, Derek, *New Collected Poems* (Loughcrew: Gallery Press, 2011), p.19.
6. Ackroyd, Peter, *T. S. Eliot* (London: Hamish Hamilton, 1984), p. 10.
7. Hamilton, Ian, *Keepers of the Flame: Literary Estates and the Rise of Biography* (London: Pimlico, 1992).
8. Eliot, T. S., *Collected Plays* (London: Faber and Faber, 1962), p. 325.

9. Cited in *The Letters of T. S. Eliot: 1898–1922*, ed. Valerie Eliot (London: Faber and Faber, 1988), p. xvi.

10. Letter to Henry Eliot, 25 May 1930, in *The Letters of T. S. Eliot. Vol. 5: 1930–31*, ed. Valerie Eliot and John Haffenden (London: Faber and Faber, 2014), p. 203.

11. *The Letters of T. S. Eliot. Vol. 3: 1926–27*, ed. Valerie Eliot and John Haffenden (London: Faber and Faber, 2012), p. 228.

12. *Letters of T. S. Eliot: 1898–1922*, p. xv.

13. Gordon, Lyndall, *T. S. Eliot: An Imperfect Life* (London: Vintage, 1998), p. ix.

14. *Letters of T. S. Eliot*, p. 75.

15. Ibid., p. v.

16. *Letters of T. S. Eliot. Vol. 5*, pp. xix–xxxvii.

17. Interview with Thomas Dozier, *Time-Life*, 3 March 1970, cited in *Letters of T. S. Eliot: Vol. 5*, p. xxxiii.

18. Letter to Robert Giroux, August 1966, cited in *Letters of T. S. Eliot: Vol. 5*, p. xxxiii.

19. *The Letters of T. S. Eliot. Vol. 2: 1923–1925*, ed. Valerie Eliot and Hugh Haughton (London: Faber and Faber, 2009), p. 627.

20. Ibid., p. 632.

21. *Letters of T. S. Eliot. Vol. 3*, pp. 711–13.

22. Eliot, T. S., *The Poems of T. S. Eliot. Vol. 1: Collected and Uncollected Poems*, ed. Christopher Ricks and Jim McCue (London: Faber and Faber, 2015), p. 9.

23. Virginia Woolf, cited in Gordon, *An Imperfect Life* (London: Vintage, 1998), p. 142.

24. See <https://muse.jhu.edu/book/32733> (accessed 30 April 2018).

25. *The Complete Prose of T. S. Eliot: The Critical Edition. Vol. 3: Literature, Politics, Belief, 1927–1929*, ed. Frances Dickey, Jennifer Formichelli and Ronald Schuchard (Baltimore: Johns Hopkins University Press), p. 91.

26. Eliot, T. S., *For Lancelot Andrewes: Essays on Style and Order* (London: Faber and Faber, 1928), p. 7.

27. Eliot, T. S., *After Strange Gods: A Primer of Modern Heresy* (London: Faber and Faber, 1934), pp. 20–1.

28. *Complete Prose of T. S. Eliot. Vol. 3*, pp. 37–8.

29. *The Letters of T. S. Eliot. Vol. 1: 1898–1922 (Revised Edition)*, ed. Valerie Eliot and Hugh Haughton (London: Faber and Faber, 2009), pp. 338–9.

30. Ibid., p. 748.

31. Eliot, T. S., *The Waste Land: A Facsimile and Transcript of the Original Drafts, Including the Comments of Ezra Pound*, ed. Valerie Eliot (London: Faber and Faber, 1971), p. 121.

32. *Letters of T. S. Eliot. Vol. 1 (Rev. Edn)*, p. 748.

33. Eliot, T. S., *Inventions of the March Hare: Poems 1909–1917*, ed. Christopher Ricks (London: Faber and Faber, 1996), p. 71.

34. Eliot, T. S., *The Poems of T. S. Eliot. Vol. 2: Practical Cats and Further Verses*, ed. Christopher Ricks and Jim McCue (London: Faber and Faber, 2015), p. 304.

35. Eliot, T. S., *The Use of Poetry and the Use of Criticism* (London: Faber and Faber, 1933), p. 154.

36. Eliot, *Inventions of the March Hare*, p. 29.
37. Eliot, T. S., 'What is Minor Poetry?', in *On Poetry and Poets* (London: Faber and Faber, 1957), p. 47.
38. *Poems of T. S. Eliot. Vol. 1*, p. 39.
39. Ennis, Stephen, *After the Titanic: A Life of Derek Mahon* (Dublin: Gill & Macmillan, 2014), p. 243.
40. Mahon Papers, Emory University, 'Scrapbook, 1996–1997'. MS 689.
41. Haughton, Hugh, *The Poetry of Derek Mahon* (Oxford: Oxford University Press, 2007), p. 271.
42. See Derrida, Jacques, *Archive Fever: A Freudian Impression*, trans. Eric Prenowitz (Chicago: University of Chicago Press, 1996).
43. Mahon, *New Collected Poems*, p. 226.
44. Stilling, Robert, *Beginning at the End: Decadence, Modernism, and Postcolonial Poetry* (Cambridge, MA: Harvard University Press, 2018). References in quotation to: Mahon Papers, Emory. MS 689. I.8.3. MARBL; MS 689 V.44.21. MARBL; MS 689. I.8.1. MARBL; MS 689. I.8.2.
45. Ennis, *After the Titanic*, p. 3.
46. Ibid., p. 258.
47. Mahon, *New Collected Poem*, p. 305.
48. Ennis, *After the Titanic*, pp. 257–8.

Chapter 3

Archival Poetics: Containing Multitudes

Mark Byers

In 1936 Ezra Pound received a request from Charles D. Abbott, Director of the new Lockwood Library at the University of Buffalo. Abbott was looking for 'worksheets' (manuscripts and notes) produced in the composition of a single poem, requests for which he was sending out to fifty contemporary poets writing in English.[1] Pound's opinion of the project – which would provide the seed of the Buffalo Poetry Collection – was not encouraging. In his view, the new Buffalo archive was exploiting 'Creative writing' in order to 'support passivity and accumulators'; it was doing nothing 'toward production'.[2] 'I don't care a damn', he added, 'about storing mss / in a safe'.[3]

The irony of Pound's cranky response to Abbott, however, was that his own work of 'production' at the time, the *Cantos*, was steering modernist poetics ever more firmly into the arms of the archive. Following closely on the citational practice of *The Waste Land*, which he famously attacked with a blue pencil, the 'Malatesta' cantos (1923) had already heralded a movement towards research-based and archival poetics. Drawing on early printed books and primary documents in libraries and archives throughout Italy, the sequence – which draws up a nearly Cubist portrait of the fifteenth-century *condottiere* Sigismondo Pandolfo Malatesta – refigures long-form poetics as a genre of both original research and textual curation.[4]

The *objet trouvé* of Dada practice, as well as the Cubist collage, suggest some parallels with Pound's creation by assembly.[5] Bibliographical precedents might also be found in the scrapbooks, commonplace books and *zibaldone* which had been popular in Europe since the Renaissance. The 'Malatesta' cantos dispense with lyric expression for a model of poetic activity as *construction*, what Charles Olson would describe as 'putting things together / which had not previously / fit'.[6] In the 'Malatesta' cantos, Pound is, as A. David Moody puts it, the 'active intelligence of his materials'; the authorial dark matter behind a constellation of disparate texts.[7] The result is an archive reproduced through violent compression and volatilisation; a cache in which historical materials speak through sheer force of juxtaposition.[8]

The long poem as miscellany, a disjunctive assemblage of found texts and original research, provided an extensible precedent for later modernist poetry, from William Carlos Williams's *Paterson* and Charles Reznikoff's *Testimony: The United States (1885–1915): Recitative* to Charles Olson's *The Maximus Poems*. A series of recent works, including the book-length poems of Susan Howe, Anne Carson's *Nox* (2010) and Claudia Rankine's *Citizen* (2014), enlarge further upon a modernist practice which conceived of the long poem as a curated *space*; a physical or bibliographical environment in which the materials of history are jammed into unanticipated relations and new frames of reference.

In so far as they represent history spatially rather than linearly – in the form of assemblage rather than narrative – these works are suggestive not only of the commonplace book or scrapbook but also of the physical archive. As Paul Stephens has recently argued, 'avant-garde poetry has been centrally concerned with technologies of communication, data storage, and bureaucratic control – not simply rejecting those technologies, but also adopting and commenting on them'.[9] The technology of the archive is prominent among these, suggesting varieties of information organisation that resist conventional narrative trajectories and reading practices. However, unlike the conventional repository, with its claims for transparency and objectivity, these assemblages do not conceal their own work of historical representation. Rather, the modernist long poem as archive foregrounds the selection, reproduction and arrangement of found and original materials as a primary form of historical interpretation.

In this way, the archival long poem – from Pound and Olson to Howe and Carson – might also be understood under the sign of modernist historiography; a practice which has been the subject of significant recent inquiries by Robert Lehman and Mandy Bloomfield.[10] In both of these accounts, modernism rejects prior traditions of history writing in order to foreground – as Lehman puts it – the 'relationship between historical representation and literary form'.[11] While Lehman recognises this in the work of Pound and Eliot, Bloomfield's exemplars are Pound and Walter Benjamin, both of whose accumulative and archival practices serve to 'rethink the philosophy and aesthetics of writing history'.[12] More particularly, Bloomfield understands the *Cantos* and the *Arcades Project* as contesting a model of history as 'continuous, progressive, and unitary'; a model closely involved with 'dominant ideologies within modernity'.[13]

As a spatial more than a narrative construction, the long poem as archive provided modernism with a medium ideally suited to historiographical critique. Whether letters from a fifteenth-century mailbag (Pound), court records from across the United States (Reznikoff) or photographs of an estranged brother (Carson), curating the historical record becomes a means of calling into question not only the facts of history but historicity itself; the framing and interpretation of the past within the present. Indeed, the spatial practices of literary modernism – parataxis, collage, 'COMPOSITION BY FIELD' – foster critical approaches to the writing of history which extend even to a critique of archival form itself.[14]

Containing multitudes

In presenting and arranging, resisting the temptation to comment or embroider, Pound's poet assumes the role of curator rather than a conventionally 'creative' writer (albeit one touched by the violent energies of Vorticism).[15] This curatorial practice favours the 'Luminous Detail' over the abstract or generic, identifying history with dynamic assemblages of specifics rather than the narratives of traditional historiography.[16] The arc of works such as Gibbons's *The History of the Decline and Fall of the Roman Empire* is replaced by a version of history writing as the disjunctive collection of high-concentration fact.

That modernism's reorganising of historical representation was explosively politicised would have been clear not only from the 'Malatesta' cantos but also from contemporary cinema, above all Sergei Eisenstein's *Battleship Potemkin* (1925). The turn to montage, assemblage or 'found' materials offered a shock to the conventions of historiography and new ways of organising the minor or colloquial detail in relation to larger historical events. These formal possibilities would continue to be explored in subsequent interwar works, particularly in the United States. In Muriel Rukeyser's *The Book of the Dead* (1938), for instance, the potential of the form for social activism is reinterpreted for the era of the Popular Front.[17]

Published in Rukeyser's second book, *U.S. 1* (1938), *The Book of the Dead* collects a range of perspectives on the 1931 Hawk's Nest Tunnel disaster in West Virginia, in which up to five thousand men died after mining silica without safety apparatus. In around half of its twenty sections, the dominant perspective or subject-position in the poem is that of an unnamed narrator, whose presence in the text recalls the voice-over in documentary film.[18] However, this narration only provides a frame for other forms of testimony, including lyrics, poetic narratives, monologues and adapted sections from original source texts. The friction between these forms makes for a polyvocality which is, however, almost unanimous; the poems mount as evidence against Union Carbide and its criminal indifference to the welfare of its (predominantly African American) workers. The most potent testimony is perhaps that of the social worker Philippa Allen before a House subcommittee of the Committee on Labor in 1932:

— You like the State of West Virginia very much, do you not?
— I do very much, in the summertime.
— How much time have you spent in West Virginia?
— During the summer of 1934, when I was doing social work
    down there, I first heard of what we were pleased to call
    the Gauley tunnel tragedy, which involved about 2,000
    men.
— What was their salary?
— It started at 40¢ and dropped to 25¢ an hour.
— You have met these people personally?
— I have talked to people; yes.
  According to estimates of contractors
  2,000 men were
    employed there
    period, about 2 years
    drilling, 3.75 miles of tunnel.
  To divert water (from New River)
  to a hydroelectric plant (at Gauley Junction).
The rock through which they were boring was of a high silica content.
In tunnel No.1 it ran 97–99% pure silica.
The contractors
    knowing pure silica
    30 years' experience
    must have known danger for every man[19]

In the total fabric of the poem, the factual power of these lines derives partly from their position immediately following 'West Virginia'; a poem which provides a snapshot history of the state from the expedition of Thomas Batts and Robert Fallam in 1671 to the Civil War. That poem had ended on a note of natural and economic resurgence: 'Live country filling west, / knotted the glassy rivers; / like valleys, opening mines, / coming to life'.[20] Coming after this, Allen's testimony – excerpted from the *Congressional Record* – represents a conspicuous shift of perspective; a turn from an abundant West Virginian landscape to a fatal one, and from 'poetic' topographic description to congressional testimony given under oath.

But the intervention of this documentary text has broader implications for *The Book of the Dead*. As Tim Dayton has shown, Rukeyser does not quite quote verbatim from the *Congressional Record*; Allen's testimony is reordered in order to establish her 'authority' as a witness.[21] Even so, the inclusion of readymade material from the congressional archive refigures not only the genre of the poem but also its textual status. That is, the incorporation of non-poetic material effectively transforms the poem from an exclusively linguistic artefact into a curated space or repository; an archive of documentary testimonies (this is perhaps why Rukeyser identifies the poem as itself a 'book' even though it is collected in *U.S. 1*).

While material from the *Congressional Record* corroborates the other testimonies in the sequence, its incorporation into the overall structure of *The Book of the Dead* also supports Rukeyser's broader experiment in history writing. More concretely, *The Book of the Dead* proposes a form of documentary witnessing in which 'history' is collected across multiple scales and written from a series of formal, institutional and social perspectives. Framing the long poem as a curated space, a repository of found material, historical narration and topographical description, the assemblage imagines history writing as both textual curation and investigative fieldwork; not a linear narrative but a gathering and compilation.[22] The long poem, from this perspective, becomes a site for multiple forms of historical documentation, evidence and voice, including those marginalised by conventional history writing.

There is then a democratic (and maybe even a populist) urge in the American archival poem after Pound, something also seen in the later modernisms of Williams, Reznikoff, Olson and Howe. The democratic, Whitmanian desire to 'contain multitudes' is approached by way of archival constructions which collect the various documentary evidence of modern experience, especially that experience often considered peripheral to mainline historical developments.[23] Whitman's expansiveness (which Pound agreed, reluctantly, to 'carve' and hone) finds expression in aggregate forms that are at once sprawling and (being fragmentary and paratactic) precise and refined.[24] The democratic multitude appears in the form of documentary constellations rather than contained within a single bardic voice.

This is, as Williams would put it, 'to make a start, / out of particulars', and the first book of *Paterson* extends (in one case infamously) the archival practice of Pound and Rukeyser.[25] In addition to cribbing prose sections from published sources including *Historical Collections of the State of New Jersey* (1844) and the *History of Paterson and Its Environs* (1901), *Paterson* also incorporates printed material as diverse as a geological survey for an artesian well and a local manifesto for finance reform. More controversially, Williams incorporated into his poem personal letters from other writers, including Pound, Allen Ginsberg and a young poet named Marcia Nardi. The effect of these inclusions is comparable to that of the letters in the 'Malatesta' cantos; the poem becomes a space or a 'flat surface' (as Marjorie Perloff describes Pound's cantos) upon which textual materials are curated and juxtaposed.[26]

Williams's published sources in *Paterson* lean heavily towards bizarrerie and the outright macabre. In the first and second books alone we encounter original or lightly edited accounts of a 'monster in human form' visited by George Washington, a seven-foot striped bass caught below Paterson's Great Falls, and a meeting of the German Singing Societies of Paterson which culminated in a shootout, barn burning and riot.[27] Clearly, Williams's practice of accumulation contests 'great man' or 'paradigm shift' views of history, turning attention to the unlikely vernacular events that constitute local historical lore. In fact, the gathering of extreme and fantastic episodes in *Paterson* recalls the folk epic or saga more closely than modern narrative historiography. Instead of waypoints on a forward narrative movement, these events exist in the simultaneous present that is the collective memory of Paterson city.

But Williams's accounts of these events are not incorporated seamlessly into the flexible structure of his free verse. Instead, they stand out conspicuously as blocks of historical documentation, foregrounding the work of collection, curation and archival reconstruction undertaken by the poem. In other words, by corralling documentary materials within the physical space of the poem, Williams proceeds by 'rolling / up the sum' of its parts not only linguistically but also *bibliographically*.[28] This is particularly apparent in the case of the geology report in Book III and the rather left-field economic leaflet. But it is also true of personal correspondence such as this accusatory letter from Marcia Nardi:

> My feelings about you now are those of anger and indignation; and they enable me to tell you a lot of things straight from the shoulder, without my usual tongue tied round-aboutness.
>
> You might as well take all your own literature and everyone else's and toss it into one of those big garbage trucks of the Sanitation Department, so long as the people with the top-cream minds and the 'finer' sensibilities use those minds and sensibilities not to make themselves more humane human beings than the average person, but merely as means of ducking responsibility toward a better understanding of their fellow men, except theoretically – which doesn't mean a God damned thing.[29]

Even more than those from Ginsberg and Pound, Nardi's letters to Williams read like foreign bodies lodged within the work, perhaps because they raise questions about the character of the author and the purpose of *Paterson* itself. In Sandra M. Gilbert's view, the inclusion of these letters is a matter of authorial and narrative mastery: Williams 'defuse[d] anxiety about Nardi as paradigmatic woman of letters by transforming her into a *character* and thus into a creature he could control'.[30] Williams's own comments on the subject tend to support this reading.[31] At the same time, there remains an aspect of self-recrimination in the inclusion; the letters call into question not only Williams himself but also the project upon which he is embarked. Perhaps *Paterson* is itself merely a 'theoretical' effort to understand Williams's 'fellow men'; a 'means of ducking responsibility' to the actual people behind its assembled texts?

Williams allows for contradictions and mixed motives of this kind in his preface to the first book: 'we know nothing, pure / and simple, beyond / our own complexities'.[32] We are always, in other words, complicit, unable to assume a position outside ourselves or outside history. This might account for the inclusion of Nardi's incriminating correspondence, but it is also a broader rationale for the practice of archival assemblage. Being inside history, the author cannot hope to provide an objective account of events. But by gathering the documentary material within his or her reach the poet may at least 'make a start, / out of particulars'. While Williams hoped to reveal the 'resemblance between the mind of modern man and a city', *Paterson*'s practice of assembly foregrounds the intersection of private and public experience and the embeddedness of historical representation *itself* within history.[33]

Charles Olson saw the *Cantos* and *Paterson* as two 'HALVES' of the same unfinished project.[34] Writing to Robert Creeley in 1951, he argued that Williams had made an advance upon the *Cantos* in so far as he rejected Pound's 'EGO-POSITION': the organisation and representation of history according to a single authorial intelligence.[35] Although Williams's materials are ostensibly more personal than those of Pound, Olson believed that Williams's representation afforded multiple subject-positions and was not filtered through a unifying authorial consciousness. However, Olson ultimately judged *Paterson* too limited in historical scope and depth: 'by making his substance historical of one city (the Joyce deal), Bill completely licks himself'.[36] Olson was looking to 'throw the materials' of history in a way which both escaped the 'EGO-POSITION' and pushed back deeper into historical time.[37]

By 1951 Olson had already made a name for himself as an archival sleuth. As a Wesleyan graduate student in 1933–4 he had reassembled a substantial portion of Herman Melville's personal library, scouring archives, family homes and second-hand bookstores across Massachusetts and New York.[38] His first book, *Call Me Ishmael* (1947), drew upon exhaustive further research at the Library of Congress, the National Archives, the Widener Library and the Nantucket Whaling

Museum.[39] Several years later, in the first volume of *The Maximus Poems* (1960), these archival attentions were brought to bear on the town of Gloucester, Massachusetts, in the first years following its founding in 1623. In a poem such as 'The Record', composed at Gloucester in the winter of 1957–8, Olson's alternative to the 'EGO-POSITION' is discovered in the *process* of research and compilation.[40] The reader here is privy not only to the author's original curation of material but to the act of discovery and selection itself:

<pre>
                         Weymouth Port Book, 873
       Here we have it – the goods – from this Harbour,
       1626, to Weymouth (England) consigned to
                         Richard Bushrod and Company
                       & Wm Derby and Company
  fr Cape An   dry fish[1]
  corfish[2]
  train oil[3]
  quarters of oak
  skins: fox
                    racons
                   martyns
                    otter
                 muskuatche
                   beaver
                 The *Amytie* arriving Weymouth 1st Aug
                 and the *Fellowship* followed 11th September
                 Capts Evans, & Edward Cribbe
</pre>

1 'so hote this time of yeare except the very fish which is laid out to be dryed by the sunne be every day turned it cannot possibly be preserved from burning' Shore fishery
2 Banks fishery, where fish are large and always wet, having no land heere to drie and were called core or green fish – split & salted
3 the oil of seal, whale or cod – undoubtedly here cod[41]

In his influential manifesto 'Projective Verse' (1950), Olson had proposed a form of 'COMPOSITION BY FIELD' which departed from 'inherited line, stanza, over-all form'.[42] In 'The Record' this 'field' incorporates a range of bibliographical possibilities, including the use of page space (indentation and centring) and internal footnotes. But unlike, for instance, the 'Malatesta' cantos, the material does not have the appearance of having been worked over, spliced and rearranged. Rather, this process is seen happening *on the page*, so that the poem presents a live record of Olson's encounter with his published sources: Frances Rose-Troup's *John White, the Patriarch of Dorchester [Dorset] and the Founder of Massachusetts, 1575–1648* (1930) and Harold A. Innis's

The Cod Fisheries: The History of An International Economy (1954).[43]

This practice of assemblage in process reflects Olson's deeply unconventional understanding of history and historiography. In *The Special View of History* (1957/1970) the poet would argue that Herodotus' term *historia* meant '"finding out for oneself" instead of depending upon hearsay'.[44] According to this view, events have significance only in so far as they are experienced concretely by individuals; an abstract narrative is less significant than a direct encounter with a 'specific pin or gold piece'.[45] At the same time, history conceived in this manner is (as Olson puts it) a verb rather than a noun; a practice of active investigation and questioning which is ongoing and ultimately inexhaustible.[46]

In the first volumes of *The Maximus Poems*, Olson's understanding of *historia* informs the formal organisation of the poems as much as their content. The arrangement of textual matter across the page governs the pace of the reader's progress and reproduces the experience of original textual inquiry. Here, for instance, the double-spaced list indented left ('corfish / train oil / quarters of oak') suddenly gives way to a dense cluster of particular detail ('fox / racons / martyns / otter'). The layout reflects the experience of research itself; the shift from narrative to illuminating, historically evocative facts. At the same time, the spatial form also allows for multiplying relations between materials that would not be available in a syntactical structure. Whereas conventional syntax might have imposed a grammatical hierarchy upon the particulars Olson presents, the spatial form foregrounds each element individually.[47]

In a sense, however, 'COMPOSITION BY FIELD' describes a broader modernist commitment to incorporating the materials of history into a textual, quasi-archival structure. The 'field' activates the spatial organisation of the text as opposed to (or in addition to) its grammatical structure. This has been typical of research-based poetics from Pound and Benjamin onwards, affording new possibilities for arrangement and organisation and radical alternatives to linear historiography. Despite marked divergences in practice, Rukeyser, Williams and Olson lever the spatial and physical properties of their work to engage critically with the conventions of historical representation.

The Skythian bowl

Towards the end of his life, Charles Olson's 'COMPOSITION BY FIELD' extended well beyond the typewritten or manuscript page. Writings are found on napkins, maps, envelopes and other paper ephemera, and even on the inside window frames of his Gloucester apartment.[48] Perhaps this was to be expected. As an environment in which documentary materials are brought into collision, the archival long poem consistently pushed against the boundaries imposed by the book form (including – prominently in the case of Pound, Williams and Olson – the need for a definitive 'final' poem or conclusion).

The limits of the book had already been recognised by the archival projects of the 1920s. In *One-Way Street*, Benjamin described the book as 'an outdated mediation between two different filing systems [:] the card box of the researcher who wrote it' and the 'card index' of the scholar who interprets it.[49] Unlike bound books, which set materials in a fixed and determinative order, cards and unbound scraps of paper resist incorporation into generalising linear narratives, preserving their singularity and integrity within a larger differentiated whole. Moreover, such texts remain capable of migration from one context into another, so that the overall structure of the texts remains permanently changeable.

While the physical aspect of poetic assemblage was anticipated by earlier archival poetics, contemporary poets have attended more self-consciously to the book form and its significance to the practice of history writing. In these works, bibliographical form itself comes under critical scrutiny, recognised as a historically specific form of representation and not a neutral physical medium. In the case of Anne Carson's *Nox* (2010), for instance, the poem as a physical archive or curatorial space is especially foregrounded. Here, the work of historical representation is inscribed in the *material* character of the published text, as well as coded in the unorthodox interpretive practice it asks of its readers.

Nox purports to be a reproduction of an original scrapbook created after the death of the author's estranged brother; a scrapbook containing (on verso pages) authorial text in addition to photographs, letters and other paper matter, usually collaged and sometimes fragmented. On the recto pages are definitions of every word in Catullus' poem number CI; an elegy written for his own brother. However, the pages of *Nox* are not bound but assembled in a single concertina and housed in a hinged box. This physical presentation of the text assumes increasing significance as the poem (literally) unfolds.

Early in the work, Carson returns – like Olson – to the example of Herodotus, and to history as verb rather than noun. Herodotus' travels among the Skythians provide an occasion for *Nox* to reflect upon the artificiality of history writing generally and its own practice of representation in particular:

1.3 Herodotos is an historian who trains you as you read. It is a process of asking, searching, collecting, doubting, striving, testing, blaming and above all standing amazed at the strange things humans do. Now by far the strangest thing that humans do – he is firm on this – is history. This asking. For often it produces no clear or helpful account, in fact people are satisfied with the most bizarre forms of answering, e.g. the Skythians who, when Herodotos endeavours to find out from them the size of the Skythian population, point to a bowl that stands at Exampaios. It is made of the melted down arrowheads required of each Skythian by their king Ariantes on pain of death. Herodotos describes the bowl, what else can he do?[50]

Writing history may be the 'strangest thing that humans do'. Like the Skythians, we are content with even 'bizarre forms of answering' so long as they offer vivid or formally compelling answers to our (perhaps unanswerable) questions. However, the Skythian bowl – like *Nox* itself – is not an entirely arbitrary figure. Both bowl and poem are forms of representation through aggregation: while the Skythians compile a census in the form of a bowl of melted-down arrowheads, *Nox* represents a long-lost brother through an assemblage of paper ephemera. Arguably, these depictions are less 'bizarre' than purely orthographic or numeric representations; they provide tangible, haptic figurations of their absent subjects.

Fittingly, the verso page facing this passage provides a gloss on the adjective 'multa' which directs us to Carson's earlier gloss on 'multas' (numerous, many). In the first line of his poem, Catullus is *'multas per gentes et multa per aequora vectus'* ('carried across many lands and many seas'). At first glance, the significance of the line for Carson's poem is that of the transhistorical parallel: like Catullus, Carson travels to a distant land (in this case, Denmark) in order to say *ave* to her dead brother (Carson's poem adopts, in this sense, the high modernist 'mythical method').[51] But Carson's definition of 'multas' also bears upon the construction of *Nox* itself and the archival poem more generally:

multas

multus multa multum   adjective

[cf. Gk μάλα, MELIOR] numerous, many, many of, many a; many people, many, many women, the ordinary people, the many especially in phrase *unus de multis*: one of many; many things, much, to a great extent, many words especially in elliptical phrases e.g. *quid multa? ne multa*: to cut a long story short; an abundance of, much, large, *multum est*: it is of value; appearing or acting on many occasions, assiduous, regular, used many times; (of persons) too much in evidence, tedious, wearisome, verbose; occurring in a high degree, full, intense, *multa dies* or *multa lux*: broad daylight, *multa nox*: late in the night, perhaps too late.[52]

The Maximus Poems had borne an epigraph which Olson overheard in a Black Mountain College kitchen: 'All my life I've heard / one makes many.'[53] And for Olson the relationship between the one and the many is both the central problem of democratic politics ('ordinary people', Whitman's 'multitudes') and the crux of epic poetry. How are the diverse evidences of human thought and action across time to be corralled within a single structure? 'Many' was also the problem of *Paterson*: 'a mass of detail / to interrelate on a new ground, difficultly'.[54] And for Pound the problem of there being 'too much' historical evidence led to the radically compressed historiography of the 'Luminous Detail'.[55]

In *Nox*, however, the problem represented by '*multas*' – the problem of containing multitudes – is coded into the book form itself. To open the box and turn the accordion pages is to sift through a welter of evidence, much of it fragmentary and incomplete (a letterhead from a Kashmiri guesthouse, for instance, or two corners of a black and white photograph). *Nox* engages the reader in the 'searching, collecting, doubting, striving, [and] testing' which Carson herself embarked upon in the wake of her brother's death, and which for Herodotus was the very definition of history. *Nox* is a personal, or rather a family, archive, gathering the paper remains of a lost brother and son. However, the material structure of the work draws the reader towards the physical, active, *embodied* investigations which for Carson (as for Olson) are the true practice of historiography.

But the book form does not need to be disassembled in order to critique the practice of history and archival collection. In certain recent texts, the very publication of a 'work' within the covers of a book activates significant questions about how history should be written and what documents the state or civil society should (and should not) preserve for posterity. The crucial works here are a series of books by conceptual writer Kenneth Goldsmith, including his American trilogy: *The Weather* (2005), *Traffic* (2007) and *Sports* (2008). Questions of inclusion and exclusion, significance and insignificance, are raised immediately by passages such as the following, taken from the 'Spring' section of *The Weather*:

> Oh, just a damp and chilly day underway. There will be some occasional light rain and drizzle, some areas of fog, and even a rumble or two of thunder, we'll have a high of just forty-four degrees, and then windy and cold, with clearing skies tonight, low thirty-six. A sunny but windy and chilly day, with a high around fifty degrees. Monday, cloudy, windy, and cold with some snow, sleet, and rain, and we're probably going to be talking accumulations north and west of the city, Monday's high just forty degrees, though. Cloudy, with a chance for lingering rain Tuesday, especially during the morning, with

a high around fifty, and partly sunny Wednesday, with a high around near fifty degrees. Battlefield forecast is as follows, we do have a partly cloudy sky with gusty winds over Saturday night, and a mix of clouds and sun, with blowing sand and dust on Sunday. It's thirty-seven degrees right now, heading up to forty-four in midtown.[56]

All is not quite as it appears. If this is a weather report for early spring in New York City ('midtown'), what is the 'battlefield forecast' and where, exactly, is it 'blowing sand and dust'? If the 'battlefield forecast' is for the US military (presumably personnel deployed to Iraq or Afghanistan) is it possible that some of these temperatures – 'thirty-seven degrees right now' – refer to *Celsius* rather than Fahrenheit?

Goldsmith assembled *The Weather* from hourly weather reports on the New York radio station 1010 WINS, with each paragraph in the work corresponding to one hourly bulletin of one minute in length.[57] Goldsmith began transcribing the forecasts on 21 December 2002 and continued for a year.[58] However, the project as originally conceived was shaken up by the American invasion and occupation of Iraq, which began on the first day of spring, 19/20 March 2003.[59] Presumably owing to the significance of the weather for military operations in the country, 1010 WINS interleaved its New York forecasts with predictions of dust and sandstorms across the Iraqi desert.

The content of *The Weather* at the level of the paragraph is, however, less significant than its actual publication. The release of the bulletins in book form represents a radical act of conservation or information storage, providing a repository for audio material that might otherwise have been lost. We might think of *The Weather* as revealing a modernist commitment to everyday life and, in the line of William Carlos Williams, to vernacular American speech ('Oh, just a damp and chilly day ...'). However, Goldsmith has distinguished his own 'uncreative' work from that of the modernist tradition.[60] In a 2004 talk entitled 'Being Boring', Goldsmith argued that writers of the digital era must negotiate a new overabundance of text:

> Faced with an unprecedented amount of available text, the problem is not needing to write more of it; instead, we must learn to negotiate the vast quantity that exists. I've transformed from a writer into an information manager, adept at the skills of replicating, organizing, mirroring, archiving, hoarding, storing, reprinting, bootlegging, plundering, and transferring. I've needed to acquire a whole new skill set: I've become a master typist, an exacting cut-and-paster, and an OCR demon. There's nothing I love more than transcription; I find few things more satisfying than collation.[61]

Originality is redundant in the context of endless textual proliferation. The contemporary writer must instead evolve into an 'information manager', refabricating texts in new locations. However, following other 'hoarding, storing, reprinting' epics before it, *The Weather* also carries an account of history and history writing; one which depends – in this case – on its own material form. Like *Nox*, *The Weather* is a mobile archive, but its physical publication lends it the specific cultural prestige associated with the printed book. The published form of *The Weather* (its 'bibliographical code', to use Jerome McGann's phrase) argues that this 'boring' material is worthy of your consideration and attention, even if it is 'just' found material transcribed from local radio.[62] A little like the Skythian bowl reported by Herodotus, *The Weather* is a work of historical assemblage which takes the measure of its time and place.

Goldsmith has sought to rationalise poetics for the Google era. But the literary practices he advocates – 'organizing', 'storing', 'hoarding', 'archiving' – were already prominent in early and mid-twentieth-century avant-garde poetry. The poet as 'information manager' is a figure found as early as Pound's 1911 essay on the 'Luminous Detail'; a method to 'govern knowledge as the switchboard governs an electric circuit'.[63] The 'unprecedented amount of available text' Goldsmith finds in the contemporary digital environment is experienced as an information surplus which the twentieth-century avant-garde had already – as Paul Stephens suggests – both replicated and parodied.[64]

If modernist poetics approached the problem of overabundant knowledge, the physical archive suggests practices of collection that reflect its experiments in information management. But these textual archives also intervened specifically in the conventions of history writing, establishing new methods of historical curation and representation. Indeed, more recent long poems 'containing history' (as Pound put it) continue to practise a variety of assemblage which earlier modernist poetics turned against traditional historiography.[65] Drawing on the material and spatial resources of the page and the physical book, these works reject the unifying and generalising tendencies of historical narrative and instead dramatise the seemingly minor and tangential; the fragment and the detail, the contradiction, ellipsis and non sequitur.

The long poem as makeshift repository has lent itself, for this reason, to alternative and revisionist histories; to the recuperation (or at least the acknowledgement) of suppressed voices, marginalised stories and neglected experiences. Containing 'multas' or multitudes, these works realise a history at once various, uncertain and multivocal. Thus, while an account of the contemporary poetry archive might chart its continuing significance to the institutionalisation of modern poetry, the structure of the archive finds its own volatilised reflection within modernist poetry itself. Assembling the *disjecta membra* of the recorded past, archival poetics witnesses to the production of history between text and space, material form and collective memory.

Notes

1. See Braddock, Jeremy, *Collecting as Modernist Practice* (Baltimore: Johns Hopkins University Press, 2012), pp. 226, 216. For more on the history of modern poetry collections see Brinkman, Bartholomew, *Poetic Modernism in the Culture of Mass Print* (Baltimore: Johns Hopkins University Press, 2017), ch. 5.
2. Quoted in Braddock, *Collecting as Modernist Practice*, p. 226.
3. Ibid.
4. Marjorie Perloff describes the 'Malatesta' cantos as a 'flat surface, as in a Cubist or early Dada collage, upon which verbal elements, fragmented images, and truncated bits of narrative, drawn from the most disparate contexts, are brought into collision'. Perloff, Marjorie, *The Poetics of Indeterminacy: Rimbaud to Cage* (Evanston: Northwestern University Press, 1999), p. 181.
5. Ibid.
6. Olson, Charles, *The Maximus Poems*, ed. George F. Butterick (Berkeley: University of California Press, 1983), p. 327.
7. Moody, A. David, *Ezra Pound: Poet. A Portrait of the Man and His Work. II: The Epic Years, 1921–1939* (Oxford: Oxford University Press, 2014), p. 49.
8. As Rainey has demonstrated, however, Pound also adapted and revised his materials. See Rainey, Lawrence, *Ezra Pound and the Monument of Culture: Text, History, and the Malatesta Cantos* (Chicago: Chicago University Press, 1991).
9. Stephens, Paul, *The Poetics of Information Overload: From Gertrude Stein to Conceptual Writing* (Minneapolis: University of Minnesota Press, 2015), p. 1.
10. Lehman, Robert, *Impossible Modernism: T. S. Eliot, Walter Benjamin, and the Critique of Historical Reason* (Stanford: Stanford University Press, 2016); Bloomfield, Mandy, *Archaeopoetics: Word, Image, History* (Tuscaloosa: University of Alabama Press, 2016).
11. Lehman, *Impossible Modernism*, p. xiv.
12. Bloomfield, *Archaeopoetics*, p. 24.
13. Ibid.
14. Olson, Charles, *Collected Prose*, ed. Donald Allen and Benjamin Friedlander (Berkeley: University of California Press, 1997), p. 239.
15. In a later essay, Pound would compare strong literary criticism to the work that 'a good hanging committee or a curator would perform in a National Gallery or in a biological museum'. Pound, Ezra, *Literary Essays*, ed. T. S. Eliot (London: Faber and Faber, 1974), p. 75.
16. Pound, Ezra, *Selected Prose 1909–1965*, ed. William Cookson (London: Faber and Faber, 1973), p. 21.

17. Rukeyser's poem is often neglected in accounts of the poem 'containing history'. An exception is Thurston, Michael, *Making Something Happen: American Political Poetry between the World Wars* (Chapel Hill: University of North Carolina Press, 2001), pp. 169–210, especially pp. 188–9. See also Hickman, Ben, *Crisis and the US Avant-Garde: Poetry and Real Politics* (Edinburgh: Edinburgh University Press, 2015), ch. 2.

18. For Rukeyser and documentary film see Gander, Catherine, *Muriel Rukeyser and Documentary: The Poetics of Connection* (Edinburgh: Edinburgh University Press, 2013), pp. 7–10.

19. Rukeyser, Muriel, *The Collected Poems of Muriel Rukeyser* (New York: McGraw-Hill, 1982), pp. 73–4.

20. Ibid., p. 73.

21. Dayton, Tim, *Muriel Rukeyser's The Book of the Dead* (Columbia: University of Missouri Press, 2003), p. 38.

22. For American poetics as fieldwork see Shaw, Lytle, *Fieldworks: From Place to Site in Postwar Poetics* (Tuscaloosa: University of Alabama Press, 2013).

23. Whitman, Walt, *The Complete Poems*, ed. Francis Murphy (London: Penguin, 1996), p. 123.

24. Pound, Ezra, *Personæ: The Collected Shorter Poems*, rev. edn, prepared by Lea Baechler and A. Walton Litz (London: Faber and Faber, 2001), p. 90.

25. Williams, William Carlos, *Paterson*, ed. Christopher MacGowan (New York: New Directions, 1995), p. 3.

26. Perloff, *Poetics of Indeterminacy*, p. 181.

27. Williams, *Paterson*, p. 10.

28. Ibid., p. 3.

29. Ibid., p. 82.

30. Gilbert, Sandra M., 'Purloined Letters: William Carlos Williams and "Cress"', *William Carlos Williams Review* 11/2 (Fall 1985), 5–15 (p. 8).

31. Ibid., p. 7.

32. Williams, *Paterson*, p. 3.

33. Ibid., p. xiii.

34. Olson, Charles, *Mayan Letters*, ed. Robert Creeley (London: Jonathan Cape, 1968), p. 28.

35. Ibid., p. 29.

36. Ibid., p. 28.

37. Ibid.

38. See Clark, Tom, *Charles Olson: The Allegory of a Poet's Life* (New York: Norton, 1991), pp. 24–5.

39. Ibid., pp. 104–6.

40. As Lytle Shaw says of this poem: 'the main *action* that emerges from this silent record is the archival, reflexive one undertaken by the poet in order to generate it'. Shaw, *Fieldworks*, p. 61.

41. Olson, *Maximus Poems*, p. 121.

42. Olson, *Collected Prose*, p. 239.

43. See Butterick, George F., *A Guide to the Maximus Poems of Charles Olson* (Berkeley: University of California Press, 1980), pp. 174–6.

44. Olson, Charles, *The Special View of History* (Berkeley: Oyez, 1970), p. 20.

45. Quoted in Butterick, George F., 'Charles Olson and the Postmodern Advance', *The Iowa Review* 11/4 (1980), 3–27 (p. 10). See also Bloomfield,

Archaeopoetics, p. 3.

46. See Olson, *Special View*, p. 26.
47. Bloomfield provides a strong reading of this aspect of Olson's historio-graphic practice. See Bloomfield, *Archaeopoetics*, p. 26.
48. See Siraganian, Lisa, *Modernism's Other Work: The Art Object's Political Life* (Oxford: Oxford University Press, 2012), pp. 139–41.
49. Benjamin, Walter, *One-Way Street and Other Writings*, trans. Edmund Jephcott and Kingsley Shorter (London: New Left Books, 2009), p. 62.
50. Carson, Anne, *Nox* (New York: New Directions, 2010), n.p.
51. Eliot, T. S., *Selected Prose*, ed. Frank Kermode (London: Faber and Faber, 1975), p. 178.
52. Carson, *Nox*, n.p.
53. Olson, *Maximus Poems*, n.p.
54. Williams. *Paterson*, p. 19.
55. Pound, *Selected Prose*, p. 21.
56. Goldsmith, Kenneth, *The Weather*, Electronic Poetry Center <http://writing.upenn.edu/epc/authors/goldsmith/goldsmith_spring.html>(accessed 14 February 2017). First published in Los Angeles by Make Now Press, 2005.
57. See Perloff, Marjorie, '"Moving Information": On Kenneth Goldsmith's *The Weather*', UbuWeb <http://www.ubu.com/papers/kg_ol_perloff.html> (accessed 14 February 2017).
58. Ibid.
59. Ibid.
60. Goldsmith, Kenneth, 'Being Boring', Electronic Poetry Center <http://writing.upenn.edu/epc/authors/goldsmith/goldsmith_boring.html> (accessed 31 May 2017).
61. Ibid.
62. McGann, Jerome J., *The Textual Condition* (Princeton: Princeton University Press, 1991), p. 56.
63. Pound, *Selected Prose*, p. 23.
64. Stephens, *Poetics of Information Overload*, p. 1.
65. Quoted in Hall, Donald, *Remembering Poets: Reminiscences and Opinions* (New York: Harper Colophon, 1979), p. 241.

Chapter 4

Digital Baedeker:
A Feminist Experiment with
Mina Loy's Archive

Suzanne W. Churchill, Linda Kinnahan and Susan Rosenbaum

Introduction: The historical avant-garde and the digital archive

Take, for example, this archival photograph, unearthed and published in the *New York Times Style Magazine* in 2016, nearly a century after the moment it records. The photograph depicts an avant-garde gathering in Constantin Brancusi's Paris studio in 1921.[1] As reproduced in *Style Magazine*, this iconic photograph typifies Mina Loy's position in the avant-garde. She is a central, animating, illuminating presence, yet she is also a ghostly spectre, mentioned only in a caption and never in the article. In this way, Loy is representative of women in the historical

From left, Constantin Brancusi at his studio in 1921, with the poet Tristan Tzara, the photographer Berenice Abbott, the poet Mina Loy, the publisher Jane Heap and the editor Margaret Anderson.
Courtesy of Paul Kasmin Gallery/©Succession Brancusi — all rights reserved ADAGP, Paris/Artists Rights Society (ARS), New York, 2016

avant-garde, a term that encompasses early twentieth-century, European, predominantly white, male-dominated art movements such as Futurism, Cubism, Dada and Surrealism. These experimental movements typically opposed bourgeois values and tastes, seeking to challenge and shock their audiences. The movements chronicled their exhibitions, publications and performances, generating their own heroic histories and archives. Although women played major parts in the historical avant-garde, they have been relegated to supporting roles in its lore – posed in a photograph, mentioned in a caption, or deposited in a slim folder in the archive of a celebrated male associate.

Artist, poet, playwright, novelist, inventor and entrepreneur, Mina Loy (1882–1966) moved in the circles of Futurism, Dada and Surrealism and migrated among major metropolitan centres of avant-garde activity, including Paris, Florence, Rome, New York, London and Berlin, from the 1910s to the 1950s. Loy's interest in avant-garde experiment was shaped by feminism, gender and sexuality, and led her to self-consciously assume a position on the margins of these movements. Her ambivalent stance of interested but critical, feminist detachment typifies the relationship of many women to the historical avant-garde, and her work in diverse media and response to the gendering of visual culture were widespread among avant-garde women artists. Her experimental writing, typified by radically new uses of language, typography and page space, garnered attention for its bold feminism and innovative forms, often activated by encounters with visual culture.

Loy published only two volumes in her lifetime, *Lunar Baedeker* (1923) and *Lunar Baedeker & Time-Tables* (1958),[2] but her work in various genres and media appeared in Paris salons, transatlantic magazines, and galleries in London, Paris, Rome and New York. The small body of her published work now includes *Last Lunar Baedeker* (1982), *Lost Lunar Baedeker* (1996), *Stories and Essays of Mina Loy* (2011) and her edited novel *Insel* (1991, 2014).[3] Loy's unpublished writings, as well as her paintings, sculptures, assemblages, lampshades and designs, comprise a larger body of work. Much of the uncollected material is held in Yale's Beinecke Library,[4] while the visual art and some manuscripts reside with a number of private collectors. The location of other work remains unknown. Carolyn Burke's biography makes tantalising reference to many works of visual art which have been lost.[5]

Though highly regarded, Loy's small body of work remains elusive. All is not lost, however: the Beinecke Library's 2017 announcement that 'the Mina Loy Papers have been digitised in their entirety' promises to remediate her precarious status in the annals of the historical avant-garde.[6] This is a tremendous boon for Loy scholarship. Hundreds of

letters, manuscripts, drawings, sketches, designs for inventions, portraits, lampshades and more can now be freely accessed in the Beinecke's
digital library. Anyone with a computer and internet connection can
read Loy's handwritten 1914 'Feminist Manifesto' to see for themselves
how the punctuation, spacing and word size affect the meaning of the
problematic 'choice between Para-sitism, & Prostitution – or Negation'.[7]

Yale's digitisation of the Mina Loy Papers is not merely an act of
preservation; it is an indication of cultural significance and institutional
value, and a recognition of the changing meaning of the archive. As
Judith Halberstam argues, an archive is not merely a repository of
documents but 'a theory of cultural relevance, a construction of collective memory, and a complex record'.[8] Digitisation makes this dynamic
understanding of the archive tangible; responding to the digital environment, Rick Prelinger argues that 'new archival practice ... needs
to be SOCIAL. PUBLIC. TRANSPARENT. COLLABORATIVE AND
DECENTRALIZED'.[9] While Loy's papers have been preserved in the
Yale Collection of American Literature since 1974, their digitisation
signals greater recognition of her cultural significance and allows
broader public access to avant-garde culture and history, allowing users
to become active participants in the ongoing production of knowledge.
This bodes well for feminist practice, since, as Kate Eichhorn comments,

> For a younger generation of feminists, the archive is not necessarily either a
> destination or an impenetrable barrier to be breached, but rather a site and
> practice integral to knowledge making, cultural production, and activism.
> The archive is where academic and activist work frequently converge. Indeed,
> the creation of archives has become integral to how knowledges are produced
> and legitimized and how feminist activists, artists, and scholars make their
> voices audible.[10]

Access to a digital archive does not guarantee that this revisionary
feminist work will be done, however. The public digital archive allows
users to see Loy's work up close, but it may distance them from the
curatorial work that selects, organises and interprets the material, and
from the materiality of the documents themselves. Digital archives can
unwittingly promote a fantasy of comprehensive coverage and unmediated contact. The digitisation of 'the Mina Loy Papers in their entirety'
may make users think they have access to all of her work in one digital
collection, but even within the Beinecke digital library, much of Loy's
writing lies in the papers of Carolyn Burke, Carl Van Vechten and
Mabel Dodge Luhan, and still more of her work remains scattered in
other archives and private collections. Even when users can access Loy's
papers in the Beinecke's digital archive, they may have difficulty finding
specific items or making sense of what they find. While the Finding Aid

describes the collections and folder contents of the digitised Mina Loy Papers, the items online are no longer grouped in carefully organised folders, but appear as a stream of 245 artefacts which can be sorted by language, genre, type of resource and date. Thus, the 'curation' appears to lie with the user, rendering invisible the larger curation of the digital collection.

Of course, combing through often disintegrating, disordered papers in a traditional print archive can be equally challenging, but as Kate Theimer points out, the 'modern digital age' increases the expectation 'that more descriptive information about materials will be made available online'. Theimer argues that it is 'critical to know the context of these collections' – who made them, what was included or excluded, where did the metadata come from? She makes a distinction between traditional archives and intellectual products that make selective use of these archival sources. According to Theimer, using 'archive' to refer to 'collections in which copies of archival materials are removed from their original context and "re-mixed" to be part of a new creation' elides the curatorial processes that led to their creation; she prefers the term 'digital historical representation' in order to emphasise those curatorial processes.[11] In distinguishing curated digital products from traditional physical archives, Theimer downplays the fact that traditional archives have also been curated, whether through the whims of the collector, the accidents of time or the hard facts of historical power (what is commemorated and what is not; who is remembered and who is forgotten). While Theimer resists the broader understanding of the 'archive' that has emerged in the digital era, her call to contextualise collections and to reflect on the curation of archival sources is nevertheless important.

The digital archive as analogue to the physical archive is a vital and necessary step towards reassessing the work of figures like Mina Loy, but it is not sufficient on its own. We need to frame the archive with narrative interpretations and explanations, that is, to develop a Baedeker for the archive – a scholarly travel guide that helps users navigate archival sights, attractions and artefacts. As William G. Thomas argues, the most pressing need in digital humanities today is for digital narratives, which he defines as 'multimodal, user-directed, hypertextual' narratives that change with each encounter and 'situate evidence, interpretation, and arguments in ways that allow readers to understand the scholarly project'.[12] When narratives change with each encounter, it means that users have been able to navigate the material according to their own interests and questions, and participate in the process of meaning making. A digital Baedeker enables such user-directed inquiry, allowing users to chart their own course through the archive, interact with the materials and seek expertise from scholars (Plate 1).

A digital Baedeker for the archive: 'Mina Loy: Navigating the Avant-Garde'

'Mina Loy: Navigating the Avant-Garde'[13] is a collection of digital narratives and visualisations that contextualise and interpret Loy's work and related artefacts. Enhancing access with interpretation, the scholarly website offers a curated, multimedia, interactive exhibit of selected works by Loy that effectively serves as a digital Baedeker for her archive. The term 'Baedeker' emerged in 1826, when German publisher Verlag Karl Baedeker began to publish travel guides for cities around the world, which included introductions, fold-out maps, travel routes, and information about important sights and destinations, all written by experts. Popularly called 'Baedekers', the guides became best-sellers, were translated into multiple languages and continue to be published today.[14] Loy, a world traveller, no doubt relied on the guides for practical advice and also drew upon them for imaginative inspiration, entitling both volumes of her work *Lunar Baedeker* – guidebooks to the moon. In adopting the term 'Baedeker' as a metaphor for our scholarly website, we acknowledge Loy's ingenious use of innovative forms to navigate real and imagined territory, as well as contemporary readers' need for a new kind of guidebook for navigating her complex archive.

While our exhibit interacts with a particular archive that has just come into digital being (the Beinecke collection), we recognise that archive as still very partial and only partially understood. Roger Conover, Senior Editor at MIT Press and Loy's literary executor, is our project advisor and has granted us permission to provide access to the material examined in our digital narratives, including unpublished work from his private collection. But even as we provide access to previously unknown works, our project seeks to disturb the notion of the complete archive, instead offering a way of navigating a broadly conceived archive, one that remains scattered in various places, both accessible and inaccessible.

Inspired by Loy's innovative uses of verbal and visual design, our scholarly website documents Loy's avant-garde affiliations and pursues new modes of textual and visual expression in order to invite a closer, more informed engagement with her work. Our goals are to:

- provide access to and interpretations of Loy's verbal and visual work, much of which remains buried in archives or private collections;

- transform close reading through multimodal tools and environments that activate verbal and visual reading practices;
- develop a crowd-sourced, flash-mob, feminist theory that accounts for the contributions of women and people of colour to the historical avant-garde;
- conduct an experiment in public humanities scholarship that involves scholars and students in transforming scholarly methods and products, tests new processes for peer review, and sets UX (user experience) design standards for digital scholarship.

Our aim is not to create a comprehensive digital archive, but to provide a platform for accessing and understanding Loy's published and unpublished writing and artwork. Through feminist methods of building a digital Baedeker for the archive, we seek not to emphasise the preservation of great authors or works, but to activate networks of interested readers and scholars engaging in ongoing conversations. Our scholarly narratives situate Loy's work in relation to the key places she lived (Florence, New York, Paris) and to the avant-garde movements centred on each locale (Futurism, Dada, Surrealism). In this way we make coherent and visible what has too often been obscured by Loy's scattered, difficult-to-access physical archive: Loy's centrality to the history of the twentieth-century avant-garde. While Marcel Duchamp's role as an avant-garde provocateur who was central to several movements but who resisted strict affiliation with any particular movement has been amply chronicled and celebrated, Loy's similar role and trajectory (fuelled by her feminist perspective) has contributed instead to her marginality. Our website places Loy at the centre of the history of avant-garde experimentation and critique, making visible a new kind of history and new ways of digitally navigating the archive.

Using Loy as a case study, our project aims to broaden understanding of the diversity of avant-garde production. Emboldened by Loy's audacious manifestoes for Futurism and feminism, we have composed our own manifesto:

MANIFESTO
for
<Mina Loy: Navigating the Avant-Garde>

<<<<<<<<<<<<<<<<<<<<<<<<<<<<<<•>>>>>>>>>>>>>>>>>>>>>>>>>>>>>>>

Digital Humanities are **EXPANDING** at a ***VELOCITY***
that defies the limits of human **CONSCIOUSNESS**.

Much of the EXCITEMENT and INTEREST congregates on possibilities for

DISTANT READII

and TEXTUAL ANALYSIS of BIG DA1

NEW digital *tools, platforms, plug-ins, and apps* allow scholars to analyze literature in **BULK**.

The opportunities are especially rich for **modernist periodical studies**,
where the **VAST QUANTITY** of data—

- THOUSANDS of magazines,
- MILLIONS of pages,
- BILLIONS of characters
  —exceeds the capacity of the individual mind to grasp the discourse in aggregate.

BUT Mina Loy's corpus is *relatively small*.

1 scholar can read **ALL** her published work—*poetry, fiction, plays, essays, artwork*—in a finite period:
a few weeks of **concentrated** study.

CONCENTRATION is key.

Loy's work defies linguistic, poetic, narrative conventions.
It is *DIFFICULT* to digest and make sense of.
It demands CLOSE READING.

This site **DEMANDS** and *DELIVERS* CLOSE READING of work by Loy that has received the least attention:

- Futurist plays
- Dada prose

- Surrealist paintings

This is **ABSURD**.

WE KNOW that online "users" do not **READ**; they *SCAN*.

BUT WE BELIEVE that *DIGITAL DESIGN* can be utilized to:

- strengthen concentration
- foster close reading
- enable the delivery of complex arguments

FEMINIST DESIGN means

breaking down hierarchies,

        fostering o p e n exchanges of expertise,

          reflecting artistic diVeRSity,

            embracing *style* & *aesthetics* as crucial to Digital Humanities

              (rather than insufficiently techy or rigorous)

We are **NOT** simply preserving or retrenching traditional scholarly practices in the digital era.

        We aim to ***TRANSFORM*** these practices for a digital environment.

We want to **DO <u>CLOSE READING</u> BETTER:**
more ***INFORMED,***
less **CLOSED.**

This site delivers a **scholarly argument** enriched by documents, maps, timelines, images, and interactive commentary.

AUTHORSHIP is neither eliminated nor crowd-sourced.
But the processes of *writing, peer review, & revision* are made **PUBLIC,**

        so that **AUTHORSHIP** becomes **PUBLIC & COLLABORATIVE**

        (rather than **PRIVATE** and **INDIVIDUALISTIC**).

We aim for a **Ux**(user experience) that is:

      ~ **IMMERSIVE** (we hope you are drawn into the design)

      ~ **GENERATIVE** (we hope you are stimulated to respond in kind)

Even more boldly, we propose a new theory of the avant-garde – one capacious enough to account for women and people of colour who have been excluded from conventional formations of the historical avant-garde. Histories and theories of the modernist avant-garde have tended to focus on male-dominated movements, erasing or marginal- ising contributions of women and people of colour. In recent years, scholars such as Paola Sica, Mirella Bentivoglio, Franca Zoccoli and Paula Kamenish have sought to clarify women's contributions, while articulating the importance of gender, sexuality and race to the avant- garde.[15] While their approaches have transformed our understanding of the avant-garde, scholars have yet to offer a theory of the avant- garde that accounts for the distinct experiences of women and people of colour, who were often ambivalent about claiming affiliation with white, male-dominated movements.

The term 'avant-garde', derived from the 'advance guard' of an army, emphasises the militant, oppositional stance of the movements. Rather than attempting to rehabilitate this term to include a broader range of artists and strategies, we propose an alternative term. Taking a cue from classical ballet rather than warfare, we offer the term *en dehors garde* to describe the strategies of writers and artists whose mode of experimentation does not conform to the oppositional stance associated with the historical avant-garde. *En dehors* means 'coming from the outside' or 'turning outward'. Rather than assuming a militant position at the forefront of culture, women and people of colour often came from the outside and operated on the margins, working strategically to transform gendered, racialised literary traditions and visual cultures.

We aim to develop forms of digital scholarship and theory commensurate with the *en dehors garde*. As Elisabeth Frost argues, to look back at history with the inclusion of female experimental writers and artists 'challenges the way in which avant-gardism itself has been conceptualized'.[16] Digital platforms offer new technologies for documenting and analysing women's negotiations with the historical avant-garde, allowing us to chart an alternative *en dehors garde* that proves to be neither a mere supplement to, nor a plea for inclusion within, the current critical models of avant-garde formation. Open-source tools enable us to transform our scholarly methods and products in the same spirit of avant-garde innovation and collaboration that animated Mina Loy's feminist designs a century ago.

Digital platforms and feminist designs

A digital platform is an ideal stage for a study of Loy and the *en dehors garde*. The non-linear, spatial affordances of a website provide more flexibility than a print monograph for mapping the co-ordinates of Loy's peripatetic career; moreover, the interchange between visual, verbal and performative dimensions of her work invites multimodal presentation and interpretation. This kind of interactive capacity underscores the specific contribution that avant-garde modernism – considered not just as a historical movement or subject but as a range of aesthetic experiments that drew on diverse media and profoundly altered the reading and viewing experience – can bring to the creation, curation and reading of online environments.

'Mina Loy: Navigating the Avant-Garde' contributes to a broader shift to digital platforms in modernist studies. The 'new modernist studies', with its expansion beyond Europe and North America and the period 1890–1940, along with its attention to diverse cultural forms, to work by marginalised social groups and to historical contexts, has been fuelled by archival research, and has helped in turn to generate digital archives.[17] As the recent digital exhibitions at the Modernist Studies Association (MSA) annual conferences demonstrate, digital archives will increasingly provide access to the material histories, texts and artefacts of modernism. Digital archives build bridges between disciplines but also consolidate disciplines, objects of study and methodologies. The development of a 'print-plus platform' for the scholarly journal *Modernism/ Modernity* signals a commitment to new methodologies. As we develop the digital Loy platform, we've been guided by the following questions: what are the difficulties and possibilities presented by the movement of modernist archives to digital platforms? How can modernist textuality and modernist aesthetics help us to reimagine the archive for the digital age? How will the work of scholarship change in the age of digital reproduction? How can modernism help us to explore the new editorial and reading practices made possible by digital platforms?

Indeed, the question of '*how* we read' remains central to our website design, which seeks to transform close reading of verbal and visual texts, rendering the practice more interactive and embedded in social, material and historical contexts. Digital tools such as StoryMap allow us to scrutinise Loy's painting *Surreal Scene* alongside an analysis of her Surrealist-inspired novel *Insel*; to examine the significance of visual spacing in her poetic sequence 'Songs to Joannes' as it originally appeared in the little magazine *Others*; to explore correspondences between her war poems and photojournalistic coverage of the Second World War; and to consider connections between Joseph Cornell's films of downtown New York and Loy's late poems set in the Bowery.[18] The WordPress platform enables users to access a typed manuscript of Loy's play *The Sacred Prostitute*, read the story of its composition, and watch YouTube videos of early cinematograph film that may have inspired its strange stage directions. Split-screen architecture will allow users to scroll through scholarly narratives on one side of the screen, while studying a primary text or image on the other, with anchoring and highlighting functions to visualise connections between the text and its interpretation. Split-screen display will enable study of the primary text alongside a close reading, each given equal weight without privileging one over the other, enabling users to examine both and form their own conclusions.

Just as the historical avant-garde used aesthetic design to disrupt conventional ways of reading and seeing, our project uses UX design to defy habits of web surfing by creating an immersive online environment for reading complex verbal-visual texts and long-form scholarly narratives. If scholarly reading and writing are to thrive in a digital age, then UX design – the process of enhancing user satisfaction by improving the usability, accessibility and pleasure provided in the interaction between the user and the resource – must move to the forefront of digital humanities scholarship. Just like any other producers of digital content, scholars must compete for, capture and hold readers' attention online. To capture and hold attention, Richard Lanham argues, requires attending to matters of style:

> The devices that regulate attention are stylistic devices. Attracting attention is what style is all about. If attention is now at the center of the economy rather than stuff, then so is style. It moves from the periphery to the center. Style and substance trade places.[19]

Of course, academic researchers should not subordinate substance to style: the accuracy of data and quality of interpretation remain paramount. Rather than adopting a commercial mindset and placing style above substance, digital scholars must wed style and substance by giving attention to matters of design.

To give design its due is a feminist act. It is not just about making websites look pretty, but about considering the audience's needs and interests, meeting them where they are, and recognising them as vital partners in the scholarly endeavour. Websites need users, just as books need readers, but websites must pay more attention to design as a mediating element of reading. Every literate reader knows how to read a book, but the conventions for reading online are still forming and changing rapidly as more sophisticated digital tools enable new modes of presentation and communication. Website design should be as intuitively navigable, immersive and even pleasurable as reading a good book. John Branch's 'Snow Fall'[20] and David Boeri's 'Bulger on Trial'[21] provide design inspiration for our project, convincing us that online reading of extended narratives is not only possible but potentially more engaging than print. Design inspiration from the academic arena comes from the innovative digital scholarship of Alex Christie et al., Whitney Trettien, Lauren Klein and Amanda Visconti. Marrying challenging content and disruptive visual formatting, the co-authored Manifesto of Modernist Digital Humanities asks, 'WHAT would a methodological modernism look like?' Christie et al. visually draw attention to matters of style, insisting they are worthy of 'attention and curiosity'. Trettien's digital journal *Thresholds* uses split-screen architecture to embody the entanglement of texts and ideas that is the essence of critical reading and writing. Her Master's thesis, 'Computers, Cut-ups, & Combinatory Volvelles', provided design inspiration for generating scholarly arguments and theory in non-linear, participatory frameworks, while Klein's 'Speculative Designs' informs our reader-interactive approach to the theory of the *en dehors garde*. Visconti's 'Infinite Ulysses' offers a dynamic, engaging, intuitively navigable site that invites users to annotate and interpret James Joyce's *Ulysses*, offering a new model for interactive close reading. As these groundbreaking projects show, feminist design means embracing style and aesthetics as crucial to the work of digital humanities, rather than insufficiently techy or rigorous.[22]

Feminist design is fundamental to our project in other ways as well. Both a noun and a verb, *design* refers not only to style and aesthetics, but also to structure and creative process. Feminist design means rethinking the processes by which we generate and disseminate knowledge. As Catherine D'Ignazio and Lauren Klein argue: 'Feminism is not (just) about women, but rather draws our attention to questions of epistemology – who is included in dominant ways of producing and communicating knowledge and whose perspectives are marginalized.'[23] Feminist design means rethinking our structures and processes to break down hierarchies, encourage open exchanges of expertise and reflect the diversity of human creative production. It involves transforming our scholarly methods and products in order to involve undergraduates, graduate students, librarians, technologists and designers as equal partners in the production of original humanities research.

Students contribute to 'Mina Loy: Navigating the Avant-Garde' as creators of original scholarship, and our UX design affords equal prominence and value to their work, while allowing for experimentation with new tools and formats for humanities research. Our team includes three faculty architects (Suzanne Churchill, Linda Kinnahan and Susan Rosenbaum); three institutions (Davidson College, Duquesne University and UGA (University of Georgia)); numerous undergraduate and graduate students; librarians, instructional technologists and a programmer/designer; and an advisory board that comprises modernist scholars and digital humanists from across the US, Canada and the UK. The project originated in 2014 as a sabbatical project proposed by Churchill and supported by Davidson College's Boswell Family Fellowship. The first prototype was developed at Davidson in collaboration with undergraduate Andrew Rikard, technology fellows Olivia Booker and Katie Wilkes, and director of instructional technology Kristen Eshleman. Supported by Mellon funding, it was further advanced by designer Greg Lord and other digital humanities practitioners at the Institute for Liberal Arts Digital Scholarship (ILiADS). When Rosenbaum and Kinnahan joined the team, UGA and Duquesne contributed significant funds and resources to the project, along with the digital humanities expertise of Emily McGinn and Gesina Phillips. In 2017, we received a generous Digital Humanities Advancement Grant from the National Endowment for the Humanities, and Jennifer Serventi and the staff at the Office of Digital Humanities now count as members of our team, contributing vision, expertise and resources. Soon to be drawing upon the ideas of a broader public, 'Mina Loy: Navigating the Avant-Garde' engenders an interactive network of participants learning from each other. In this way, it demonstrates how digital tools can transform humanities scholarship from the traditional model of a lone scholar writing a monograph to a team of researchers collaborating on a 'multigraph' – an interactive, multi-authored, multimodal resource that sets UX design standards for digital humanities scholarship.

Feminist design is a form of avant-garde feminism. In our project, feminist design pivots on the notion of 'turning outward', as we seek to engage readers – whom we imagine as students, scholars and the general public – not only in Loy's work, but also in the ongoing work of reimagining the historical avant-garde as a more inclusive *en dehors garde*. A collaborative project involving students at Davidson, Duquesne and the University of Georgia unfolded in the autumn of 2018, as each of the directors involved undergraduate and graduate students in their classes in writing short biographies of participants in the historical avant-garde and other figures connected to Loy for the digital platform. A second collaboration between graduate students at Duquesne and University of Georgia working on the short biographies transpired in autumn 2018. Students entered data they had collected for their biographies to help generate a preliminary visualisation of Mina Loy's social and artistic network in Florence, New York and Paris. As they neared completion of their biography projects, students engaged in peer review and editing across institutions, and the finished biographies were uploaded to the site in 2018.

Our born-digital theory of the *en dehors garde* turns outward conceptually and methodologically. In the summer of 2018 we used social media to orchestrate a flash mob, inviting Loy scholars, feminist poetry scholars, MSA members, students, poets and visual artists, and the interested public to register on our platform and contribute digital post(card)s of varying lengths, media and formats. Answering Kathleen Fitzpatrick's recent call for 'generous thinking' in the humanities, we invited our readers to 'think with' us and participate in the ongoing work of reimagining the historical avant-garde as a more inclusive *en dehors garde*.[24] We received sixty-eight post(card)s from the USA,

Canada, the UK and France, and watched our site stats grow from a monthly average of 50 to a record high of 4,450 in September 2018. The post(card)s are displayed in a Pinterest-style masonry grid, and users can select and arrange them in their own theoretical formations. Via this production process, theory is not a fixed, unified or finished argument, but a plural, elastic and ongoing process. Yet what we imagined participants producing and recombining may not be so different from what we do when we read what we typically think of as theory – dense, complex, abstract arguments in very small print. When we grapple with that kind of theory, we typically underline the passages that we deem most important and rearrange them according to our own interests, often combining them with other texts. Our feminist method simply makes this process of selecting and arranging more tangible and explicit, so that readers may become more conscious of their active role in theorizing.

Despite the success of the flashmob, the experiment failed to produce anything resembling theory as we know it. Few of the post(card)s took the form of 'position statements' or arguments that could be assembled into any kind of theoretical narrative. The most popular form of entry was collage. But this failure to produce theory as we know it may be the mark of the experiment's greatest success: it invites us to think of theory in new ways, and to recognise that our feminist theory of the *en dehors garde* resides in the process rather than the product. Many of Mina Loy's own artworks and inventions similarly 'failed' in the sense of being unfinished, unproduced, unsellable, overlooked or lost, precisely because she ventured outside norms, conventions and proven results. The 'aim of the artist is to miss the absolute – the only possible creative gesture', Loy declared.[25] With similar chutzpah, we might say that the aim of the feminist designer is to miss the absolute – to fail to produce a total, complete theory may be the only possible creative gesture worthy of the *en dehors garde*.

Using open-source tools to chart a course outside traditional academic hierarchies and institutional boundaries, our team is continuing to collaborate publicly in communication with experts in the field. To that end, we have partnered with ModNets, and will submit the completed project to their vetting process for double-blind peer review. We are also working with the developers of the web annotating tool Hypothes. is, asking our advisory team to test out this tool as a means of offering public commentary on the platform. Although there are professional risks involved in working outside traditional vetting processes for print scholarly publication, the principal faculty architects of the project have tenure at our respective institutions, so we can afford to risk testing alternative processes for assessing the quality and value of digital scholarship in ways that might eventually benefit junior scholars and help transform institutional standards for hiring, tenure and promotion. Upon completion, the platform will remain available to the public as a scholarly resource and model, hosted and sustained by the University of Georgia Libraries and DigiLab. Students and scholars will be permitted to use and adapt the scholarly content based on terms set in a Creative Commons licence.

Although we envision the platform as a finite experiment with a clear end date, we hope to inspire new research and contribute to an expanding network of digital scholarship on the women and people of colour of the *en dehors garde*, including new websites, digital exhibits and curated digital archives that use and adapt our code and proof of concept. Our white paper will be downloadable as a PDF, making our methods, tools, processes and lessons learned freely available to the public. We will also use GIThub to share our WordPress theme. In sum, Mina Loy serves not only as a representative of women in the historical avant-garde, but also as a model for what digital humanists can and should be, if, like Loy, we dare to risk doing things in radically different ways.

Notes

1. <https://www.nytimes.com/2016/09/22/t-magazine/art/impasse-ronsin-artists-montparnasse-constantin-brancusi.html> (accessed 24 October 2018).
2. Loy, Mina, *Lunar Baedecker* (Paris: Contact Editions, 1923); *Lunar Baedeker & Time-Tables* ed. Jonathan Williams (Highlands, NC: Jargon Society, 1958).
3. Loy, Mina, *The Last Lunar Baedeker*, ed. Roger Conover (Highlands, NC: Jargon Society, 1982); *The Lost Lunar Baedeker: Poems of Mina Loy*, ed. Roger Conover (New York: Farrar, Straus and Giroux, 1996); *Stories and Essays of Mina Loy*, ed. Sara Crangle (Champaign: Dalkey Archive Press, 2011); *Insel*, ed. Elizabeth Arnold (Santa Rosa: Black Sparrow Press, 1991; Melville House Publishers rev. edn 2014).
4. Mina Loy Collection, Beinecke Rare Book and Manuscript Library, Yale University (YCAL MSS6).
5. Burke, Carolyn, *Becoming Modern: The Life of Mina Loy* (Berkeley: University of California Press, 1997).
6. <https://beinecke.library.yale.edu/about/blogs/room-26–cabinet-curiosities-yale-collection-american-literature/2017/12/05/mina-loy> (accessed 24 October 2014).
7. <https://brbl-dl.library.yale.edu/vufind/Record/3483102> (accessed 24 October 2018).
8. Halberstam, Judith, *In a Queer Time and Place: Transgender Bodies,*

Subcultural Lives (New York: New York University Press, 2005), pp. 169–70.

9. Prelinger, Rick, 'We Are the New Archivists: Artisans, Activists, Cinephiles, Citizens', Keynote presentation, 'Reimagining the Archive' Conference, UCLA November, 2010 <https://www.slideshare.net/footage/reimagining-the-archive-keynote-presentation> (accessed 1 February 2018).

10. Eichhorn, Kate, *The Archival Turn in Feminism: Outrage in Order* (Philadelphia: Temple University Press, 2013), p. 3.

11. Theimer, Kate, 'A Distinction Worth Exploring: "Archives" and "Digital Historical Representations"', *Journal of Digital Humanities*, 3/2 (2014), n.p. <http://journalofdigitalhumanities.org/3–2/a-distinction-worth-explor ing-archives-and-digital-historical-representations> (accessed 1 February 2018).

12. Thomas, William G, 'Plenary Address', Digital Humanities Symposium, UGA DigiLab. Athens, GA, 17 April 2015.

13. <https://mina-loy.com> (accessed 24 October 2018).

14. See <https://en.wikipedia.org/wiki/Baedeker> (accessed 21 January 2019).

15. See Sica, Paola, *Futurist Women: Florence, Feminism, and the New Sciences* (New York: Palgrave Macmillan, 2016); Bentivoglio, Mirella and Franca Zoccoli, *The Women Artists of Italian Futurism: Almost Lost to History* (New York: Midmarch Arts Press, 1998); Kamenish, Paula, *Mamas of Dada: Women of the European Avant-Garde* (Columbia: University of Southern Carolina Press, 2016); Sawelson-Gorse, Naomi, ed., *Women in Dada: Essays on Sex, Gender, and Identity* (Cambridge, MA: MIT Press, 2001); Rosemont, Penelope, ed., *Surrealist Women: An International Anthology* (Austin: University of Texas Press, 1998); Caws, Mary Ann, Rudolf E. Kuenzli and Gwen Raaberg, eds, *Surrealism and Women* (Cambridge, MA: MIT Press, 1991); Chadwick, Whitney, *Women Artists and the Surrealist Movement* (Boston: Little, Brown, 1985).

16. Frost, Elisabeth. *The Feminist Avant-Garde in American Poetry* (Iowa City: University of Iowa Press, 2003), p. xv.

17. Mao, Douglas and Rebecca L. Walkowitz, 'The New Modernist Studies', *PMLA*, 123/3 (2008), 737–48.

18. *Others: A Magazine of the New Verse* was founded in New York by Alfred Kreymborg in 1915 and ran until 1919. It published, amongst others, T. S. Eliot, Ezra Pound, Marianne Moore, Wallace Stevens and William Carlos Williams. See Churchill, Suzanne, *The Little Magazine Others and the Renovation of Modern American Poetry: Modernism's Others* (London and New York: Routledge, 2006).

19. Lanham, Richard, *The Economics of Attention* (Chicago: University of Chicago Press, 2006), pp. xi–xii.

20. <http://www.nytimes.com/projects/2012/snow-fall/index.html#/?part=tu nnel-creek> (accessed 24 October 2018).

21. <http://bulger.wbur.org/story/1977/?location=14098> (accessed 24 October 2018).

22. Christie, Alex et al., 'Manifesto of Modernist Digital Humanities', <http://www.shawnaross.com/manifesto/> (accessed 24 October 2018); Trettien, Whitney, <http://openthresholds.org/home> (accessed 24 October 2018); <http://www.whitneyannetrettien.com/thesis/#thesis> (accessed 24 October

2018); Klein, Lauren, 'Speculative Designs', <http://threedh.net/lauren-f-klein-speculative-designs-lessons-from-the-archive-of-data-visualization> (accessed 24 October 2018); Visconti, Amanda, <http://infiniteulysses.com> (accessed 24 October 2018).

23. D'Ignazio, Catherine and Lauren F. Klein, 'Feminist Data Visualization', presented at and published in the workshop proceedings from the Workshop on Visualization for the Digital Humanities at IEEE VIS Conference 2016: <http://www.kanarinka.com/wp-content/uploads/2015/07/IEEE_Feminist_Data_Visualization.pdf> (accessed 24 October 2018).

24. Fitzpatrick, Kathleen, 'Generous Thinking: The University and the Public Good – Planned Obsolescence', <https://generousthinking.hcommons.org> (accessed 24 October 2018).

25. *Stories and Essays of Mina Loy*, ed. Sara Crangle (Champaign and London: Dalkey Archive Press, 2011), p. 228.

Chapter 5

Louis MacNeice and His Archives

Jonathan Allison

Recent critics have spoken of the archival turn as one of a series of critical manoeuvres taken in the past two decades, perhaps associated with the new bibliography, or with certain kinds of new historicism. Such turns are often characterised as new although they are frequently a turning back, a rediscovery, or a reaffirmation of a traditional, neglected practice. Proponents of the archival turn urge us to consider the order, the pleasure, the allure and even the fever of the archive. In the early 1980s, Pierre Nora wrote that 'the obsession of the archive is a mark of our times ... Now that historians have put an end to their cult of the document, society as a whole recites the credo of conservation and archival productivism.'[1] Helen Freshwater describes the idea of the archive as 'long-neglected textual territory: mountainous piles of paper bundled together; corridors of catalogued files; dusty, disintegrating letters; musty records; obscure lists'.[2] She makes it sound something in between appealing and its opposite, but definitely an idea inviting renewed attention.

> The archive is also an increasingly contested space in terms of its ability to be all things to all people: a space for scholars to pursue 'serious' research; a place for the general public to find out more about their own personal history or a favorite topic; a place of access and education; but also a place in which things are guarded and kept safe, both from the ravages of time and rough treatment.[3]

The archive, especially if housed in a distinguished library, is likely to be a pleasant enough place, possibly even a bit like Philip Larkin's church, 'a serious house' which may be felt to be 'proper to grow wise in, / If only that so many dead lie round'.[4] However, attached to the allure, the pleasure and the fever, archival research presents significant challenges of access, organisation and interpretation. My own extended experience of literary archives was prompted by my being commissioned to prepare an edition of the letters of Louis MacNeice, resulting in publication of a volume of letters by Faber and Faber. The first task was to identify the locations of the author's correspondence, for which C. M. Armitage and Neil Clark's *Bibliography of the Works of Louis MacNeice* was insufficient, and indeed had not been updated in many years.[5] Consequently, the advice of librarians as well as the 'Location Register of English Literary Manuscripts and Letters' proved indispensable.[6]

When W. B. Yeats died, W. H. Auden wrote in his well-known elegy that 'By mourning tongues / The death of the poet was kept from his poems', as if the author's language continues to hold the life of the man, and at the moment of his death his posthumous reputation has its beginning.[7] The poet 'became his admirers' and his language continues to live in the minds of his readers. Yet he has been broken into parts. There has been a scattering: 'Now he is scattered among a hundred cities / And wholly given over to unfamiliar affections.' Auden is referring to the afterlife of literary influence as a continuing cultural presence, but his words might as well be applicable to the posthumous fate of authorial manuscripts and personal writings, as diaries, notebooks, textual fragments and scribbled notes on envelopes, letters and fair-copy manuscript pages – not to mention revised or amended galleys and proofs – become disseminated among libraries, archives, book dealers and private collectors, among friends and family members, at home and abroad. No doubt this holds true of most authors, and the work of MacNeice (hereafter FLM, except in titles) is no exception, with major holdings of his papers in the UK, Ireland and the USA.

In America, the largest body of manuscripts is kept at the Harry Ransom Center, University of Texas, in twenty-two boxes (catalogued as MS-02632), including manuscripts of poems and plays, notebooks, correspondence, and papers from schooldays and Oxford. Much of this collection had been purchased in 1964 from T. E. Hanley but added to later by the MacNeice family. Two boxes of material acquired in 2013 had previously been on loan to the Bodleian Library.[8] The Berg Collection, New York Public Library, has a very substantial body of manuscripts and typescripts, notebooks (1945–59) and correspondence (1934–7) (Berg Coll MSS MacNeice).[9] There are smaller holdings of correspondence elsewhere, such as Columbia (Bennet Cerf, Frederick Dupee), Delaware (John Malcolm Brinnin), Emory (Basil Barr, Adrian Green-Arymtage, John Lehmann, Melville Hardiment), Morgan Library & Museum, New York (Geoffrey Grigson), Ohio State University (Mark Van Doren), Penn State University (Marguerite Caetani), Princeton (Allen Tate), Sarah Lawrence College (Harold Taylor), SUNY Buffalo (Lockwood Memorial Library), Tulsa (Graham Greene), Wellesley

College (Elizabeth Mainwaring) and Yale.[10] The list is incomplete and doubtless will change.

In Britain, there is a very substantial body of documents, including many radio and television scripts, programme notes and many hundreds of internal memos, at BBC Written Archives Centre, Caversham.[11] A much smaller, though significant collection of correspondence with Anthony Blunt and his family is housed at King's College, Cambridge. There are small collections of letters, sometimes just a handful, in other libraries in the UK and Ireland – in Aberdeen, in Belfast (the McCann correspondence at the Linenhall Library; the W. R. Rodgers papers at the Public Record Office of Northern Ireland), University of Birmingham (Charles Grant Robertson), the British Library (John Betjeman), Eton College (Brian Howard), University of Hull (Philip Larkin), the Brotherton Library at the University of Leeds (Jon Silkin), Royal Holloway, University of Sussex (John Freeman and the *New Statesman*), the Victoria and Albert Museum (Arts Council), West Sussex Record Office (Walter Hussey), the National Library of Scotland (Hector MacIver), National Library of Wales (Dannie Abse), and (despite the fact MacNeice had written of Dublin 'she will not / Have me alive or dead') Trinity College Dublin has letters to Desmond Hawkins, F. R. Higgins, Denis Johnston and H. O. White, and University College Dublin has a letter to Patrick Kavanagh.[12]

However, by far the largest collection of MacNeice papers is at the Bodleian Library, Oxford. The collection comprises some boxes of uncatalogued material as well as collections, including the following:

1. Papers of John Frederick MacNeice [the poet's father], including diaries, exercise books, correspondence and printed books (1890–1940), (Dep. c. 757–9; Dep. d. 807.) From this collection two boxes of correspondence by FLM written while at school and at Oxford, as well as various literary papers, were withdrawn by the depositor Dan MacNeice in 1995 (they had been on loan), taken to New Jersey, and not returned (Dep. c. 755–756.)
2. Papers gifted by John R. Hilton, including three boxes of manuscript materials, and copies of undergraduate magazines *The Heretick* and *Sir Galahad* (MS. Don. c. 153/1–3.)
3. Correspondence: fifty-nine letters written by FLM to E. R. Dodds and his wife A. E. Dodds (MS. Eng. lett c. 465.)
4. Literary manuscripts by and relating to FLM (MS. Eng. c 5893.)
5. The Stallworthy Working Papers (restricted and uncatalogued), comprising approximately six boxes of material used by Jon Stallworthy when he was researching his life of MacNeice. They include Stallworthy's correspondence with former friends and

acquaintances of the poet, as well as a great deal of Xerox copied material from other collections, including from other libraries.

6. A significant archive of MacNeice material dating back to his time at the BBC and acquired in 1997, including radio scripts, notes and letters written home while travelling overseas on BBC assignments.[13]

7. Letters and photographs of Louis MacNeice, 1911–40, purchased from Didi Hopkins, including letters to family, a list written by John Frederick MacNeice of schools, colleges attended, family illnesses and vaccinations, a triptych photograph of Louis and Elizabeth (1910) and a studio portrait of Louis as an undergraduate (MSS. Don. c. 197; MS. Photo b 15.)

8. Material from the Carrickfergus Louis MacNeice Centenary, including printed ephemera from the conference, exhibition and outreach programme (10 September–14 December 2007) (MS. Eng. c. 7379.)

9. Letter from FLM to Herbert Davis, purchased 27 September 2005, from Prof. Graham Falconer (MS. Eng. c. 6859, fols. 44–5).

10. Louis MacNeice Letters to Nancy Coldstream, 1939–43 (MS Eng. c 7381), 78 leaves, purchased from Philip Spender, 28 February 2007.

11. Papers relating to Louis MacNeice and Mary Wimbush (four boxes) purchased from Mark Todd, 2006–7, including letters from FLM to Wimbush (MS Eng. c 7879), letters of condolence after his death (MS. Eng. c. 7880), Miscellaneous MacNeice papers, 1937–63 (MS. Eng. c. 7881), and MacNeice books and two pocket diaries (MS Eng d 4007).

12. Two letters from FLM to Stephen and Natasha Spender (MS Spender 56). (12) Letters and Related Material from Louis MacNeice to Nancy Spender (MS. Res.c.1441).

A large body of previously uncatalogued material, formerly cased in 70 large boxes, has now been catalogued under shelfmark MSS. 10641/1-75.[14] These include personal, general and professional correspondence (1928–63), literary papers (1926–89), diaries and person papers (1917–63), and include the papers of Hedli MacNeice (1931–89). They were catalogued in late 2018 by Svenga Kunze, based on lists by Judith Priestman, and the cataloguing was completed with the support of private donors. This material was formerly accessible to visitors but recent cataloguing throws light on a large archive which had been under the radar.

Jon Stallworthy kindly guided me around the Bodleian when I first went there and showed me the materials he had accrued in his Working Papers, as well as pointing me towards the other sources in the main collection. It soon became clear that the two boxes withdrawn from the

John Frederick MacNeice collection would pose a problem, since they contained over 300 early letters written by the poet to his family, from childhood through his undergraduate years. I contacted the depositor himself, Dan MacNeice, son of Louis and Mary, who invited me to his home near Egg Harbor, New Jersey, where he lived with his wife Charlotte and son Adam. I arrived in the evening but next morning at 9.00 a.m. sharp we sat opposite each other at the dining room table, surrounded by boxes which had emerged from a closet, and started to read the letters in chronological order. As I scanned them using a portable scanner, Dan read them, or rather re-read them, after many years, because many of them were familiar to him, pausing to read aloud a humorous passage or to point out something unusual or witty his father had written, or to comment on people to whom he referred. He explained the importance of someone, or what he had said when Dan had last met him. He explained how he had been sent to Ireland out of London during the war, and stayed initially with his grandparents in Belfast and then with the Clements family in Cootehill, County Cavan, when there was a threat of Belfast being bombed. He talked at length about his grandparents, Bishop MacNeice and his wife Georgina Beatrice Greer, and of her family the Greers of Tullylagan, County Tyrone, and of Seapark, Carrickfergus (the setting for the late MacNeice poem, 'Soap Suds').[15] It was extremely helpful to have the letters put in context by the author's son, and it was not late in the afternoon when he suggested we open the bottle of bourbon which I had brought him from Kentucky. We worked on the letters that day until midnight, and all the next day. I visited a second time in order to scan every letter, and our conversation continued by phone and email for some time after. Dan's assistance was indispensable, as was that of Corinna MacNeice, daughter of Louis and Hedli Anderson, whom I also came to depend on for information about her father and his work. As a result of their cooperation, it was possible to have some of their commentary on their father as annotation to the letters, thus framing the correspondence with the voices of his children in footnotes in the space below the main text.

Inevitably, MacNeice must have known his papers would be kept, and he appointed E. R. Dodds as his literary executor (who in turn appointed Jon Stallworthy). In a letter of 17 November 1940, two weeks before he was to make an Atlantic crossing, MacNeice warns Dodds that he will come to Oxford to 'dump some belongings & Mss on you', and proceeds to give 'instructions to you as my literary & general executor'. Thinking carefully about how he might be seen by posterity, he offers a series of warnings about using his letters to his parents in any future publication, and warns against using family members as sources of information in case anyone comes to write his biography:

(1) In case any mug wants to publish any of my letters (my solicitor in London kept mentioning that possibility), I do not want any letters to my father or stepmother to be published as they nearly always contain some falsity. I also regret most of my undergraduate letters (esp. to Anthony Blunt) which are nearly always v. affected & forced but I suppose they might be amusing to social historians.

(2) Poems: I have a new book of poems which I am bringing back from Fabers. In case the book & I vanish, all the new poems are included in a collected book being done by Random House, New York, in the coming spring & can be extracted from that & compiled separately.

(3) If anyone does a Collected Poems of me in England, I do not want any prose bound in with it.

(4) With regard to prose in general I have no interest in the potboiling stuff being preserved. If anyone, however, gathers together the literary criticism (the 2 O.U.P books & various reviews etc. – some of which have their points) I hope he or she will add a few notes giving the attendant circumstances of their writing.

(5) In case any super-mug wants to do a life of me I would warn him against accepting, without careful scrutiny, any alleged information from my family (including Elizabeth). The best authorities (though each only from a certain angle) are Graham Shepard, Nancy Coldstream, yourself, Eleanor Clark. &, I suppose, Wystan. (How mortuary-egotistical all this sounds).[16]

In the face of an Atlantic crossing during wartime, he was thinking ahead about how he would be seen and how his work would be interpreted. How he would have reacted if he had known the vast quantities of what he calls his 'potboiling stuff', as well as his most personal correspondence, would be hoarded in archives from Oxford to Texas is anybody's guess. He was conscious of having half-written papers disposed hither and thither and he had many ideas about how he might write his memoirs (eventually published as *The Strings are False*, but edited posthumously by Dodds), and he had an unpublished study of Latin humour, a manuscript on Greek literature, and fragments of a collection of essays entitled *The Character of Ireland*, which never came to anything more than a much-revised table of contents. He wrote to Charles Monteith at Faber several times for ideas on how to publish and recirculate and republish his work, as for instance a book on travel and places, which Monteith refused to publish.[17] It is appropriate that so many of his papers are in the Bodleian, but he might have been surprised to learn how much ended up in Texas. He would have been pleased that the correspondence with George and Mercy McCann was kept in Belfast.

George McCann had done a death mask of the poet, which is now kept at the Bodleian and which on one occasion I requested to see. Next day, a librarian asked me to accompany him to a back room, where the head was exhumed from a grave of polystyrene chips in a large cardboard box. It was of course the spitting image of the poet's head, and looked very lifelike, as death masks do, so to speak. The death mask is a peculiar genre, since it is representational but not imitative in that the shape and form are not dependent on the artist's (the mask maker's) intentions or imagination. It's just a mould, but it seems to have a kind of artistic status because it resembles a sculpture. Someone behind me let out an audible intake of breath, and wept openly, saying it reminded her of her father who had recently died. There was a momentary pause when we all felt as if we were in the company of the dead. In an archive, one can feel close to the author's writing, but also in a clear sense – especially perhaps with diaries and letters – to a personality. If, in a sense, scholars try to see the author face to face, staring at a death mask seems to literalise that metaphor. The visitor may feel like an intruder, as if the encounter is not wholly appropriate. Yet that feeling of inappropriateness is in tension with the wish to find out more, read more, for this is the job we are supposed to be doing.

Archival research may require travel, and if you want to visit all of MacNeice's manuscript pages you are in for a considerable amount of that. John Brereton suggests the travel can involve a degree of serendipity:

> David Gold, calling on Linda Ferreira-Buckley, uses the term *immersion* to describe such work. These journeys rely on happenstance, the often serendipitous or quirky physical discoveries of trunks, boxes, scrapbooks, images, or stories, and on extended close encounters with people, houses and hotels, cemeteries, and landscapes.[18]

On one occasion, a brown envelope appeared before me, with what appeared to be the contents of the author's pockets when admitted to hospital, a week before his death. These included identity cards, club memberships, a driving licence, a comb, a hand mirror. Unexpectedly, I found my image in the author's mirror, which he used when combing his hair. I was probably one of a long line of researchers who found the mirror in the envelope, but it felt like a trespass, as if I had no right to look in that mirror. On the other hand, it might be a metaphor for what we do in archives, bringing our own assumptions to bear on another life, another textual life, perhaps imposing our own sense of what it all means on all of these fragments. Considerations like these might not seem wholly appropriate for an academic account, but they are part of the picture.

In a review of the letters of Elizabeth Bishop, Tom Paulin wrote: '[W]hat we demand of a letter is writing rather than the written, speaking not the spoken, the mind in action not the mind at rest.'[19] We might quibble with the distinction – doesn't all poetry show the mind in action, what Wallace Stevens called 'the poem of the act of the mind'?[20] But perhaps the basic point is clear: there is an element of the casual and even accidental in the voice of a letter, to a greater degree than in the voice in the poem, and what comes across frequently is the informal, unpolished and unfinished, the casual and spontaneous flow of thought and impulse, rather than the polished achievement of the crafted poem. We might remember Yeats's remark about the difference between the poem and the everyday self:

> A poet writes always of his personal life, in his finest work out of its tragedy, whatever it be, remorse, lost love, or mere loneliness; he never speaks directly as to someone at the breakfast table, there is always a phantasmagoria . . . even when the poet seems most himself . . . he is never the bundle of accident and incoherence that sits down to breakfast; he has been reborn as an idea, something intended, complete.[21]

It could also be argued that the author seldom writes a letter directly 'as to someone at the breakfast table', since there are conventions involved with this scene of writing as with any scene of writing. On the other hand, the letters of MacNeice often possess an immediacy and spontaneity not found in the same way in the more composed voice of the poems, and it might be claimed that the letters – often written on the hoof, or on the go – are closer in spirit and tone to what Yeats outlines as the self of accident and incoherence.

MacNeice's letters seldom address his poems directly and more commonly refer to his personal business, his friendships and affairs, and the body of letters as a whole is dominated by roughly ten long sequences of his letters composed at particular stages of life, to his parents, to his first wife Mary Beazley and to his second wife Hedli Anderson, to friends Anthony Blunt, John Hilton, E. R. Dodds and his wife, and to the American author Eleanor Clark. He wrote many hundreds of missives to Laurence Gilliam and other employees of the BBC, but many of these take the form of memos regarding broadcast programmes rather than personal revelation and gossip. He also wrote passionate letters to his lovers Nancy Coldsream and Mary Wimbush, and staid accounts of his work to his Faber editors T. S. Eliot and Charles Monteith, and to many other editors with whom he negotiated for writing and work. The style of writing varies from person to person, and clearly the youthful excesses and high camp of his letters to Blunt (which he found on later reflection to be highly affected) give way to a steadier tone. His letters home from India, which he asked Hedli to preserve as a record of his travel and research, can read like detailed reportage. MacNeice was a keeper of lists, and the number of lists that appear in his diaries, letters and notebooks, particularly in childhood, but persisting later in life, is striking. Sometimes he lists his reading, as in childhood letters where he discusses the Robert Louis Stevenson novels received as gifts from his Aunt Eva, or the latest novel by D. H. Lawrence he mentions in undergraduate letters to Anthony Blunt, or when he recommends a novel about South India by R. K. Narayan in a letter home to Hedli while travelling in the subcontinent, or when he writes to Corinna at the end of his life, just before he is taken to hospital, about his 'mixed bag of reading'.[22] Perhaps his lists are themselves attempts at archiving names, people or places. As a schoolboy, he would send lists of names and nick-names, examination marks, sports results, book lists, insects and daily occupations – as, for example, when he sent a list of boys' nicknames in his class or made a list of 'Prep things', a glossary of slang words used in Sherborne, such as '"Snails" (cabbage sometimes, always cauliflour [*sic*])' or '"Fleas in the bolster" a pudding';[23] or when at the age of four-teen he makes a list of animals seen in the zoo, thirty-five animals listed non-alphabetically and seemingly at random, in three distinct columns, ranging from lions to giraffes to dromedaries.[24] At other times he listed a sequence of letters with Morse code translation, transcribed his marks in the Common Entrance Examination, or listed the titles of books in a bookcase provided by his English teacher, from Coleridge to *A Child's Garden of Verses* by Robert Louis Stevenson.[25] Writing lists was a way of conveying detailed information to his parents and also, perhaps, a way of filling up the page to make the letter seem substantial – a way of having rhetorical authority on the page, with minimum effort. He uses lists and catalogues as a rhetorical device in later letters where he would list grievances or intellectual points, or where he would send lists of ideas to a potential publisher when he was trying to pitch a book idea.

When he was in boarding school at Sherborne he became restive as the holidays approached and he began to visualise his return to Carrickfergus, and many of the schoolboy letters are illustrated with marginalia, thumbnail sketches which throw light on or offer a comic perspective on the subject. But even if they don't directly illustrate content, they figure in a marginal and speechless way his growing excitement about coming home, and a painful sense of physical dis-tance between school and Ireland (he once wrote he wished there was an aeroplane which could fly him home). I was grateful to Faber for agreeing to print images of some of these drawings in several letters in spring 1919, depicting Carrickfergus railway station as the name 'Carrickfergus' written in block capitals on a rectangular sign, with tiny carriages travelling on a track sketched below.[26] There is a sketch of the boat from Holyhead to Kingstown, smoke faintly emanating from a smokestack, and the carriages of a train snaking between Sherborne and London. There is another sketch of the Carrickfergus station with a stiff, upright figure wearing a dark hat and a clerical collar, carrying a Gladstone bag (his father is waiting for him at the train), and another sketch of a church spire at Sherborne and a train heading northeast (to London) and then northwest (to Holyhead). These busy images capture the fantasy life of the boy as he imagines the journey by train and boat, a journey he describes (involving train stations and connections) in many other letters.

Critics have properly focused on MacNeice's sense of a mingled identity, as an Irish (or even Northern Irish) writer born in Belfast, educated in England and raised in a Church of Ireland rectory, but imbued with a sense of ironic distance from the Protestant heritage into which he was cast – 'born to the Anglican order, / Banned for ever from the candles of the Irish poor'.[27] This sense of entanglement and complexity haunted him but also invigorated his writing, and is present in his poetry, his prose and indeed his letters, not only in letters from school or from Oxford but as a thread that appears throughout, as when he argues with Eleanor Clark that she completely misunderstands him because she doesn't understand his 'peasant' background (he was capable of exaggerating for effect). In this letter as in many of his letters to Clark, you can see him thinking things through as he wrote, compounding arguments on the hoof and exploring ideas and taking up positions with fluency and deliberation, by turns angry and joyful and celebratory, but delivered in an inventive, passionate and spontaneous flow:

> If you want a formula for me (which will also explain our discrepancy much more nearly) it is that I am a peasant who has gate-crashed culture, & when I say that I am a peasant this isn't a figure of speech or an inverted snob romanticism, it is just a statement of fact, though very few people can see it except some people who have come from your 'lower classes' themselves &, having also gatecrashed culture, realise my curious position.[28]

He cottoned on early to his own complexity, and made light of it in a revealing letter to his mother, when he reflected comically on the difficulties of things being so various. Explaining to her that his friends have attributed many different strains to him, he fears he might fall apart:

> I must really be very polyglot: John and I were counting up yesterday the racial qualities which people claim to have found in me:

American	Indian
French	Japanese
Spanish	Negro
Italian	(Russian?)
Jewish	German.

This heterogeneity is very painful. I expect to fall to pieces like a jigsaw. Well, I hope the garden is full of milk and honey and William is sufficiently restrained and all the birds are jargoning.[29]

Notes

1. Nora, Pierre, 'Entre mémoire et histoire: La problématique des lieux', in *Les lieux de mémoire*, Vol. I: *La République*, ed. Pierre Nora (Paris: Gallimard, 1984). Quoted in Arvatu, Adina, 'Spectres of Freud: The Figure of the Archive in Derrida and Foucault', *Mosaic*, 44/4 (2011), 141–59 (p. 142).
2. Freshwater, Helen, 'The Allure of the Archive', *Poetics Today*, 24/4 (2003), 729–58. Quoted in Dorney, Kate, 'The Ordering of Things: Allure, Access, and Archives', *Shakespeare Bulletin*, 28/1 (2010), 19–36.
3. Dorney, 'Ordering of Things', p. 19.
4. Larkin, Philip, 'Church Going', in *Collected Poems*, ed. Anthony Thwaite (London: Marvell Press and Faber and Faber, 1988), pp. 97–8.
5. Armitage, C. M. and Neil Clark, 'The Manuscript Collections', in *A Bibliography of the Works of Louis MacNeice* (Edmonton: University of Alberta Press, 1973), pp. 104–5.
6. <https://www.reading.ac.uk/library/about-us/projects/lib-location-register. aspx> (accessed 10 January 2019). This description of catalogued material was correct at the time of writing.
7. Auden, W. H., 'In Memory of W. B. Yeats', in *Selected Poems*, ed. Edward Mendelson (New York: Random House, 1979), pp. 80–3.
8. Stoddard, F. G., 'The Louis MacNeice Collection', *Library Chronicle of the University of Texas*, 8/4 (1968), 50–5. But see also 'Louis MacNeice: An Inventory of His Collection at the Harry Ransom Center',<http://norman.hrc.utexas.edu/fasearch/findingAid.cfm?eadid=01208> (accessed 12 December 2018). Correspondents in this collection include Alexis Crosthwaite, Geoffrey Grigson, Knopf Inc., Ellen Borden Stevenson, Terence Tiller, John Lehmann and others.
9. At the Berg, correspondents include Rupert Doone, Geoffrey Grigson, Michael Roberts and Edward Sackville-West.
10. Armitage and Clark, 'Manuscript Collections', pp. 104–5.
11. Correspondents include Laurence Gilliam, F. L. Hetley, Stella Hillier, P. H. Newby, Gerard Ryan, Peter Albyn Thorogood, Philip Vaudrin, Lindsay Wellington and other staff members.
12. FLM, 'Dublin', in *Collected Poems of Louis MacNeice*, ed. Peter McDonald (London: Faber and Faber, 2007), p. 179.
13. Acquired with the help of Merton College, Sir Christopher Bland, the Friends of the Bodleian, the Museums and Galleries Commission/Victoria & Albert Purchase Grant Fund, and Friends of the National Libraries.

'Bodleian Acquires Louis MacNeice Archive', *Oxford University Gazette*, 27 June 1997.

14. Priestman, Judith, 'Frederick Louis MacNeice (1907–63): A List of Uncatalogued Papers at the Bodleian Library', 6 September 2000; revised 11 July 2003 and 5 February 2010. Email from Colin Harris, 27 October 2014. The Bodleian Library are currently raising money to catalogue the archive. On the website 'Giving to the Bodleian Libraries', the Head of Development at the Bodleian invites donations 'towards enabling the Bodleian to catalogue and make available the Denis Healey, Janet Stone and Louis MacNeice archives for the first time'. 'Support the Bodleian Healey, Stone and MacNeice Archives', *Oxford Thinking: The Campaign for the University of Oxford*, 2017 <https://www.campaign.ox.ac.uk/bodleian-libraries> (10 January 2019).

15. FLM, 'Soap Suds', in *Collected Poems of Louis MacNeice*, p. 577.

16. FLM to E. R. Dodds, 17 November 1940, in *Letters of Louis MacNeice*, ed. Jonathan Allison (London: Faber and Faber, 2010), p. 415.

17. FLM to Charles Monteith, 15 September 1961, in *Letters of Louis MacNeice*, p. 681.

18. Brereton, John, 'Learning from the Archives', *College English*, 73/6 (2011), 672–81 (p. 672).

19. Paulin, Tom, quoted in Kermode, Frank and Anita Kermode, eds, *The Oxford Book of Letters* (Oxford: Oxford University Press, 1995), p. xxii.

20. Stevens, Wallace, 'Modern Poetry', in *The Collected Poems of Wallace Stevens* (New York: Knopf, 1971), p. 239.

21. Yeats, W. B., 'A General Introduction for My Work', in *Essays and Introductions* (New York: Macmillan, 1961), p. 509.

22. FLM to Corinna MacNeice, 20 August 1963, in *Letters of Louis MacNeice*, p. 707.

23. FLM to Georgina Beatrice MacNeice, September 1918, in *Letters of Louis MacNeice*, p. 22.

24. FLM to Georgina Beatrice MacNeice, Easter 1922 (date conjectural), in *Letters of Louis MacNeice*, pp. 65–6.

25. FLM to Georgina Beatrice MacNeice, 5 March 1921 and March 1921 (date conjectural), in *Letters of Louis MacNeice*, pp. 44, 47.

26. See letters to Georgina Beatrice MacNeice of 16 March and 13 and 18 April, in *Letters of Louis MacNeice*, pp. 33–8.

27. FLM, 'Carrickfergus', in *Collected Poems of Louis MacNeice*, p. 55.

28. FLM to Eleanor Clark, 21 May 1940, in *Letters of Louis MacNeice* pp. 394–5.

29. FLM to Georgina Beatrice MacNeice, 30 June 1927, in *Letters of Louis MacNeice*, pp. 172–3.

Chapter 6

On Efficiency:
John Updike's Poetry Archives

Jo Gill

This chapter reflects on the experience of working with the archives of the American poet, novelist, short-story writer and art critic John Updike (1932–2009). Held at Harvard University's Houghton Library, with additional materials among the New Yorker Records at the New York Public Library, the papers prove to be a curiously mixed resource.[1] The primary holdings at the Houghton Library are beautifully catalogued, and as clear, comprehensive and accessible as one might expect from a close familiarity with his poetry. The New Yorker Records offer a wonderful insight into the modus operandi of the periodical, and of Updike's relationship with it. There is, nevertheless, something rather disappointing about these fonds. And although I concede, with Carolyn Steedman, that scholarly frustration is part of the story of working with archives, I would add that such 'everyday disappointments' are usually counterbalanced by the reward of unexpected discoveries.[2] In Updike's case, I suggest, we are denied these small pleasures. Or, more properly, our pleasure comes from an enhanced sense of the complexities (the limitations and the possibilities) of the archiving process and an appreciation for his skill as a self-curator, rather than from any striking insight into his work.

Unlike the archives of many of his peers (Anne Sexton's and Elizabeth Bishop's spring to mind), Updike's papers – specifically those relating to his poetry – reveal few signs of extensive drafting, revision or correction, and little that has not been carefully considered before deposition. We look in vain for moments of personal reflection or revelation; a few pencil lines from 23 October 1975, headed 'reasons for depression' and listing work and divorce, are the only ones to offer a glimpse of intimacy.[3] In a rather chastening move, then, his archive thwarts any attempt on our part to read it as a 'place of singular embodiment and intention'.[4] As a consequence, we are left with an impression not of the richness of his oeuvre, but of the efficiency of his self-curation. Where Jacques

Derrida, in a point to which I'll return, speaks of the compelling attraction of the archive – of 'archive fever', of a 'disorder' manifested in the hot and heady pursuit of originary knowledge – I want to suggest that the effect in Updike's case tends rather towards the chilling and aseptic.[5] To reiterate, this is not to propose that his archives are devoid of interest. Rather, it is to suggest that their distinctiveness and value lie in their knowing manipulation of archival conventions and their playful anticipation and exploitation of scholarly desire.

In what follows, I outline some of the key features of Updike's papers with particular attention to what the evidence tells us about his writing process and the place of his poetry in its material contexts. I discuss the trails – perhaps even traps – he lays for his readers in the curation of his own record and I suggest some ways of reading Updike's poetry in relation to both the established and 'alternative' (Marsha Bryant's term) archives.[6] I conclude with some reflections on Updike's approach to his own legacy and its implications for the scholar of poetry and of archives alike.[7]

John Updike: poet

Although best known, and almost exclusively studied, in terms of his fiction, Updike began and ended his career as a poet (he makes much of the symmetry in a late letter to Judith Jones, his editor at Knopf, where he explains: 'My first book was poems; it would be nice to end with another').[8] That first book, *The Carpentered Hen and Other Tame Creatures*, was published in 1958, a year before his first novel, *The Poorhouse Fair*, and two years before the work of fiction for which he is best known, *Rabbit, Run*.[9] A poem from *The Carpentered Hen*, 'Ex-Basketball Player' (originally, 'Ex-Basketball Player with Gasoline Station'), itself a second attempt at the theme, after the early and uncollected draft poem 'To a Boy Playing Basketball by Himself', provided the character of Harry Angstrom and thus what Donald Greiner has called the 'ur-text' for the *Rabbit* series.[10] In 1954 Updike entered into what was to prove a mutually rewarding, five-decade relationship with *The New Yorker*, quickly acquiring a reputation as a precocious talent, particularly in the light and occasional verse that dominated his first two collections (*The Carpentered Hen* and *Telephone Poles*) and continued to be an important strand throughout his career.[11] He also forged often lucrative working relationships with other periodicals, from the *Ladies' Home Journal* to *Scientific American*. The latter accepted his 1968 poem 'The Dance of the Solids' with some enthusiasm: 'We have always dreamed of publishing poetry, but everything that came our way either was not sufficiently related to scientific culture or was aggressively critical of it. Your verses strike exactly the right chord.'[12] In his middle years, he adopted a more sombre and at times experimental idiom (see, for example, *Midpoint and Other Poems* of 1969) and then turned to poems about travel, art and environmental themes (*Tossing and Turning*, 1977; *Facing Nature: Poems*, 1985) and observations about the state of the nation (*Americana*, 2001) before emerging in his last book, *Endpoint*, published posthumously in 2009, as a distinguished poet of witness and a powerful elegist.

The efficiency that I see as a hallmark of Updike's archiving practice is of a kind with his self-conscious self-fashioning as a poet. Jack De Bellis observes that he 'considered himself a "professional writer"' and he was widely reported as treating writing as a job like any other, and as imposing on himself the routine of the white-collar worker.[13] A 1966 interview in *Life* magazine notes that he 'reports six mornings a week to his [rented] office . . . on South Main Street in downtown Ipswich, Mass.'.[14] The following year, in an interview with the *Paris Review*, he invokes this practice as important to the projection and defence of his public persona: 'I work downtown, above a restaurant, and can be seen plodding up to my office most mornings, and I think Ipswich pretty much feels sorry for me, trying to make a living at such a plainly unprofitable chore.'[15] The archival evidence, though, rather unsettles this image, certainly as far as his poetry is concerned. Clearly he did use the office time and space to conscientiously type up drafts and mark up proofs (Judie Newman suggests that he aimed to write fiction in the mornings, and to work on poetry and reviews and deal with administration in the afternoons), but prior to this, many of the poems were composed on the hoof – or at 'odd moments' as Updike explained – and drafted in a range of places and on a variety of different media.[16] As we will see shortly, these included a golf score card, an airplane boarding pass and an exhibition catalogue. Other poems appear on pages from small notebooks, the versos of proofs of essays, reviews or novels (see, for example, *Endpoint*, much of which was drafted on the discarded proofs of the 2006 novel *Terrorist*) or, more usually, on standard office pads. The Houghton archive in particular tells us much about the larger story of modern and contemporary poetry publishing – an industry that, across Updike's lifetime, saw a move from hand-drawn book designs on onionskin paper with copious manuscript amendments at every stage (*The Carpentered Hen*) to clean, digitally set proofs (*Endpoint*). In the case of the former, the typeset copy shows that the concrete poem 'Pendulum', which has each of its four short lines placed at alternate diagonal angles on the page, as though to represent the swinging strap of a commuter train, is literally cut with scissors and then glued onto the page.[17] In the case of the latter, Updike never quite reconciled himself to digital typesetting and towards the end of his career refers rather tentatively to the work of computer wizards and keyboarders.[18] As befits a writer with a keen interest in the visual arts (Updike studied for a year at the Ruskin School of Drawing and Fine Art in Oxford, and wrote well and often about the topic – see his 1989 book *Just Looking: Essays on Art*), he was keen to be involved in design decisions relating to his collections of poetry.[19] He was writing in a period when the value of the literary archive – and in particular of a poet's papers – was being newly recognised, and monetised. Documents in his own archive, for example marked-up newspaper clippings from 2007 and 2008 featuring the valuation and/or sale of Harold Pinter's and Cormac McCarthy's papers (the latter annotated in red ink, 'minor writer') for $2.3m and $2m respectively, signal Updike's awareness that poetry manuscripts and other personal papers might have financial as well as intellectual worth.[20]

Working and reworking

One of the most striking features of Updike's archive is how few poems show signs of extensive drafting, revision or final amendment. A thoroughly worked and reworked poem in Updike's case may stretch to five or six drafts at the most; many have just one manuscript (MS) version and a typescript (TS) or two – the latter usually showing only minor subsequent changes. 'Movie House', from 1962, for example, has one two-page pencil draft and just one TS draft which shows only one MS amendment (the word 'pealing' is deleted from line 14) and one revised line before the poem achieves its final form.[21] The 1974 poem 'Sleepless in Scarsdale', drafted in pencil on plain paper, finds its title, form (seven stanzas) and almost all of its twenty-eight lines in its initial draft. Only two lines show any change in the only TS: 'are weeded' in stanza four becomes 'look arranged', and in stanza six, 'floods the tunnel' is amended by hand to become 'pollutes the tunnel'. There are only minor and primarily typographical corrections between the TS and the final published version. For example, 'beyond' in line two becomes 'beneath', and 'drains fatigue dry' in line three becomes 'has drained off fatigue', while 'A step somewhere' at the beginning of stanza five is inverted to become 'Somewhere, a step'.[22] 'Sunday in Boston' from 1975 has one MS and three TS drafts. The crucial exclamation at the beginning of the final stanza: 'Brick Boston, city of students and drunks! / In Godless doggy righteousness we bask' appears only in the final TS draft.[23] Some twenty years later, 'Slum Lords' begins as a pencil draft, this time on a half-sheet of plain paper, and again shows few if any changes between first MS, first TS and final published version. The shape and, notably here, the jaunty rhythm (an iambic tetrameter line) are present from the outset.[24] The only significant difference comes in line ten where in the MS draft, Updike has left a blank ('Or _____ after the [illegible] had fled') which is amended in the TS – presumably after Updike had taken the opportunity to do some research – to read 'Or Tombstone after the silver boom went bust'. This becomes 'Or Tombstone once the silver boom went bust' in the published version.[25] From the same period, 'São Paulo' has one MS draft (blue pen on lined paper torn from a composition pad) and two TS versions showing only small alterations made some ten days apart (7 and 17 March 1992).[26]

We might compare the paucity of Updike's drafts with the evidence of Elizabeth Bishop's archive, wherein a poem like 'One Art' goes through some sixteen carefully worked drafts before it reaches its final form.[27] 'The Moose', famously, went through multiple drafts over some twenty-five years until Bishop was satisfied with it.[28] Phyllis McGinley, Updike's near-contemporary, correspondent and fellow light-verse (and *New Yorker*) poet, would work and rework a poem – even a piece of apparently 'occasional' verse – ten or more times.[29] In Updike's case, of course, it may be that earlier drafts were discarded, and only finished or polished versions retained for the archive. Unlike in Bishop's archives, there are only a small number of unpublished and/or incomplete drafts in Updike's files. Either everything he wrote was completed, and good enough to publish, or he discarded large numbers of incomplete poems. I suspect the former. This was, in other words, his writing practice. Many poems, particularly in his early and middle periods, came to him in a state very close to their final form or in 'one sitting' as he explained in a 1987 interview.[30] In a letter to Alice Quinn, then poetry editor of *The New Yorker*, of 25 September (1990?), he writes 'a day's visit to your stimulating city sprang two sonnets, of my careless sort'.[31] The apparent insouciance should not, though, be mistaken for a lack of care. The New Yorker Records in particular show Updike's deep commitment to his poetry and his tenacity in reaching for (or defending) the right title, or line, or word, or punctuation.

His engagement with his editors there, as played out in the drafts and correspondence in the archive, shows him first gratefully accepting, then, as he gained confidence as a poet, beginning to resist, their interventions. In January 1959, for example, he responds with some irritation to poetry editor Howard Moss's query about the correct names of rockets featured in the poem 'Deities and Beasts':

> I don't really know what to say to the sundry objections to Deities and Beasts. That is, it seemed so obvious to me that, the first stanza being about rockets, the second would be too. I mean, what would the point of the poem be if they were, say, submarines or types of perfume?[32]

In May 1961, he takes exception to Moss's reservations about the final two lines of the poem 'Earthworm', which Moss finds opaque. Updike writes:

> When I wrote them their burden of meaning seemed very clear. What I meant was that, just as the earthworm is immersed in the earth, so we are immersed in facts that make us claustrophobic. . . . If these lines continue to be a stumbling-block, you might consider omitting the last stanza, though I hope it will not come to this.[33]

In fact, it did, and the poem appeared with just three stanzas on 12 May 1962.[34] *The New Yorker* liked it enough, though, to feature it again in the commemorative selection from Updike's work that appeared in their 9 February 2009 issue shortly after his death.[35] Updike restored the final stanza in the *Telephone Poles* and *Collected Poems* settings.[36]

Archiving

Both archives demonstrate how important particular occasions or settings were to the emergence of the poems. Updike is assiduous in preserving, and thus making available to us, contextual information that will help us see this, to the extent that, on occasion, we cannot help but feel, perhaps, manipulated – or at least overly under Updike's control – as he steers us towards the 'ur' text (a plumber's bill or a wedding announcement or a newspaper cutting). We are denied, we might say, the kind of chance discoveries, or connections, that are available to us in other poets' archives. In *Archive Fever*, Derrida reflects on Freud's preference for archaeology over the archive; the former promises us the 'nearly ecstatic instant' of discovery, the latter only 'laborious deciphering'. Arguably, Updike's archive offers neither; instead we have a set of remains that – to continue Derrida's metaphor – have been deliberately buried so that we might excavate them. It's a discovery, of sorts, but one that has been pre-prepared such that, to cite Derrida again, we 'run after the archive, even if there's too much of it, right where something in it anarchives itself'.[37] Of course, this says as much about the scholar's desires and preconceptions as it does about Updike (we are reminded of Henry James's cautionary tale *The Aspern Papers*, where the thrill of the chase is soured by the realisation that its object has the upper hand). And to make this observation about Updike's careful and obvious editorial control is not to deny that there is much of note in the evidence that he does choose to leave. Neither is it to suggest that the material paratexts provide the best or only explanation of the final poems. But it is to propose that we need to read the supplementary material carefully and with an eye to its possible limitations.

In the case of the holdings for the early poem 'Blkd', for example, Updike obliges us in our quest for the poem's originary moment by archiving the plumber's bill that provides the poem's source and epigraph:

Labor-gas tove	$28.00
4 ¾ female ells	2.60
1 ¾ blk union	.80
4 ¾ X 2′ cplings	1.14
2 ¾ male tees	.72[38]

Filed alongside the bill is the pencil draft of stanza one of the poem, the first three lines of which are retained in the published version. The bill itself, though, is slightly different. And although Updike has fun in the poem with some of the terms from the account ('cplings' and 'union') and with the potential rhyme of 'blk' and 'milk', 'tove' and 'love', there is much that he foregoes. The actual bill has '6′ blk nipples', providing a source and internal rhyme for the assertion that 'love's language ripples through' in stanza two. It also has a 'gas cock' and much more. In providing the primary source, then, Updike gives us a starting point but not a complete explanation of how the poem works.

The file for the affectionate 1962 poem 'Miss Moore at Assembly' comprises two sheets of MS drafts (blue ink on plain paper), several TS drafts, and a marked-up clipping of *The New York Times* article to which the poem's subtitle, as set in *Midpoint*, refers: 'Based, with a derived scrupulosity, upon an item in the *New York Times*, describing Marianne Moore's lecture appearance before the students of a Brooklyn high school'.[39] The *Collected Poems* setting changes 'with a derived scrupulosity' to 'finically'.[40] The latter arguably better captures Moore's linguistic virtuosity.[41] The news article, by Nan Robertson, from *The New York Times* of 22 March 1962, headlined 'Gum-Popping Youths Yield to Marianne Moore: Poet Stills "Cool" Audience in Brooklyn High School', is headed with a photograph of Moore speaking, apparently rather anxiously, from behind seated rows of high-school students. Updike has underlined key lines from the article in the same blue pen he uses for the MS draft, including the lines 'a chattering, gum-snapping audience', 'gigantic white orchid fluttering at her shoulder' (both of which are quoted in stanza one of the poem) and 'I've always wanted to play a snare drum' – the final line of the article, which also serves as the last line of the poem. Other observations from the cutting find their way into the text, for example an allusion to Moore's tricorn hat and her Bollingen Prize. The distinctive epithet 'tobacco-eschewer' in stanza two derives from Robertson's report of Moore's response to lines about marijuana, wine and whiskey in one of the high-school student's poems: 'The 74-year-old poet, who does not smoke and who eschews alcoholic beverages and coffee, said she "would have liked it just as well if he had left out the narcotics".'[42] Very unusually, the MS in this case shows Updike deliberately, and in homage to Moore's preferred style, working out and marking the syllabic count of each line (10, 7, 8, 8, 5, 9, 11). The only other MS in his archive to do anything like this is 'Two Hoppers', where the attempt to work out a rhyme scheme commensurate with the plainness of the scene depicted in the paintings is evident in pencil inscriptions on the page.[43]

Similarly, the file for 'Epithalamium' – a poem first published in the *Paris Review* in 1995 – provides the wedding announcement from *The New York Times* of 30 December 1956 ('Miss Terriberry Wed in Suburbs') to which the poem refers and a first TS draft with pencil amendments.[44] These include a change of title from 'Miss Terriberry to Wed in Suburbs' to the more elegant, and also less specific, 'Epithalamium'. Of note here is the apparent length of time between the 1956 date of the wedding (and newspaper clipping) and the presumed writing of the poem. The draft gives 31 May but doesn't give a year, but the quality of paper and the typeface would suggest a date much closer to the 1995 publication than to the 1956 wedding which is the poem's starting point. The question of what prompted Updike to turn to this source at a distance of almost forty years is left unanswered – and it is here, where, as Derrida might say, 'the archive slips away', that our attention is, tantalisingly, most engrossed.[45] There are other holdings, too, where the material evidence suggests a moment of origin or inspiration that seems some distance from the text itself. Here there is more room for conjecture; first, about the poem's meanings, and second, about Updike's purpose in preserving the proof of its conception. Across the Houghton archive, in particular, a playful spirit seems to have guided his curatorial hand – a delight in the many and varied ways in which poetry might suggest itself to the poet. The notes to Updike's *Collected Poems* provide brief accounts of sources and contexts for many of those collected while the Index provides a fairly comprehensive, and accurate, list of dates of composition. Even so, in the case of the former, the archival evidence doesn't always substantiate the information in the note. In the case of the 1981 poem 'Small-City People', the *Collected Poems* note tell us that it was 'inspired by Lawrence, Massachusetts . . . Lawrence always reminds me of Reading, Pennsylvania, a city where I always feel excited and childlike.' But the first draft, in the Houghton archive, is jotted – apparently with some urgency – on both sides of a folded and partially completed Beverley Golf and Tennis Club score card. The crammed writing, which is squeezed horizontally, vertically and on the diagonal on all available areas of space, including across the map of the course, suggests that the poem was 'inspired' not by Lawrence, but by a game of golf on his home course, and that Updike could not wait until he had clean paper on hand to record the poem's initial lines. Here, as in the poems discussed earlier, much of the poem as first drafted makes it through into the published version. The original draft opens 'I love small-city people' and this slightly patronising preamble is sensibly omitted from the finished text. Nevertheless, the rest – including the highly effective enjambement suggesting a gushing enthusiasm – is there from the start even if this enjambement is, at least in part, determined by the dimensions of the card (with a width of c. 10 cm) on which the poem was written. See the first stanza as drafted, and then as published:

> I love small-city people,
> They look shabby and crazy but not
> in the campy big-city way
> [illegible] who really would kill you
> who really did
> have a million dollars in the safe at home –
> Dudes of the absolute, show pieces.

> They look shabby and crazy but not
> in the campy big-city way of those
> who really would kill you or really do
> have a million dollars in the safe at home –
> dudes of the absolute, swells of the dark.

Stanza four, too, is present in the MS draft in pretty much the same form as the final version, from the alliteration and the striking metaphor of the circus: 'the girls look tough, the men look tired, / the old people dress up for a circus called off', through to the image of the 'genetic pool' which, in both versions, 'confluxes to cast up a rare beauty / a boy full of brains', but in the original draft also offers the possibility 'or a priest'.[46]

That Updike was deliberately placing this material on the record is evident from the file for 'The Overhead Rack', which contains the TS of the poem, the first MS version, written on a US Air boarding card, and a copy of a letter to his editor where he explains the connection between the two. Dated 25 January (1994), the letter reads: 'I left a book for review, and the scraps of paper on which I had written yet another air-travel poem, on the plane; but fate was with us, and the kindness of USAir, and here is the poem.'[47] In the poem itself, the speaker's frustration is evoked in relentless run-on lines, emphatic alliteration, and hyperbolic questions:

> Why don't the smug smooth bastards check
> their preening polyester wardrobes and
> proliferating printouts, sheaf on sheaf,
> at the ticket counter [?]

By archiving the boarding card and the explanatory note alongside the TS, Updike lets us see both the anger of the moment (as evident in the heavily scrawled lines in the MS) and the refining effects of subsequent reflection and modification. In other words, while valuing and preserving the instant of origin, he also reminds us that poetry is an art that often (always?) benefits from later work.

'Alternative archives'

'The Overhead Rack' indicates that some of the most interesting drafts – and, arguably, some of the most successful complete poems – are those that came to Updike while he was travelling. In a 1975 interview, he explains that 'Writing in airplanes is a great poetry-writing time.'[48] The first MS draft of 'Flight to Limbo', for example – which started life as 'Flight to Hell' and then became 'Airplane to Hell' – was written on two pages of adverts (including one for Bacardi) torn from an in-flight magazine.[49] 'Thin Air' was first drafted on a paper napkin from the Trump Shuttle.[50] With these and many other examples (including 'Blkd' and 'Epithalamium', discussed above), we see Updike deploying material objects (the bill, the clipping, the napkin) as a way of guaranteeing the authenticity of the poem. Equally, and perhaps more generously, he is sharing with us the novelty of the moment and his sense of astonishment that chance encounters with the ephemera of life can become part and parcel of poetic production and are worth placing on the archival record. Updike came to prominence at the time of the so-called 'culture wars', and his embrace of the daily details of life both in light and in more serious verse provides a defence of the ordinary and quotidian in a context where the borders between low and high art were anxiously being policed.[51] *The New Yorker* archive in particular prickles with consternation about poetry's proper place in an increasingly commercialised and globalised world. See, for example, an exchange of lengthy memos in December 1952 and March 1953 between Katharine White, William Shawn and Gus Lobrano, debating the acquisition and placing of poems.[52] The juxtaposition of high and low culture (poetry and advertisements) in *The New Yorker* caused Wallace Stevens to caution younger poet Richard Wilbur against publishing there: 'He did say he felt it would be impossible for me to write over a period of years for a chic magazine that carried advertisements for Black Starr and Frost Gorham without adapting myself to their expectations.'[53]

If we extend our definition of the archive beyond the holdings of specific institutions and begin reading Updike's poetry against the backdrop (the supplementary or 'alternative' archive) of other texts and contexts – in other words, if we read his *New Yorker* poems in the setting in which they were first published and read – we begin to see new tensions and meanings. To take just one example, the 1959 poem 'In Praise of $(C_{10}H_9O_5)_x$,' which appeared in *The New Yorker* on 16 May 1959, had first gone through lengthy editorial correspondence, fascinating enough in its own right, about grammar, the title (*The New Yorker* preferred 'In Praise of Terylene'), the correct rendering of the chemical formula, and the spelling of the Latin term 'aeternum' ('eturnum' in Updike's TS draft).[54] But if we read the poem in relation to the launch first of Dacron (the US term) and then of 'Terylene' – a distinctively British brand – into a voracious American market, as evidenced in advertisements and even a short story in contemporary issues of *The New Yorker*, we can see that the poem is more than simply a humorous quip about the fabric's miraculous properties.[55] Instead, it registers something about the poverty of post-war desire (are wipe-clean ties the best we can hope for?), about masculinity (did we fight for this?), about the rise of the much-maligned 'egghead' scientist, and about British hubris.[56] The poem is set in *The New Yorker* just a few pages after one of the first of a series of advertisements over successive months and years for the new-fangled fabric. While some US retailers were happy to promote Dacron, those with Old World roots, or who were trying to appeal to an Anglophile consumer, made much of Terylene's native origins. The Brooks Brothers advert in the 16 May 1959 issue heralds its 'exclusive light weight suits' in 'washable Irish Linen and "Terylene"'; these, like the tie in Updike's poem, are said to be suitable for all weathers – 'cool, comfortable, practical' and seemingly indestructible. A month later, Dunhill Tailors advertise 'New Summer Slacks of English Terylene'.[57]

A further example of this kind of 'cultural configuration' (providing an opportunity to consider, in Marsha Bryant's terms, 'not only alternative materials but new ways of reading') is to be found in the files for Updike's poem 'Shipboard', especially when read in conjunction with the wider archive that is the pages of *The New Yorker*.[58] Originally drafted as 'Shipbored', the title was changed by *The New Yorker* to 'Shipboard' when it appeared on 15 January 1955 (in a letter of 4 October 1954 to Katharine White, Updike notes wryly: 'I can't resist a pun myself, and am glad to know *The New Yorker* can').[59] He reverted to the original title in the *Collected Poems* version. The poem sits in the magazine alongside advertisements for various ocean liners – including the United States Lines, the Grace Line and the Canadian Pacific Line's *Empress of Scotland*.[60] Each emphasises the leisurely relaxation to be found on an ocean crossing – an ideal that Updike's poem gently undermines. He was speaking from experience, having sailed to Europe on the Cunard ship the RMS *Caronia* the previous year. The *Caronia* was a frequent *New Yorker* advertiser; a full-page advertisement the week after 'Shipboard' was published promises 'Getting there is half the fun!'[61]

Endpoint and beyond

The impression one gains from working with these archives (and certainly with the Houghton collection) is that Updike's papers have been left knowingly, and in good order. His approach is invariably professional and efficient – both in terms of his poetic practice and in terms of what we might regard as the curation or collection management of his own materials.[62] In a sense, though, his archive forecloses on our ability to find what Derrida describes as the 'place of absolute commencement'.[63] The traces he leaves are sufficient up to a point; but don't entirely satisfy. In this respect, Updike sits in what Derrida identifies as a 'double relationship' with the archive – simultaneously avowing and denying its potential.[64] To go back to the pathological metaphors that seem inevitably (if not always accurately) to underpin discussion of the archives, Updike's self-curation, in other words, what he chooses to leave, and how his fonds operate to order our understanding, might be understood as a type of inoculation. He gives us just enough to stave off the 'mal d'archive' that would otherwise present as a 'compulsive, repetitive, and nostalgic desire . . . irrepressible'.[65]

Where a recent trend in archival studies has foregrounded uncertainty, instability and indeterminacy, Updike's archive seems to want to close this down – to secure, rather than to liberate, meanings: here is a poem ('Blkd', say) and here is its source.[66] The paradox, of course, is that this very gesture – the attempt to designate origin and thus meaning – and our response (resistance) to this manoeuvre become, in themselves, proof of what Derrida describes as the archive's irreducibility.[67] As Steedman argues, to say that there is nothing else to see is itself an invitation to read that space – that nothingness – as potentially and tantalisingly replete with meaning: 'If we find nothing, we will find nothing in a place; and then, that ... absence is not *nothing*, but is rather the space left by what has gone.'[68]

I turn in closing to 'Oblong Ghosts', a poem from Updike's final collection, *Endpoint* – a book that he knew he would not live to see into print (his letter of 31 December 2008 to Judith Jones in effect entrusts the book to her care).[69] *Endpoint* is caught on the cusp between past and future; between the immediacy of the present moment, the traces of history and the inevitability (which is also the unknowability) of what will follow. *Endpoint* looks back on moments from Updike's childhood, his adult life and his recent diagnosis and treatment. But it also looks forward: to his own death, to the unknown future of family, friends and the American nation, and most importantly, to the afterlife of these poems which in the very moment of being published join their own proofs and drafts in forming his archive. For Derrida, future and past are irrevocably connected in and through the archive: 'The archive is never closed. It opens out of the future.' The archive is 'a movement of the promise and of the future no less than of recording the past'. It provides, and this I think is what Updike seeks, 'salvation and indemnity'.[70]

The seventeen poems of the first and eponymous sequence of *Endpoint*, of which 'Oblong Ghosts' is one, offer a loose narrative of the progression of Updike's terminal illness over some six years from 2002 ('March Birthday 2002, and After') to December 2008 ('Fine Point 12/22/08').[71] On its first publication in *The New Yorker*, though, on 16 March 2009, the sequence was curtailed such that only the final ten poems were used, with a time span of just eight months (April to December 2008); the effect is to emphasise the elegiac tone and the sense of urgency that seems to drive this act of self-commemoration. 'Oblong Ghosts', the eleventh in the complete sequence, shows us that the past is always there. It lives with us (the shadow on the lung), is present in spectral traces (the 'Ghosts' of the title), awaiting its moment to determine the future. It is the relationship between what has been and what will be that is the poem's crucial – and saving – concern. The opening eight lines of the sonnet reflect on the immediacy of the diagnosis (the shock of the 'wake up call'), moderated by a characteristic attempt at levity: pneumonia is risky for the very young 'or 'very old (over 75)'. The closing sestet changes direction, sets the present prognosis aside, and looks instead to signs of hope for the future. In its original draft, it reads:

> Meanwhile, our President Obama waits
> downstairs to be unwrapped and I, a child
> in air as bright as that on Christmas day
> in Shillington – a touch of snow outside,
> the rushing traffic hushed, on holiday –
> inhale the scent of fresh-cut evergreens.
> Downstairs to be unwrapped. A child in air [illegible]

The draft brings past and present, self and other, the personal and the political, into productive alignment. The scene is both familiar and unfamiliar; ordinary and startling. It reminds us of the comforts of the habitual (the Christmas rituals, the turn of the seasons) and of the certainties of history, but it also alerts us to the thrill of the unknown, to the possibilities of the future.

The final version in both *The New Yorker* and *Endpoint* retains these qualities but concentrates – crystallises – them by slowing down and shortening the stanza. There is no need now for the mention of 'rushing traffic hushed', for the hush is embodied in the soft assonance and the lengthened lines and further confirmed by the (posthumous) circumstances in which the poem appears. The distance implied in the direct simile of the first draft ('I, a child / in air as bright as that on Christmas day') is broached by the removal of the simile in the final version: 'I, a child / transposed towards Christmas day'. More properly, perhaps, the metaphor of 'transposed' takes away one form of distance (child / air / Christmas) and replaces it with a closeness (transposition) that brings with it both immediacy and, curiously, ineffability. For a while, Updike plays with further amendments to the second draft of the final couplet: 'pause here, ^small^/~~one~~ hand upon the banister, / and ^scent^/~~breathe~~ the ^smell^/~~scent~~ of fresh-cut evergreens'. He finally rejects these variants and settles on the lines as they appear in *Endpoint*: 'pause here, one hand upon the banister, / and breathe the scent of fresh-cut evergreens'.[72] It is a good call, I think. It drops the otherwise too-obvious sibilance and half-rhyme ('small', 'scent', 'smell') and the sentimentality of 'small hand', and thus renders the poem less private (this is not only or necessarily a poem addressed to a particular child) and more open. The authenticity of the utterance in 'Oblong Ghosts' is, as this brief discussion of the revisions shows, hard won, carefully wrought, and further refined until it reaches its final form.

It is a poem in which Updike both looks back to the past and paves the way for the known and unknown things to follow; it signals an 'endpoint' which is also a new beginning. It offers, to quote Derrida again on the capacity of the archive, 'the affirmation of the future to come'. It is, Derrida continues, 'nothing other than the affirmation itself, the "yes", in so far as it is the condition of all promises or of all hope, of all awaiting, of all performativity, of all opening towards the future'.[73] Updike's poem is poised on this threshold, one part of an archive whose full and final meaning remains to be known.

Notes

1. John Updike Papers, 1940–2009 (MS Am 1793). Houghton Library, Harvard University. Hereafter, Updike Papers. The finding aid provides an overview of the collection. Available at <http://oasis.lib.harvard.edu/oasis/primo?id=hou01365> (accessed 2 August 2017). The New Yorker Records, Manuscripts and Archives Division, the New York Public Library, Astor, Lenox and Tilden Foundations. Hereafter, New Yorker Records. Finding aid available at <http://archives.nypl.org/mss/2236#descriptive_identity> (accessed 2 August 2017).
2. Steedman, Carolyn, *Dust* (Manchester: Manchester University Press, 2001), p. 9.
3. Updike Papers, 2014–M 140 (John Updike Additional Papers), 23 October 1975.
4. Helle, Anita, ed., *The Unraveling Archive: Essays on Sylvia Plath* (Ann Arbor: University of Michigan Press, 2007), p. 3. Updike writes to Leslie Morris of the Houghton Library on 18 January 2004 expressing concerns about the possible accessibility of personal letters once archived. Updike Papers, 2014–M 140 (John Updike Additional Papers).
5. Archive fever means 'to burn with a passion. ... It is to have a compulsive, repetitive, and nostalgic desire for the archive, an irrepressible desire to return to the origin, a homesickness.' Derrida, Jacques, *Archive Fever: A Freudian Impression*, trans. Eric Prenowitz (Chicago and London: University of Chicago Press, 1996), p. 91. Steedman, glossing Derrida, calls it 'a feverish desire – a kind of sickness unto death' (*Dust*, p. 1).
6. Bryant, Marsha, 'Ariel's Kitchen: Plath, *Ladies' Home Journal*, and the Domestic Surreal', in Helle, *Unraveling*, pp. 212, 214.
7. My focus here is on materials relating to Updike's poetry. For more on Updike's prose archives, see Begley, Adam, *Updike* (New York: HarperCollins, 2014).
8. Updike, John, letter to Judith Jones (Knopf), 31 December 2008, Updike Papers, box 196, folder 2465.
9. Updike, John, *The Carpentered Hen and Other Tame Creatures* [1958] (New York: Knopf, 1982); the book was published in a slightly revised form in England under the title *Hoping for a Hoopoe* (London: Gollancz, 1959).
10. Katharine White wrote to Updike on 2 August 1954 to accept, with some corrections, 'Ex-Basketball Player with Gasoline Station', New Yorker

Records, box 732, file 20. 'To a Boy Playing Basketball By Himself', Updike Papers, box 6, folder 303. The undated TS has the postal address for his adolescent home in Plowville at the top left-hand corner (R.D. 2, Elverson, PA), indicating that the poem probably pre-dates his departure for Harvard in 1950, and even if written during a holiday visit home, pre-dates his graduation in 1954. A second note on the TS indicates that Updike had intended it for *Collier's*. Greiner, Donald, *The Other John Updike: Poems/ Short Stories/Poems/Play* (Athens: Ohio University Press, 1981), p. 201.

11. As a young boy writing for his school magazine, *Chatterbox*, and a student working on the *Harvard Lampoon*, he had wanted to be a cartoonist. One of the earliest of his five decades of letters to *The New Yorker*, dated 21 March 1949, asks for information about the editors' commissioning policy for filler drawings: 'for I would like to try my hand at it'. New Yorker Records, box 484, file 18. For more on Updike's apprenticeship, see De Bellis, Jack with David Silcox, *John Updike's Early Years* (Bethlehem: Lehigh University Press, 2013). On his early engagement with *The New Yorker*, see Thomas Karshan, 'Portrait of the Rabbit as a Young Beau: John Updike, *New Yorker* Humorist', in *Writing for the New Yorker: Critical Essays on an American Periodical*, ed. Fiona Green (Edinburgh: Edinburgh University Press, 2015).

12. Flanagan, Dennis, *Scientific American*, letter to John Updike, 3 December 1968, Updike Papers, box 271, file 5946; collected in Updike, John, *Midpoint and Other Poems* (London: André Deutsch, 1969).

13. De Bellis, Jack, *The John Updike Encyclopaedia* (Westport, CT: Greenwood Press, 2000), pp. xviii–xiv. De Bellis continues: 'Updike has long considered himself a "professional writer", one capable of writing about baseball, Hindu religion, computers or car dealers – whatever was assigned. So a study of Updike as journeyman writer is in order' (p. xix).

14. Howard, Jane, 'Can a Nice Novelist Finish First?', *Life* Magazine, 61 (4 November 1966), reprinted in *Conversations with John Updike*, ed. James Plath (Jackson: University Press of Mississippi, 1994), p. 12.

15. Samuels, Charles Thomas, 'John Updike, The Art of Fiction, No. 43', *Paris Review*, 45 (1968) <https://www.theparisreview.org/interviews/4219/john-updike-the-art-of-fiction-no-43–john-updike> (accessed 1 October 2010).

16. Newman, Judie, *John Updike* (Basingstoke: Macmillan, 1988), p. 5; McNally, T. M. and Dean Stover, 'An Interview with John Updike', *Hayden's Ferry Review* (1988), reprinted in Plath, *Conversations*, p. 195.

17. Updike Papers, box 190, file 2402.

18. Updike, John, letter to Judith Jones (Knopf), 31 December 2008, Updike Papers, box 196, file 2465. In his *Paris Review* interview he notes: 'The miracle of turning inklings into thoughts and thoughts into words and words into metal and print and ink never palls for me; the technical aspects of bookmaking, from type font to þinding glue, interest me.'

19. In a letter to Judith Jones of 8 October 1984 about *Facing Nature*, he makes a series of astute observations and recommendations about the placing of the poems on the page. Updike Papers, box 196, file 2475.

20. Updike Papers, 2014–M 140 (John Updike Additional Papers). Begley records that the papers, after a period on loan to Harvard University, were acquired for $3m after the author's death (*Updike*, p. xiii).

21. Updike Papers, box 199, file 2572; collected in Updike, John, *Telephone Poles and Other Poems* (New York: Knopf, 1963) .

22. Updike Papers, box 201, file 2682; collected in Updike, John, *Tossing and Turning* (New York: Knopf, 1977).

23. Updike Papers, box 201, file 2713.

24. In his essay 'Rhyming Max', Updike asserts 'Tetrameter is the natural light verse line.' Updike, John, *Assorted Prose* (London: André Deutsch, 1965), p. 149.

25. Updike Papers, box 201, file 2683; collected in *Americana and Other Poems* (London: Penguin, 2001).

26. Updike Papers, box 201, file 2668.

27. Bishop, Elizabeth, *Edgar Allan Poe and the Juke-Box*, ed. Alice Quinn (New York: Farrar, Straus and Giroux, 2006), pp. 223–40.

28. Goldensohn, Lorrie, *Elizabeth Bishop: The Biography of a Poetry* (New York: Columbia University Press, 1992), pp. 252–9.

29. See, for example, the drafts of 'A Girl and her Room', Phyllis McGinley Papers, Special Collections Research Centre, Syracuse University Library, box 30.

30. McNally and Stover in Plath, *Conversations*, p. 193.

31. Updike Papers, box 202, file 2723.

32. Updike, John, letter to Howard Moss, 22 January 1959, New Yorker Records, box 773, file 14.

33. Moss, Howard, letter to John Updike, 10 May 1961; Updike, John, letter to Howard Moss, 12 May 1961. New Yorker Records, box 789, file 28.

34. *The New Yorker*, 12 May 1962, 145.

35. *The New Yorker*, 9 February 2009, 64–79. See also Adam Gopnik's 'The Talk of the Town' tribute in the same issue (pp. 35–8).

36. Updike was not the only poet to accede to *The New Yorker*'s requests for changes. Other poets, notably Sylvia Plath, showed themselves willing to bend, either because they trusted the editor's judgement or because they were so gratified to gain acceptance there. See Freedman, Linda, 'Sylvia Plath and "The Blessed Glossy *New Yorker*"', in Helle, *Unraveling*.

37. Derrida, *Archive*, p. 91.

38. Updike Papers, Box 200, file 2635; collected in Updike, John, *Collected Poems 1953–1993* (London: Penguin, 1993), p. 298.

39. Updike, *Midpoint*, p. 93

40. Updike, *Collected Poems*, p. 323.

41. Elizabeth Bishop's 1948 poem 'Invitation to Miss Marianne Moore', which would almost certainly have been known to Updike, alludes to the poet's 'priceless set of vocabularies'. Bishop, Elizabeth, *Poems* (New York: Farrar, Straus and Giroux, 2011), p. 81.

42. Robertson, Nan, 'Gum-Popping Youths Yield to Marianne Moore', *The New York Times*, 22 March 1962, p. 37. Updike Papers, box 199, file 2566.

43. Updike, John, *Facing Nature: Poems* (London: André Deutsch, 1986), p. 49; Updike Papers, box 203, file 2756. The poem was first drafted as 'Two Hoppers on Display at the National Gallery' but becomes 'Two Hoppers', with the subtitle 'Displayed in the Thyssen-Bornemisza Collection', in the published version.

44. Updike, John, 'Epithalamium', *Paris Review*, 37/136 (1995), p. 73.
45. Derrida, *Archive*, p. 91.
46. Updike Papers, box 1793, file 2684; collected in Updike, *Facing Nature*.
47. Updike Papers, box 199, file 2614; collected in Updike, John, *Americana and Other Poems* (New York: Knopf, 2001), pp. 12–13.
48. Stout, Elinor, interview with John Updike, *Sunday Pantechnicon* (WGBH-FM/Boston), 4 May 1975, reprinted in Plath, *Conversations*, p. 82.
49. Updike Papers, box 197, file 2488; collected in Updike, *Americana*.
50. Updike Papers, box 202, file 2723; collected in Updike, *Americana*.
51. See the special issue of the *Partisan Review*, 19/3 (1952), which opened the debate; responses in *Mass Culture: The Popular Arts in America*, ed. Bernard Rosenberg and David Manning White (New York: Free Press, 1957); and, for a critical overview, Lazere, Donald, '"Partisan Review": Our Country and our Culture', *College English*, 67/3 (2005), 296–310.
52. Memos of 10 December 1952 and 4 March 1953. New Yorker Records, box 132, Fiction and Poetry Reports. See also Yagoda, Ben, *About Town: The New Yorker and the World it Made* (London: Duckworth, 2000), pp. 171–3, 256.
53. Brazeau, Peter, *Parts of a World: Wallace Stevens Remembered, an Oral Biography* (San Francisco: North Points Press, 1985), p. 197. Black Starr & Gorham was an upmarket jewellery and gift company on 5th Avenue at 48th Street. For an example of their advertisements, see *The New Yorker* of 13 December 1958 (p. 13). Updike's poem, 'Party Knee', features in the same issue (p. 46).
54. *The New Yorker*, 16 May 1959, p. 44. Updike had previously taken the precaution of suggesting that *The New Yorker*'s famous fact-checkers might 'pay especial attention to the formula for Terylene (dacron in America), which I figured out myself from this Chemistry book and may be wrong'. New Yorker Records, letter to Howard Moss, 29 January 1959, box 773, file 14. See also Howard Moss, letter to John Updike, 13 March 1959, box 773, file 14. Updike had dressed his 'Small-City People' in 'Dacron' in his earlier poem.
55. Terylene was first referred to in a *New Yorker* advertisement for Brooks Brothers on 17 May 1958 (p. 13). Prior to this, Dan Jacobson's story 'A Long Way from London' had marked it out as a distinctively British fabric (*The New Yorker*, 10 December 1955, 50–6). For more on the relationship between poetry and advertising at this time, see Chasar, Mike, 'The Business of Rhyming: Burma-Shave Poetry and Popular Culture', *PMLA*, 125/1 (2010), 29–47.
56. For more on the figure of the 'egghead' in contemporary American culture, see Lecklider, Aaron S., 'Inventing the Egghead: The Paradoxes of Brainpower in Cold War American Culture', *Journal of American Studies*, 45/2 (2011), 245–66.
57. Advertisement for Brooks Brothers, *The New Yorker*, 16 May 1959, 11; advertisement for Dunhill Tailors, *The New Yorker*, 20 June 1959, 92.
58. Bryant, 'Ariel's Kitchen', p. 212.
59. *The New Yorker*, 15 January 1955, 93; New Yorker Records, box 732, file 20.
60. *The New Yorker*, 15 January 1955, 47, 1, 91.

61. *The New Yorker*, 22 January 1955, 53. See Green, Fiona, 'Elizabeth Bishop in Brazil and the *New Yorker*', *Journal of American Studies*, 46/4 (2012), 803–29, for more on the relationship between poetry, advertising and travel.
62. Adam Gopnik's *New Yorker* tribute praises Updike's reliability, punctuality and accuracy and the consistent quality of his contributions to the magazine over decades (p. 35).
63. Derrida, *Archive*, p. 91.
64. Ibid., pp. 55, 58.
65. Ibid., p. 91.
66. See, for example, the essays collected in Helle, *Unraveling*, and in Smith, Carrie and Lisa Stead, eds, *The Boundaries of the Literary Archive: Reclamation and Representation* (Farnham: Ashgate, 2013).
67. Derrida, *Archive*, p. 68.
68. Steedman, *Dust*, p. 11.
69. Updike, John, letter to Judith Jones (Knopf), 31 December 2008, Updike Papers, box 196, file 2465.
70. Derrida, *Archive*, pp. 68, 29, 26.
71. Updike, John, *Endpoint and Other Poems* (London: Hamish Hamilton, 2009).
72. Updike Papers, box 195, file 2464; Updike, *Endpoint*, p. 22.
73. Derrida, *Archive*, p. 68.

Chapter 7

Sylvia Plath's Library:
The Marginal Archive

Amanda Golden

Writers' libraries are often on the margins of archives, secondary to more prominent manuscript drafts, correspondence, journals and other private writings. But the items in Sylvia Plath's personal library are an important addition to other archival holdings, providing a record of her responses to the world in which she lived and the texts that she read. The majority of these books are held in two repositories, Smith College, comprising 162 books that Plath had in England, taking some to London, where she died in 1963, and Indiana University's Lilly Library, holding 150 more books which Plath left with her mother in Massachusetts before departing for England in 1959.[1] Plath's books document the history of her own reading. By considering Plath's library and those of other writers, we learn that their annotating can be a means of engaging in larger conversations, responding to critical contexts and writers' own social and political landscapes.[2]

While scholars of twentieth- and twenty-first-century literature are less familiar with writers' libraries per se, marginalia in reading libraries have been a subject of interest in earlier literary periods.[3] As Richard W. Oram stresses in his introduction to *Collecting, Curating, and Researching Writers' Libraries: A Handbook*:

> It is extremely important that reference staff should make manuscripts researchers aware of the existence of the author's books in the same reposi-tory during the course of a reference interview; in many cases I have found that this comes as a complete surprise and results in additional research visits.

As Oram adds, a writer's library presents an intellectual terrain, with some paths taken and others overlooked. He frames his piece with an epigraph from Robert Darnton:

> a catalogue of a private library can serve as a profile of a reader, even though we don't read all the books we own and we do read many books that we

never purchase. To scan the catalogue of the library in Monticello is to inspect the furnishings of Jefferson's mind.[4]

Scholars have introduced readers to some of the books that Plath annotated,[5] and other critics continue to cite the underlining and annotating in her personal library. However, understanding how Plath read also means, as Oram and Darnton suggest, examining the scope of her library and the ways she navigated it in relation to other materials, including the literary criticism with which she was familiar, the notes she recorded as a student and the teaching notes she prepared.

Plath left evidence for detectives, inscribing her name and possibly a year in some of her books, and occasionally leaving stickers from bookshops inside the back covers.[6] Her copy of *Hawthorne's Short Stories* (edited by her professor, Newton Arvin) carries the inscription 'Library 59'; this was her office in Neilson Library while teaching first-year English at Smith College from 1957 to 1958.[7] Marking her books in this way reflected the thoroughness that shaped her work as a student. As H. J. Jackson has observed, annotating is a student practice, and Plath was the consummate student, reading with pen in hand.[8] She tended to underline the introductions to books as she read, at times transferring their contents to corresponding passages.[9] In the case of *The Sound and the Fury*, Plath consulted William Faulkner's 'Compson Appendix' (1945), included at the beginning of the Modern Library edition (and described by Faulkner as 'the key to the whole book').[10] Plath studied Faulkner's work in Alfred Kazin's twentieth-century fiction course during her final term at Smith in 1955, and the appendix makes its way into Plath's margins.[11] We see her underline that Benjy was '[g]elded [in] 1913', including this detail at the beginning of the Benjy chapter in her list of years and ages that the novel chronicles.[12] Elsewhere in her library, Plath's annotations are the result of connections she has made to other texts and her own poetry.

The annotations left by writers like Plath remain (in the words of Leon Edel and Adeline R. Tintner) a 'silent witness' to the moment of reading. The more familiar a scholar becomes with a writer's personal library, however, the less silent these lines, symbols and words become. Edel and Tintner describe the annotations and marks in the library of Henry James as an 'entire signal system':

> hundreds of informal little messages written to himself now become messages to us. Important for posterity is the way in which James used his books. They were auxiliary to his writing; and this gave them importance. ... A line drawn down the page, a single word and page number, set down in the front of a book, a tiny cross at the beginning of a paragraph to enable him

to find the place when he wanted it – an entire signal system exists in his library.[13]

By adding symbols and comments, James documents his responses to his predecessors and contemporaries. Similarly, the libraries of James's contemporaries and successors present scholars with a vast resource for tracing the reading and reception of his texts.

The greatness – in size and complexity – of James's oeuvre is characteristic of the writers whom Plath held in high regard, and critics frequently cite Plath's admiration of James's fiction alongside that of other writers she read as a student, including Virginia Woolf, D. H. Lawrence and James Joyce. While Plath read these writers earlier in her academic career, she may not have encountered James's short fiction before Newton Arvin's American literature course during her junior year in the spring of 1954. In Arvin's course, Plath studied *The American*, *The Portrait of a Lady*, *The Ambassadors* and James's short fiction, including 'The Beast in the Jungle' and 'The Pupil'. After entering Cambridge University as a Fulbright Scholar in 1955, she attended the lectures of Dorothea Krook, who later published *The Ordeal of Consciousness in Henry James*.[14] Returning to Smith in 1957 as an instructor, Plath followed Arvin's example, teaching 'The Beast in the Jungle' and 'The Pupil'. The following spring she worked as his grader, reading and revisiting several James novels, including *What Maisie Knew*, *The Wings of the Dove*, *The Bostonians* and *The Golden Bowl*.

We can see the remnants of Plath's attention to James's prose style as she worked on the novels, pausing over words and phrases that strike a curious or perplexing note. In her copy of *The Portrait of a Lady*, she marked particular combinations of words that may also suggest the language of her later poetry, demonstrating a sarcastic admiration for grave, grotesque or unusual phrases.[15] For instance, following Edward Rosier's confession that he sold his 'bibelots!' in order to marry Pansy, Plath admired James's description of Isabel's reaction: 'It was as if he had told her he had all his teeth drawn' (*Portrait* 341 V2). Using a combination of question mark and exclamation point, Plath also lingers over James's description as he recounts that Henrietta Stackpole's 'eyes, lighted up like glazed railway-stations' (282 V2). Later, Plath flags with a line in the left margin Isabel's catalogue of the objects in Pansy's sterile convent in Rome. Plath learns of the 'new-looking furniture; [and] a large clean stove of white porcelain, unlighted', and reacts in the left margin, 'ugh', as Isabel mentions 'a collection of wax flowers under glass' (375 V2). In the process, we see Plath candid and repulsed as she encounters an image she will come to adapt in her novel *The Bell Jar* (1963).

In *Portrait*, Isabel's response to the decline of her marriage and Osmond's character reminds Plath of lines from a poem she had composed the previous year, '"Never Try to Know More Than You Should"', its title from Book Seven of Milton's *Paradise Lost*. Annotating James's novel in the spring of 1954, Plath inscribes her lines in the margin: 'The suave dissembling cobra wears a hood and swaggers like a proper gentleman' (196 V 2).[16] Momentarily, it seems as if James is alluding to Plath's poem. Plath's gesture is powerful. It also reflects the extent to which she saw her own words as part of the same literary economy. If someone else picked up this book, they would not know this reference, rendered like others in a private code to the annotator. The reader might think that they were from another text to which James was alluding, or on which he was drawing, rather than one by a college student. Plath published '"Never Try to Know More Than You Should"' in the *Smith Review* in the spring of 1954 and had sent a fair copy of it to her friend Enid Epstein the previous year.[17] The closing stanza begins, 'For deadly secrets strike when understood', suggesting the outcome 'trying to know more than you should' also echoes the dire conclusion at which Isabel has arrived.

It is also in the margins that Plath critiques James's world using the terms of her own. Annotating *The Ambassadors*,[18] Plath writes 'momism' beside the word 'eminent' during Strether's observation that: 'the society, over there, of which Sarah and Mamie – and in a more eminent way, Mrs. Newsome herself – were specimens, was essentially a society of women, and that poor Jim wasn't in it.[19] He himself, Lambert Strether, *was*, as yet, in some degree.' Plath read Philip Wylie's *Generation of Vipers* in the summer of 1951. Her reading of the term 'momism' into James's novel both documents its circulation at mid-century and illustrates her understanding of it. Wylie had explained in *Generation of Vipers*:

> MOM IS THE END PRODUCT OF SHE. *She* is Cinderella . . . the shining-haired, the starry-eyed, the ruby-lipped . . . of which there is presumably one, and only one, or one-and-only for each male, whose dream is fixed upon her deflowerment and subsequent perpetual possession.[20]

Plath later refers to *Generation of Vipers* in her 1961 poem 'The Babysitters' (CP 175), and in doing so, as Jacqueline Rose argues,

> Plath situates herself – or her memory of herself – firmly within the framework of popular culture. The book, written by Philip Wylie, was a massive bestseller . . . It is most famous, however, for its creation of the concept of

'Momism', the image of a deadly middle-class American female who is ultimately responsible for the collapse of the culture, for sapping the manhood of America from within.[21]

Plath also used the term in this way to assess others whom she knew, asking in her college journal about one of her boyfriends:

> <u>Why</u> is he so afraid of my being strong and assertive? . . . Just what is his relation toward his mother anyway? She has become a matriarch in the home – a sweet, subtle matriarch, to be sure, but nonetheless, a 'Mom'. (cf. Phlip Wylie – 'Generation of Vipers'). She has become ruler of finances, manager of the home, '<u>mother</u>' of her husband.[22]

In this case, the margin presents a space in which contemporary social anxieties merge with the interpretation of texts. A reader a decade later would not necessarily interpret James using the same terminology.

Annotations allow us to know things we otherwise would not. Underlining too is a means of knowing, of keeping up with a text and maintaining focus. As in the case of 'momism', attending to the reference means for us revisiting Plath's reading of James and Wylie, and considering how she may have connected the two. H. J. Jackson has compared the experience of reading marginalia to that of eavesdropping:

> A metaphor I like to use for the experience of coming upon handwritten notes in printed books, when you expect to be communing only with the author, is of a phone call in which suddenly another voice comes on the line, and you have to attend to it as well.[23]

As Plath approached her slim paperback copy of *What Maisie Knew*, with Edward Gorey's wary Maisie on its cover, Plath underlined and left lines in the margin attending to the young protagonist's awareness of her parents' and step-parents' relations.[24] As Arvin's grader during the spring of her teaching year at Smith, Plath acquired a copy of F.W. Dupee's *Henry James*, underlining that

> <u>What Maisie knows at last is that she is being used by her elders</u> for <u>their own disreputable ends;</u> <u>that she is in fact an-strument of badness among them</u> <u>and a not unwilling</u> <u>one so long as she goes along with them in her desire</u> <u>for support and affection.</u>[25]

This instance sheds light on what Plath's library can witness, including her engagement with critical conversations.

As a grader for Newton Arvin, Plath 'read till …[she] finished' *The Bostonians* near the close of her teaching year at Smith in 1958, attending her former professor's lectures to 'hear roughly the same things' she had as a student. The novel also depicts the city to which she would soon be moving with Ted Hughes (*UJ* 374, 375). Born in Boston, Plath spent her childhood near the sea in Winthrop, Massachusetts, before moving to the suburb of Wellesley, where her mother commuted to teach at Boston University. Plath had also spent a summer at Harvard University in 1955, living in Cambridge, and she would have recognised features of the landscape as she read James. Beginning with her underlining of Irving Howe's introduction in the Modern Library edition of the novel, we can see the ways she learned to read it, fostering some of the connections with her own experience.

In Howe's introduction to *The Bostonians*, Plath underlined that both this novel and *The Princess Casamassima* 'deal ambitiously, though rather furtively, with the public world, with the fluid contours of society and the tempting dangers of politics'.[26] The shape of Plath's underlining and where she lifted her pen reflect what caught her attention and where she moved on. Significantly, Howe would later critique Plath's own late poems, arguing that her inclusion of the Holocaust to dramatise her private struggles was inappropriate.[27] In his introduction to *The Bostonians*, Plath learns of the contours of James's representation of political and social content. She accentuated with an exclamation point Howe's observation, underlining it in part, that '[f]or a writer who is often said to shy away from physical experience, James, in *The Bostonians*, seems remarkably aware of the female body' (*Bostonians* xix). James was attentive to the complexity of his world. In a note at the bottom of the page, Howe warns sceptics:

> It is sometimes asked whether James 'really knew' how thoroughly he had drawn a lesbian type. The question is relevant only if we suppose that because people in an earlier age did not use our vocabulary they necessarily understood less than we do'.[28]

Howe cautions readers not to underestimate James's perceptiveness, which distinguishes his prose.

While contemplating the previous year which writers to select as 'masters' for her fiction, Plath hesitated, considering 'James too elaborate, too calm & well-mannered' (*UJ* 274, 274–5). Reading *The Wings of the Dove* in May of 1958, Plath found that

> Henry James teaches me hourly – he is too fine for me – but then, I am so crude and loud that his lesson can only serve to make me less crude, not more fine – teaches me how life is circuitous, rich, sentences and acts laden all with riches of meaning and implication. (*UJ* 382)

The following year, during her residency at Yaddo, an artists' colony in Saratoga Springs, New York, Plath noted in her journal that she

Read pound [*sic*] aloud and was rapt. A religious power given by memorizing. Will try to learn a long and a short each day. Best to read them in the morning first thing, review over lunch and chatechize [*sic*] at tea. I would have him as a master. The irrefutable, implacable uncounted uncontrived line. Statement like a whiplash. God. (*UJ* 514–15)

Raising the pitch, Ezra Pound is far from delicate.

It was the meeting of Pound and James which Hugh Kenner turned to at the opening of *The Pound Era*, beginning his reading of modernism with Pound at the centre.[29] Plath attended Smith in more of an Eliot era than a Pound one, which is all the more reason to investigate what Plath knew about Pound. It also draws into relief what authors' libraries can teach us.[30] Plath's professor, Elizabeth Drew,[31] gave a lecture during what was probably the spring of Plath's final year of college, and Plath recorded that Pound's efforts in championing others' work were more significant than the quality of his poetry and noted his aphorism that 'artists are the antennae of the race'.[32] This sense of the artist, attentive to what others are not, is also present in the connections she drew in the margins of her books.[33]

Annotating Edmund Wilson's *Axel's Castle*, Plath exclaimed, 'yes! Cf. Pisan Cantos!' beside the following line which she underlined: 'Pound's work *has* been partially sunk by its cargo of erudition.'[34] Wilson was drawing a distinction between Pound's *Cantos* and Eliot's *The Waste Land*, noting that the latter, even with the range of its language and allusion, may have been more accessible to readers. Plath's remark is one of the indications of what she knew of *The Pisan Cantos*. While she received a copy of Pound's book as a gift in 1951, two years after the decision to award it the Bollingen Prize despite Pound's arrest for treason,[35] she did not underline, annotate or mark her copy.[36] While scholars often note that Plath read and admired poets including Eliot, W. H. Auden, W. B. Yeats, and Wallace Stevens,[37] *Axel's Castle* teaches us that she not only attended to Wilson's chapters on Eliot, Yeats, and James Joyce, but also to those on Gertrude Stein, Arthur Rimbaud, and Tristan Tzara's 'Memoirs of Dadaism'. The fact that Pound himself appears in the margins, accompanying these figures, raises questions about Plath's knowledge of the political controversies surrounding Pound and the extent to which his poetry and poetics may have shaped her own.[38]

Plath, however, had started college in the autumn of 1950, the year after the decision to award the Prize to Pound. In the notes that Elizabeth Drew prepared for her overview of Joseph Conrad's *Lord Jim* in the twentieth-century literature course that Plath completed during the spring of her sophomore year in 1952, Drew stated that Pound had been 'brought to trial for treason'.[39] Even though Plath may not have heard this detail, or this version of the lecture, others on the Smith campus had voiced opinions on the issue. Robert Gorham Davis, with whom Plath would study creative writing during her junior year, had argued against giving Pound the prize. He found the content of *The Pisan Cantos* offensive and the poems not worthy of an award.[40] Even though Davis found Pound's behaviour objectionable, he qualified this, saying that 'poetry has to be judged as poetry and not as something else; poetry is not patriotism; the poem is not the same as the poet'.[41]

In March of 1958, Plath and Hughes visited academics from nearby Mount Holyoke College. Within a month, Pound would be released from St. Elizabeths Hospital.[42] In Plath's account, the evening with colleagues was awkward, made further so by the arrival of poet Peter Viereck, who 'raved: politics, Ezra Pound: we agreed a man was all of a piece, couldn't really compartmentalize himself, airtight' (*UJ* 353).[43] The key here is in the final image; despite efforts on behalf of poet and reader to separate their politics from their art, the two have a way of intersecting.[44] This detail offsets the point that Plath and her contemporaries had ostensibly been taught about poetry. On what was probably an earlier occasion, Plath had added two exclamation points in the margin of her copy of Edmund Wilson's *Axel's Castle* as she encountered Eliot's familiar explanation of the genre as 'not the expression of personality, but an escape from personality'.[45] In some ways, the trial turned this issue on its head, and the particular circumstances of Pound's offence, namely his anti-Semitism, made it impossible to ignore. But one could also entertain the possibility that Plath was not just agreeing with Viereck, but also beginning to move away from what she had been taught, anticipating the more personal direction that her later poetry would take.

Plath's 1962 poem 'Lesbos' returns to her early reading of modernism and transforms it. Rewriting lines from Eliot's 'The Love Song of J. Alfred Prufrock', Plath's persona proposes that: 'I should sit on a rock off Cornwall and comb my hair / I should wear tiger pants, I should have an affair. / ... Me and you'.[46] In a poem whose title alludes to Sappho's island and begins with the line 'Viciousness in the kitchen', she is refashioning an earlier standard for a new generation (*CP* 227). Readers can hear Plath turning over Eliot's 'Let us go then, you and I', and spicing up his rolled trousers.[47] Stylistically, 'Lesbos' veers towards Pound's *Cantos* in its uneven stanzas that vary in length from thirty-two lines to seven lines and adopt a collage style when splicing in her nod to Eliot.[48] When Plath experiments in this way, we see that the material of her reading can have a more vital purpose, beyond what Darnton called the 'furnishings' of Jefferson's mind. Poems like 'Lesbos' give new purpose to what Pansy's 'furniture' signifies; Plath's feminist speakers have greater agency, redefining both modernist poetics and women's roles in society.

Plath's library demonstrates the particularity with which she responded to fiction and poetry, from James and Faulkner to Pound and Eliot. Her imagination travels between margin and poem, incorporating and transforming the language of her social landscape. As a result, her library provides a case study for considering the value of such resources for literary scholarship. Far from marginal, the texts writers underline and annotate are sites where language and culture intersect. These materials chart where writers' reading and writing strategies meet, enabling new considerations of their creative practices and the archives that they leave behind.

Notes

I thank Elizabeth J. Donaldson, Anita Helle, Margaret Konkol and Peter K. Steinberg for their feedback. An early version of this chapter took shape as a presentation on the Henry James Society panel at the Modern Language Association Convention in Philadelphia in 2005.

1. Books Plath owned and annotated have surfaced in other collections, including a selection in Ted Hughes's personal library in Emory University's Stuart A. Rose Manuscript, Archives, and Rare Book Library and several in the Rare Book Library, University of Virginia; and individual volumes remain elsewhere, such as her copy of Virginia Woolf's *Orlando* at the University of Louisville and F. Scott Fitzgerald's *The Great Gatsby* at the University of South Carolina. Regarding Hughes's library see <http://discovere.emory.edu/primo_library/libweb/action/search.do>, searching with the phrase, 'Former Owner Ted Hughes'. Regarding Indiana's collection, see <http://www.indiana.edu/~liblilly/guides/plath/materials.shtml>. Peter K. Steinberg has catalogued Plath's library and cited the locations of her books on LibraryThing <http://www.librarything.com/profile/SylviaPlathLibrary> (all accessed 13 June 2018).

2. Regarding writers' marginalia and their relationship to cognitive thought, see Van Hulle, Dirk, *Modern Manuscripts: The Extended Mind and Creative Undoing from Darwin to Beckett and Beyond* (London: Bloomsbury Academic, 2014).

3. See H. J. Jackson's *Marginalia* for a historical consideration of annotation practices, including a survey of strategies readers use as they write in library books. Jackson, H. J., *Marginalia: Readers Writing in Books* (New Haven: Yale University Press, 2001). For historical considerations of marginalia, see Grafton, Anthony, *The Footnote: A Curious History* (Cambridge, MA: Harvard University Press, 1997), p. 30. For functions of marginalia, see Hauptman, Robert, *Documentation: A History and Critique of Attribution, Commentary, Glosses, Marginalia, Notes, Bibliographies, Works-Cited Lists, and Citation Indexing and Analysis* (Jefferson: McFarland, 2008),

p. 74. For medieval studies of marginalia, see Camille, Michael, *Image on the Edge: The Margins of Medieval Art* (London: Reaktion Books, 1992); Greetham, David, ed., *The Margins of the Text* (Ann Arbor: University of Michigan Press, 1997); and Sherman, William H., *Used Books: Marking Readers in Renaissance England* (Philadelphia: University of Pennsylvania Press, 2008).

4. Oram, Richard W., 'Introduction', in *Collecting, Curating, and Researching Writers' Libraries: A Handbook*, ed. Richard W. Oram and Joseph Nicholson (Lanham: Rowman & Nicholson, 2014), pp. 2, 1.

5. Brain, Tracy, *The Other Sylvia Plath* (New York: Longman, 2001).

6. See Golden, Amanda, 'Sylvia Plath on Charing Cross Road', *Plath Profiles* 3 (2010), 113–19 <https://scholarworks.iu.edu/journals/index.php/plath/article/view/4512/4137> (accessed 16 January 2018).

7. Hawthorne, Nathaniel, *Hawthorne's Short Stories*, ed. Newton Arvin (New York: Vintage Books, 1955). Library of Sylvia Plath, Smith College, Northampton, MA; hereafter referred to in the notes as 'Smith'.

8. Jackson, *Marginalia*, p. 21. Plath underlines and annotates a wide range of introductory and what Genette calls 'paratextual' materials throughout her library at Smith. Genette, Gerard, *Paratexts: Thresholds of Interpretation* (1987; New York: Cambridge University Press, 1997).

9. One instance is Plath's copy of *The Portable Blake*, ed. Alfred Kazin (New York: Viking Press, 1953), Smith.

10. Quoted in Blotner, Joseph, *Faulkner: A Biography* [1973] (Jackson: University Press of Mississippi, 2005), p. 475.

11. Regarding Kazin's approach to the novel, see Kazin, Alfred, 'The Sound and the Fury', in *Alfred Kazin's America*, ed. Ted Solotaroff (New York: Harper Perennial, 2003), p. 208.

12. William Faulkner, *As I Lay Dying* (New York: Modern Library, 1946), pp. 19, 23, Smith.

13. Edel, Leon and Adeline R. Tintner, *The Library of Henry James* (Ann Arbor: University of Michigan Press, 1987), p. 2.

14. Krook, Dorothea, *The Ordeal of Consciousness in Henry James* (Cambridge: Cambridge University Press, 1962). See also Krook's reminiscence of Sylvia Plath: 'Recollections of Sylvia Plath', in *Sylvia Plath: The Woman and the Work*, ed. Edward Butscher (New York: Dodd, Mead, 1985).

15. James, Henry, *The Portrait of a Lady* (New York: Modern Library,1951), Smith. Hereafter cited in the text as *Portrait*.

16. Plath, Sylvia, '"Never Try to Know More Than You Should"', *Smith Review* (Spring 1954), p. 17. A later version of his poem was published as 'Admonitions' in Plath's *Collected Poems*, ed. Ted Hughes (London: Faber and Faber, 1981), p. 319. A typescript of the poem containing Plath's address while living in Northampton from 1957 to 1958 is in Plath, 'Admonitions', 1953–8. Box 6, Folder 2, Sylvia Plath Collection, Smith. *Collected Poems* hereafter cited in the text as *CP*.

17. Plath, 'Admonitions', 1953–8. Holograph copy dated 15 April 1953. Box 6, Folder 2, Plath Collection, Smith.

18. James, Henry, *The Ambassadors* (New York: Harper, 1948), p. 258, Smith.

19. Steinberg, Peter K., *Great Writers: Sylvia Plath* (Philadelphia: Chelsea House, 2004), p. 28. Sandra Gilbert and Susan Gubar first drew my atten-

tion to the significance of 'momism' in *No Man's Land: The Place of the Woman Writer in the Twentieth Century*, vol. 2 (New Haven: Yale University Press), pp. 5–6.

20. Wylie, Philip, *Generation of Vipers* (New York: Rinehart, 1942), p. 184.
21. Rose, Jacqueline, *The Haunting of Sylvia Plath* (Cambridge, MA: Harvard University Press, 1992), pp. 165–6.
22. Plath, Sylvia, *The Unabridged Journals of Sylvia Plath*, ed. Karen V. Kukil (New York: Random House, 2000), p. 106. Hereafter cited in text as *UJ*.
23. Jackson, H. J., 'Editing and Auditing Marginalia', in *Voice, Text, Hypertext: Emerging Practices in Textual Studies*, ed. Raimonda Modiano, Leroy F. Searle and Peter L. Shillingsburg (Seattle: University of Washington Press, 2004), p. 72.
24. James, Henry, *What Maisie Knew* (Garden City: Doubleday, 1954), p. 68, Smith.
25. Dupee, F. W., *Henry James: His Life and Writings* (New York: Doubleday, 1956), p. 167, Smith. The breaks in Plath's underlining reflect the margins of the page.
26. James, Henry, *The Bostonians: A Novel* (New York: Modern Library, c. 1956), Library of Ted Hughes, Emory, p. v. Hereafter cited in the text as *Bostonians*.
27. Howe, Irving, 'The Plath Celebration: A Partial Dissent', in *Modern Critical Views: Sylvia Plath*, ed. Harold Bloom (New York: Chelsea House, 1989). In response to Howe, Ann Keniston has underscored the significance of Plath's temporal distance from the atrocities that inform her poems. See Keniston, Ann, 'The Holocaust Again: Sylvia Plath, Belatedness, and Limits of the Lyric Figure', in *Unraveling Archive*, p. 147.
28. Howe, 'Plath Celebration', p. xxiv.
29. Kenner, Hugh, *The Pound Era* (Berkeley: University of California Press, 1971), p. 3.
30. Plath, Sylvia, '20th Century Miss Drew', Notes, Box 20, Folder 17, Smith. Plath completed this course in 1952, in the spring of her sophomore year. I thank Anthony Cuda for dating these notes. Plath studied Modern Poetry with Elizabeth Drew during her junior year in the autumn of 1953.
31. Drew, Elizabeth, *T. S. Eliot: The Design of His Poetry* [1949] (New York: Charles Scribner's Sons, 1950), Smith.
32. Pound, Ezra, *ABC of Reading* [1934] (New York: New Directions, 1960), p. 73.
33. See also Janet Malcolm's discussion of a passage in Plath's journal in which Plath compares herself to James's character Maggie Verver in *The Wings of the Dove*. Malcolm, Janet, *The Silent Woman: Sylvia Plath and Ted Hughes* (New York: Norton, 1993), pp. 152, 155.
34. Wilson, Edmund, *Axel's Castle: A Study in the Imaginative Literature of 1870–1930* (New York: Charles Scribner's Sons, 1950), p. 111, Smith.
35. Alan Golding cites Robert Lowell's distinction between 'raw and cooked' poetry of the post-war era. Adapting Levi-Strass, Lowell separates the poets that continued in the experimental tradition of Ezra Pound, Gertrude Stein, and William Carlos Williams from the poets that wrote more conservative, epigrammatic lines reminiscent of T. S. Eliot. Critics often place Plath's poems in the Eliot category. *From Outlaw to Classic: Canons in*

American Poetry (Madison: University of Wisconsin Press, 1995), p. 28. One early essay describes Plath's poetics as Poundian and interprets several late poems in terms of the Imagist aesthetic of T. E. Hulme. Calvin Bedient, 'Sylvia Plath, Romantic...' *Sylvia Plath: New Views on the Poetry*, ed. Gary Lane (Baltimore, MD: Johns Hopkins University Press, 1979).

36. Pound, Ezra, *The Pisan Cantos* (New York: New Directions, 1948). Plath's copy is in the Lilly Library.

37. For example, see Alexander, Paul, *Rough Magic: A Biography of Sylvia Plath* (New York: Penguin, 1991); Axelrod, Stephen, *Sylvia Plath: The Wound and the Cure of Words* (Baltimore: Johns Hopkins University Press, 1990); Hammer, Langdon, 'Plath's Lives: Poetry, Professionalism, and the Culture of the School', *Representations* 75 (2001), 61–88.

38. For further exploration of the ways Plath's writing reflects her awareness of the surrounding political and literary climate see Peel, Robin, *Writing Back: Sylvia Plath and Cold War Culture* (Madison: Fairleigh Dickinson University Press, 2001).

39. Drew, Elizabeth, 'Lecture Notes: The Novel II', box 770.1, folder 19–21, Elizabeth A. Drew Papers, Smith College Archives, Northampton, MA.

40. Davis argues that the *Cantos* 'are a test case for a whole set of values, and stand self-condemned. They are important documents; they should be available, they should be read. But they deserve no prize.' Davis, Robert Gorham, 'The Question of the Pound Award', *Partisan Review* (May 1949), reprinted in *A Casebook on Ezra Pound*, ed. William Van Connor and Edward Stone (New York: Thomas Y. Crowell, 1959), pp. 56–7. See also Coley, Lem, '"A Conspiracy of Friendliness": T. S. Eliot, Ezra Pound, Allen Tate, and the Bollingen Controversy', *The Southern Review*, 38/4 (2002), 809–26.

41. Davis, Robert Gorham, 'Pound: The Poem and the Poet', *New Leader*, 11 December 1950.

42. Regarding the *Pisan Cantos* see Bush, Ronald, 'Modernism, Fascism, and the Composition of Ezra Pound's *Pisan Cantos*', *Modernism/Modernity*, 2/3 (1995), 69–87; Williams, David Park, 'The Background of the Pisan Cantos', *Poetry* (January 1949), reprinted in *Casebook on Ezra Pound*; Allen, Robert L., 'The Cage' and 'A letter in *Esquire*, February 1958', reprinted in *Casebook on Ezra Pound*; Kenner, *Pound Era*, pp. 460–96.

43. Plath may have read Canto XLV, 'With Usura'. The *Modern American Poetry* anthology that she purchased upon arrival in London in 1955 is at Smith: Moore, Geoffrey, ed., *Modern American Poetry* (London: Penguin, 1954).

44. Before leaving, Viereck gave Plath 'pamphlets on poetry & politics' (*UJ*, 354). They may have included *Dream and Responsibility: Four Test Cases of the Tension between Poetry and Society* (1953). This collection includes a version of his earlier essay on the Bollingen Controversy, 'Pure Poetry, Impure Politics, and Ezra Pound' (1951), which briefly asks 'to what extent his [Pound's] chichi "anti-usury" gospels are catching on among the more "advanced" English students and the *avant-garde*'. Viereck, Peter, *Dream and Responsibility: Four Test Cases of the Tension between Poetry and Society* (Washington, DC: University of Washington Press, 1953), p. 8.

45. Wilson, *Axel's Castle*, p. 123. See Buurma, Rachel Sagner and Laura

Heffernan, 'The Classroom in the Canon: T. S. Eliot's Modern English Literature Extension Course for Working People and *The Sacred Wood*', *PMLA*, 133/2 (2018), 264–81. While a copy of Eliot's *The Sacred Wood* does not remain in Plath's library, she notes its ideas in *Axel's Castle*. This too reflects a sense of distance from the initial centrality that the text may have had.

46. Plath, Sylvia, 'Lesbos', in *The Collected Poems*, ed. Ted Hughes (New York: Harper & Row, 1992), p. 228, lines 29–32.
47. Eliot, T. S., 'The Love Song of J. Alfred Prufrock', in *The Complete Poems and Plays* (New York: Harcourt Brace, 1971), p. 33. Plath underlined these words in her copy of the book (a 1952 printing) at Smith.
48. Plath notes Pound's definition of free verse in Marianne Moore's prose collection, *Predilections*: 'As for free verse, "it is not prose", Mr. Pound says. It is what we have "when the thing builds up a rhythm more beautiful than that of set metres".' Moore, Marianne, '"Teach, Stir the Mind, Afford Enjoyment"', in *Predilections* (New York: Viking Press, 1955, Smith.

Chapter 8

'Library of Opaque Memory': Spectral Archives in Brandon Som, Mai Der Vang and Bhanu Kapil

Sarah Howe

Once called the 'Ellis Island of the West', the immigration station on Angel Island in the San Francisco Bay began to operate in 1910. Unlike at Ellis Island, the majority of immigrants passing through Angel Island came from Asian countries, its main purpose being enforcement of the Chinese Exclusion Acts passed by Congress from 1882. Designed to stem the flow of Chinese labourers increasingly regarded as a threat to low-waged jobs, the 1882 Act was the first federal immigration policy in US history to target a specific nation or race. In 1970, thirty years after Angel Island was abandoned, a park ranger doing his rounds of the buildings, then marked for demolition, stumbled across several walls covered in Chinese calligraphy. During their detention on the island, which could last anything from a few days to three years, the Chinese émigrés had composed poems in their native tongue and inscribed them on the barrack walls. These unsigned verses mostly employed classical Chinese forms, echoing ancient poetic themes to speak of modern sufferings that included homesickness, filthy conditions, and unfair treatment at the hands of the authorities. Paradoxically, the poems survived partly thanks to the commissioner's orders to cover up what was considered graffiti. After the earliest inscriptions were repeatedly painted over, the Chinese poets, unperturbed, stopped writing on the walls in ink or pencil and began carving their words with a knife. Maintenance crews reacted by filling the indentations with putty before painting the walls again, helping seal their wooden surface against further decay. With passing decades, the putty shrank and the paint peeled, making the poems legible once more.

The ranger's find eventually came to the attention of local researchers and community activists who recognised the inscriptions' significance and petitioned successfully for their preservation.[1] Study of the poems precipitated the wider scholarly recovery of Angel Island's immigration history, leading finally to the station's opening for visitors as a historical monument and museum. In their precarious journey from erasure to monumentality, the Angel Island poems point towards the shifting material and social conditions that influence a nation's sense of what is worth preserving from the past. Joseph Harrington reflects, after Derrida, on the political decisions archiving inevitably entails:

> For Derrida, archive fever denotes the mania to define what's in and what's out. 'But where does the outside commence? This' Derrida asserts, 'is the question of the archive. There are undoubtedly no others'. ... The job of the archivist is not only to prevent documents from leaving the archive, but, perhaps more importantly, to keep out those that don't belong there. This is, of course, a political decision that involves repression and destruction, even as it involves preservation.[2]

In the context of the Angel Island poems, Derrida's emphasis on borders and boundaries draws an unexpected parallel between the archivist's power to select documents and the immigration officer's to decide who to admit or reject at the border. Both are bound up with race and the history of racial exclusion; in this respect, America has and has not changed. In the last two decades, archivists and historians have become increasingly interested in the role archives play in determining what kinds of histories can be told – the way their holdings privilege some stories and marginalise others. 'This represents enormous power', Terry Cook and Joan Schwartz explain, 'over memory and identity, over the fundamental ways in which society seeks evidence of what its core values are and have been, where it has come from, and where it is going'.[3]

What kind of archive are the inscribed walls of Angel Island? Derrida's account of the archive as a site of political authority begins with the word's derivation from the Greek *arkheion*: the 'house' of the magistrate or *archon*, where records generated by the processes of power were stored.[4] Another kind of 'house', the Angel Island barracks were unquestionably a symbol of power, but power *over* their unwilling inhabitants. Asian American literature had its origins in the carceral, offshore, ambiguous space of the immigration detention centre, waiting in a limbo between admission and deportation. If the archive is, according to one recent formulation, 'an institutional space enclosed by protective walls', then the barrack walls at Angel Island reveal the 'official' archive's shadowy inverse.[5] A spectral archive, Angel Island was a bounded space devoted not to the preservation of authorised documents, but to the suppression of its inmates' attempts to create through poetry a record for posterity. The materiality of that record is strikingly foregrounded by the detainees' détournement of their means of imprisonment, the walls themselves, as the physical substrate for their writing: their incised marks carry an affect at once elegiac and defiant. At the same time, those flaking and overpainted walls are, like Freud's mystic writing pad, a figure for consciousness: they embody one group's collective memory and another's collective forgetting overlaid in the same space.[6]

I begin with the Angel Island poems for the historical grounding they offer this chapter, which explores ideas of the archive in recent books by three contemporary Asian American poets. In their work, the archive recurs as both theme and source, an intractable problem and a haunting ideal. Engaged with questions of memory, documentation, and the racial imaginary as its own species of archive, these poets open a window onto Asian American identity in some of its diverse contemporary constellations. Their poems reflect on the experiences of first- to third-generation Asian Americans who might variously self-define as immigrants, refugees, expatriates, exiles, mixed-race, among other possible labels, and whose diasporic links to communities in Asia or Europe complicate a paradigm of Asian American identity focused solely on the United States.[7] Brandon Som's *The Tribute Horse* (2014) retraces his Chinese grandfather's passage to America via Angel Island in fractured lyrics and Oulipian experiments that 'Burrow straight through song'. In its mission to preserve the 'embers of the book' of inherited memory, Mai Der Vang's *Afterland* (2017) confronts the culpability of her natal America for the Secret War in Laos, the little-known conflict that displaced her Hmong parents in 1974. Part experimental novel, part ritual performance, Bhanu Kapil's *Ban en Banlieue* (2015) compulsively circles the body of 'Ban', 'a brown girl on the floor of the world', lying down in the midst of a race riot in the London suburbs of Kapil's childhood.[8]

The concept of the archive looms large for these poets as they explore and commemorate lost histories. Their work confronts the power of the archival record's exclusions and erasures to dictate what can be recovered. Derrida traced the lure of the archive to 'an irrepressible desire to return to the origin, a homesickness, a nostalgia for the return to the most archaic place of absolute commencement'.[9] For immigrants and their descendants growing ever further from an 'original' culture and language, the 'homesickness' of archive fever is cast in especially sharp relief. The historian Carolyn Steedman ties this aspect of archive fever to its role in identity formation:

> the past is searched for something (some one, some group, some series of events) that confirms the searcher in his or her sense of self . . . It seems that we do this quite obdurately, in the face of the hard and clear advice from psycho-analysis, which tells us that the quest is impossible, that what we are searching for is for a lost object, which really cannot be found.[10]

Undergirding these poets' engagement with the archive is an awareness that any promise it might hold of defining an essential identity, of return to a pristine point of origin, is ultimately a mirage.

A debt of sound: Brandon Som

The Tribute Horse opens at the grave of its author's grandfather, with his name – Som – incised in two scripts, one of 'silent' strokes, the other with its 'stowaway vowel'. A prose prologue of sorts, 'Elegy' imagines the circumstances of his passage to America:

> A Chinese immigrant, on his Pacific-crossing, carried coaching papers for the memorizing. Approaching the island station, these pages were tossed to sea. A moon's light in a ship's wake might make a similar papertrail. My grandfather, aboard at twelve, practiced a paper-name. What ensued was a debt of sound. (p. 15)

The term 'paper-name' alludes to the faked papers purchased by Chinese immigrants stating they were blood relations – 'paper sons' and 'daughters' – of Chinese Americans who already held US citizenship. The poet's grandfather was an illegal immigrant, then, his surname a false identity designed to evade the ban on Chinese immigration by 'claim[ing] himself son of a citizen, / "a crooked path", avoiding exclusion' (p. 53). This lucrative business in fraudulent documents was made possible by the San Francisco earthquake and fire of 1906, which had destroyed the city hall along with most public records, including those registering births. In response, Angel Island inspectors devised gruelling interrogations, demanding obscure details about family trees and the layout of ancestral villages which supposedly only genuine applicants would know: '"Island" interrogators had translators . . . & listened to catch // men quoting other men's lives / for their papers' (p. 69). Aware of what awaited them, Chinese immigrants bought 'coaching papers' along with their new names, which schooled them in the minutiae of their fictitious identities. They would spend the weeks of their Pacific passage committing the crib sheets to memory, so that their interview answers would tally exactly with those of their Chinese American sponsor: any slip could mean deportation for both.

As their ship approached the US harbour, 'these pages were tossed to sea'. In 'Elegy', Som defamiliarises the idiom of the 'paper trail' – that is, the written record left behind in the course of one's activities – to describe the coaching books' dispersal into the sea: 'A moon's light in a ship's wake might make a similar papertrail.' History here depends not on the survival of written records – the paper sons must leave no traces to betray them – but on a 'debt of sound'. A debt of sound: an absence or lacuna in the archive, not simply silence but sound's palpable deficit; also, the debt a descendant feels he owes a pioneering patriarch, including perhaps the obligation to tell a previously hidden story. The same phrase echoes in the long sequence that follows, 'Coaching Papers', whose eight-line poems reprise and rearrange the co-ordinates of the sea voyage introduced in 'Elegy': 'A paper-name ensures a debt / of sound' (p. 20). Thanks to the new line break, the echo is not an exact repetition. Just below its surface tremble other, half-heard words and meanings: thanks to the watery setting, 'sound' threatens to transform into a channel or inlet, while beneath 'debt' I can't help hearing 'depth' – and also possibly 'death' – as the drowned papers sink under the waves. The sea distorts and anagrams the poem's submerged words even as the tossed coaching papers dissolve.

Throughout *The Tribute Horse*, Som's poems display a loving attention to sonic effects, to the fluid mutability and almost tactile physicality of language sounded aloud. Led by the ear rather than narrative logic, the poems advance through associative strings and clusters of sounds:

> A ship's bow's shape writes an A
> To mark the indefinite way. A name
>
> is a persona, per son, per song.
> Sonar searches the sea by singing
>   (p. 28)

One descendant of Angel Island immigrants described how her illiterate mother memorised her coaching book by turning it into a song.[11] The attenuating echoes of 'persona, per son, per song' (a game of Chinese whispers?) make sonic play coincide with meaning to stunning effect. In an interview of 2015, Som traces 'Coaching Papers' back to the intuition that his grandfather's shipboard efforts to memorise, recite and perform his new name and identity were themselves a form of 'poetic practice'.[12] His answers show Som thinking around *The Tribute Horse*'s wider engagement with archives. This poem's focus on the disintegrating crib sheets 'allowed [him] to imagine the sea as a kind of archive, absorbing sound but also receiving and churning up these pages in the Pacific Ocean'.[13] An exercise in 'impossible recovery', Som's poems stand in for those lost documents:

> I asked my family about this coaching book, and they assume that my grand-father had one. But of course, like with so many other immigrants', it had been lost. . . . So my book is interested in this kind of impossible recovery. I

can't get to that coaching text, so I get to that text through other texts. I can't get to that sound, so I get to that recited sound through other sounds[.][14]

In the absence of 'paper-name' history's self-destructing archive, 'other texts' and 'other sounds' become his poetic means of accessing a lost family history.

In the same interview, Som attributes a further 'disconnect' to his own failure to talk to his grandfather about his experiences before he passed away in the poet's twenties:

I couldn't go to a primary source to learn about this history. Instead I learned about this history through coursework, through history books, through scholars. I had to come up with invented ways to get at this history, to get at these archives. As a poet, sounding out this history was one way that I was able to explore it.[15]

Here 'sounding out this history' seems to mean voicing it aloud, with a hint of sounding its depths, but also carries the tentativeness of 'sounding out' in the sense of making enquiries, asking careful questions of it. That such stories were considered shameful is stressed by the editors of the Angel Island poems, who movingly describe the cathartic effect for former detainees of publishing their 1980 anthology:

By openly airing the dark secrets of racial exclusion and illegal immigration, the book served as a catharsis as well as an exoneration of those who had been imprisoned on Angel Island. It legitimized the Angel Island experience to the degree that our immigrant parents no longer felt ashamed or afraid of sharing their stories.[16]

'Sounding out this history' could also mean openly airing the unspoken, and hitherto unspeakable, secrets of past generations.

The watery archive imagined in 'Coaching papers' is caught between the written and the aural, almost to the point of synaesthesia:

The sea types in italics voices
analogged in the archive: soundbytes

shipsank or shore tossed – babble
for the gleaner.
                 (p. 21)

The sea hovers somewhere between typist, manuscript amanuensis, and sound recorder: 'At sea, a boy recites a name. / The sea records it in waves' (p. 24). The Pacific's tidal motion seems to promise that the soundwaves Som imagines it absorbing will continue to reverberate forever. And yet the confluence in 'analogged' of logged/analogue suggests the sea's spectral archive will be no less subject to degradation or distortion than any other: noise akin perhaps to the hiss and pops of the period's waveform-etched phonograph cylinders. By contrast, the digital-era 'soundbytes' imply a different kind of distortion, with their nod to the excerpted journalistic 'sound bite' and its potential to mislead. Both punning coinages prepare for the idea that the archived 'voices' carried on the waves will be reduced eventually to 'shore tossed' static, so much 'babble / for the gleaner'. The image is no less apt as a characterisation of more conventional archives, whose unstable, incomplete and fragmentary contents depend on the subjectivity of historians to shape them into narratives.

A longer piece in nine numbered sections, 'Bows & Resonators' is the poem where *The Tribute Horse* addresses 'the barrack wall at Angel Island' most directly. Som's own words are interspersed with a tissue of extracts from other texts set in quotation marks. These include verses and individual words from the Angel Island poems (in the revised English translation of 1991), as well as material drawn from a variety of historical and theoretical works listed in an endnote. By sampling the various ambient and atmospheric sounds that appear in the Angel Island poems, Som seeks to recreate the soundscape that would have met his grandfather on reaching America in 1928:

> The wind outside
> is recorded
>
> 'faintly' also & 'whistling.'
>
> The insects
> beneath the moon
> tether its line
>
>   & 'chirp'
>   (p. 59)

The quotation marks underline the borrowed words, lending them the force of testimony, but at the same time denaturalise the scene they evoke. 'Bows and Resonators' draws a parallel between the detainee poets scratching their graffiti ('from the Italian *graffito*, "a scratch"') and the island's crickets, whose song is actually the rubbing or scratching together of their legs: 'There waiting // on Angel Island, / a poet recorded, // "The insects chirp outside the four walls"' (pp. 59, 63). The comparison offers a quiet commentary on migration and transculturality: cricket song was a favourite theme of the Tang dynasty poets, but the chirring bugs immortalised on the wall belong to the American West Coast. 'I felt like I was actually listening to that wall', Som has said, 'a kind of close listening to the history represented or contained within that

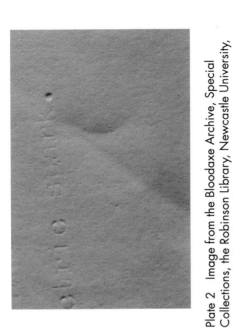

Plate 1 Home page of mina.loy.com. Designer Suzanne W. Churchill with technical and artistic assistance from Olivia Booker.

Plate 2 Image from the Bloodaxe Archive, Special Collections, the Robinson Library, Newcastle University, copyright Phyllis Christopher

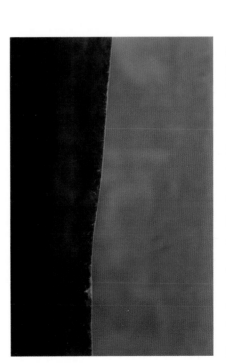

Plate 3 Image from the Bloodaxe Archive, copyright Phyllis Christopher

Plate 4 Images from administrative documents, the Bloodaxe Archive, copyright Kate Sweeney

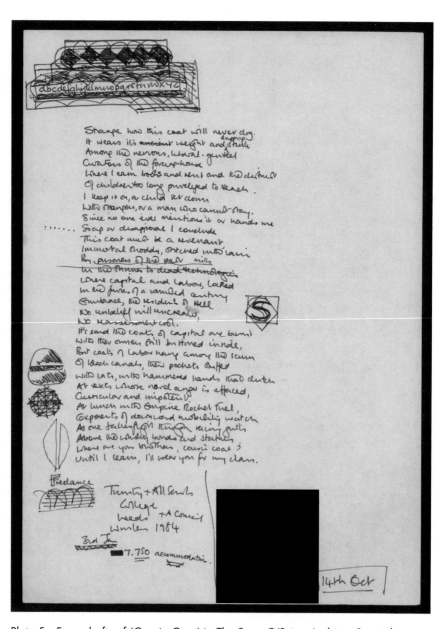

Plate 5   From drafts of 'Cousin Coat' in The Sean O'Brien Archive, Special Collections, the Robinson Library, Newcastle University

Plate 6 'This cube represents in bulk 1000 grams of sea-water of SP. Gr 1.0?? taken at Sheerness at half-flood.' (All captions in this chapter are quoted from Ashford-Brown's exhibition.)

Plate 7 'Coal from Mompson, 14 shillings and two pence per ton, charged £1 per ton, October, 1876'.

Plate 8 '91. Powdered Notre Dame'.

Plate 9 '94. Light'.

Plate 10   '101b. Bottle having once contained the smoke from a Gauloise cigarette bottled 18th Feb.1985.'

Plate 11   '105. Chewed Shakespeare, "The Taming of the Shrew", chewed by myself on a Sunday evening in March, 1985.'

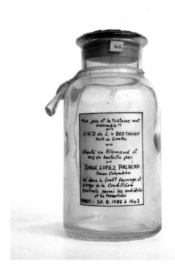

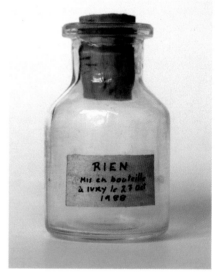

Plate 12   '145. "Joy and Sadness go together" – LIED by L.v. Beethoven, text by Goethe. Sung in German and bottled by LOPEZ PALACRO', Columbian tenor – Paris 20/08/1988 at 16.03.'

Plate 13   '147. Nothing, bottled in Ivry 27th October 1988'.

TÊTE DE PINCEAU MERITANT REPOS APRÉS DE
NOMBREUSES ET LOYALES ANNÉES AU SERVICE
DE LA PEINTURE
1991

Plate 14   '221. The Head of a paintbrush deserving a rest after many loyal years in the service of art. 1991.'

Plate 15   '231. Mysterious fragment. I cannot remember what it is, where it comes from or why it is in this museum.'

Plate 16   '242. Mineral object resembling a chicken's head.'

MORCEAU D'UNE CUILLÈRE
SANS HISTOIRE

Plate 17   '244. Part of a spoon about which nothing is known - October 1993'.

Plate 18 '251. Egyptian Pot. First Dynasty. 3000 BC. Bought by my mother from VENESSA BELL [*sic*] of Cleeve House Seend – (artist and sister to Virginia Woolf) – back in the 50s. Pot identified and restored by archeologists at Cambridge University. The pot was once again broken by a starling having flown down the chimney in 1987 – Re-stored by my own efforts in 1993.'

Plate 19 '254. Cigarette dating from the 1930s picked up on 1st August 1991.'

wall'.[17] The result is an act of poetic resurrection. By working them into his own poem – one which addresses modern speakers of English – Som lends voice and breath to the silent inscriptions, and through them their silenced authors: '"The inmates," // the poem in the wall / continues, // "often sigh"' (p. 65).

From the barrack wall 'filled with putty, painted, written on / & painted', Som leaps back five millennia to introduce the legendary creator of Chinese characters:

> To invent writing,
>
> 'Ts'ang-Chieh, if certain ancient
> books are to be believed,
>
> observed the marks
>
> of birds' claws
> and animal's foot-prints upon the ground,
>
> the shapes of shadows cast
> by trees,
>
> . . . and engraved . . .
>
> their forms upon the sticks'
> (p. 60)

The text within quotation marks is a modified extract from an academic history of Chinese calligraphy not listed among the sources in Som's note.[18] The engraved 'sticks' refer to the form taken by Chinese books prior to the invention of paper: made from slips of wood or bamboo tied together with silk or leather thongs, these bundles or *cè* remained in use until around the fourth century CE. From here, the poem's next hop across oceans and centuries is no less dizzying. Som places these ancient wooden books in resonant juxtaposition with the Californian redwoods that supplied the Angel Island barracks' 'timbered walls'. Those 'felled Sequoias', the poem continues, were 'named for the Cherokee scholar / who devised for his tribe // an alphabet' (p. 60). Setting in dialogue two cultures either side of the Pacific and the origins of their written scripts, the poem travels back to the advent of the very technology – writing – that made archival record-keeping possible. Derrida's archive fever as a search for origins becomes, in Som's hands, a search for the origins of archiving itself. Set in the same frame as the mythic inventor of Chinese ideograms, the Angel Island poets are cast as originators by association: though not (yet) American at the point of writing, they helped bring into existence the art form we now call Asian American literature.

Our bodies will be books: Mai Der Vang

In 1962, seven years into the Vietnam War, the US signed an international treaty to respect the neutrality of Laos, then proceeded to launch a covert war there while preserving the fiction of compliance. The so-called Secret War comprised over a decade of clandestine operations in which the CIA armed Hmong fighters against the North Vietnamese:

> the library of opaque memory
> inside a canefield.
> > The verb for neutrality,
> > they say,
>
> is to aim covertly.
> > (p. 19)

In these lines from 'Lima Site 20', Mai Der Vang skewers the hypocrisy of the era's American foreign policy. The poem's ironies hinge on the gap between what those on the ground know and what the official record will admit: 'This is the phantom attack / that never happened, but our fallen know it did' (p. 19). Even the poem's title points to the dissonance between Hmong and American perspectives: Lima Site 20 Alternate was the CIA code name for Long Tieng, a secret military airbase in the Laotian highlands from which the US launched their operations. The 'library of opaque memory' alludes then to American obfuscation of their involvement in Laos, which had the effect of burying the war's lost history except in classified military files. The library's jarring location – not within a pillared facade or shelf-lined room, but 'inside a canefield' – conveys how swiftly a landscape will belie eyewitness memory, once the sugar cane grows back and no visible trace of past atrocities remains.

The metaphor of memory's 'opaque' library reaches beyond its significance here to speak to one of the driving concerns in Vang's work: the difficult, intergenerational movement of memory's oral archive from Hmong refugees to their American-born children, the first generation to seek to memorialise the conflict in English. Unafraid of being opaque or riddling themselves, Vang's poems often create grammatical structures that feel wrested from another language, as if their syntax had come under the contorting pressures of cultural dislocation and historical trauma:

> > I go to funerals to meet the ancients.
> I go to funerals
> > to keep.
> > (p. 88)

Left hanging but for the concluding full stop, the speaker's intent 'to keep' – to save, preserve, maintain – is unlimited by an object, as the transitive verb would usually require. What kind of closure is available to the refugee? What kind of return? Poetry is Vang's medium of choice in her mission to preserve an uprooted culture: 'Ask me to build our temples / So rooted, so stone, we won't ever die out' (p. 62). Stone temples, 'an iron jar', 'a bone room', 'a dusty gallery', 'cloister', 'container', 'vessel', 'bowl': these enclosed and protected spaces are some of the figures for memory that lend a tangible shape to the book's efforts to 'keep' the past. These efforts are underwritten by a poignant awareness that such shrines have their cost for the living. In the final line of 'Progeny', home becomes a reliquary or monument charged with remembrance, but suggests the airless sterility of somewhere no longer habitable: 'Home is container is memorial' (p. 69). When another poem issues the injunction, 'Go on living, but never say / the names of the dead' (p. 58), we infer that the two are incompatible – that survivors cannot both remember and carry on.

Afterland develops what we might call a poetic ethnography of the archive, weighing the storytelling of oral tradition against written documents and histories as ways for societies to transmit a record of the past. Vang is interested in similar questions around orality and literacy, ephemerality and permanence, voice and page, to those that preoccupy Som's 'sounding out' of the archive, but with a difference born of Hmong's distinct history vis-à-vis the development of writing. 'Mother of People without Script' is one of several poems in *Afterland* that reflect on what is gained and what sacrificed in writing down a family of languages whose traditions appear to have been exclusively oral until the mid-twentieth century:

> *Paj* is not pam is not *pab*.
> Blossom is not blanket is not help.
>
> ...
>
> To *txiav* is not the *txias*.
> To scissor is not the cold.
> (p. 60)

For readers unfamiliar with Hmong, its orthography and tones – that is, the very readership which requires this language lesson – it is difficult verging on impossible to know how to sound these lines aloud, without hearing a speaker of the language recite them. What writing gains in permanence, the poem hints, it loses in immediacy and human presence compared to speech – 'Catch in the throat. Hollow breath'

– turning communication into a silent, solitary matter. In her poems, Vang employs the Romanised Popular Alphabet, or RPA, the most widespread Hmong script in use in the West. Contemplating the fraught power relations that accompanied the arrival of literacy, 'Original Bones' compares the invention of RPA 'for' the Hmong by Christian missionaries in 1952 to the emergence of an indigenous, 'phantom script', said to have been revealed to the farmer Shong Lue Yang in a series of divine visions in 1959. Honoured as the *'mother of writing'*, he began teaching his messianic script to followers across Laos, before his assassination by government soldiers in 1971.[19] Vang brings this mixed legacy to bear on her own early ventures into writing: '1986 when I drew / The letters of mai der' (p. 29). The end of 'Mother of People without Script' elliptically narrates Yang's demise and the weight of hope he bore: 'When they could take no more, / when all that you had was given, / you lined your grave with paper' (p. 60). For a hitherto oral culture, Vang implies, there is something deathly about writing and its unchanging permanence. For the trace it bears of the human body, combined with its ability to out-survive it, writing resembles a death mask: 'The obsidian mask / will make its own sleep' (p. 60).

Afterland also invokes an alternative, folkloric history of Hmong writing. According to oral tradition, their female ancestors concealed a lost written language in the intricate embroidered motifs of *paj ntaub*, or 'flower cloth', whose geometrical imagery would be unreadable by their Chinese oppressors. Today such designs still decorate traditional Hmong clothing, but without any discernible semantic meaning.[20] In 'Cipher Song', Vang imagines how these textiles turned 'our bodies', wearing their encoded legends and cultural beliefs, into 'books':

> It's come to this. We hide the stories
> on our sleeves, patchwork of cotton veins.
>
> Scribe them on carriers for sleeping
> babies, weave our ballads to the sash.
> (p. 42)

Vang's poems aspire to serve as a similar store of cultural memory. Yet the ending of 'Cipher Song' recalls the material vulnerability of such archives at times of conflict – 'When the words burn, all that's left is ash' – obliquely summoning the horror of people burning too. Stitching its poetic flower cloths and building its temples of words, *Afterland* assembles an archive of Hmong artisanal, linguistic and spiritual traditions, all the while considering how – and if – that way of life continues in the American present.

Vang's poems recognise the obstacles facing a second generation who wish to 'return [their] footfalls' (p. 88) to Laotian soil while it remains clogged with unexploded ordnance: 'forty years of debris / turning stale, and submunitions // still hunt inside the patina of my mud' (p. 54). In a piece for the *New York Times*, Vang writes about the ongoing intergenerational impact of a trauma like the Secret War:

> How does one memorialize a failed war that most people don't even know about or would rather forget? How will my generation attempt to retain the memories of that war so that future generations will know? . . . But I do know that many of us are innately tied to this trauma as if it were strung into our DNA. For the Hmong, to retain history and identity means also to retain trauma and loss. I carry the afflictions of this war even though I have never heard a bomb explode or feared my footsteps might trigger a mine. This war is my inheritance.[21]

Vang considers what it means for second-generation Hmong to 'retain' testimony of a war they did not experience first-hand. If the Secret War is archived in the 'DNA' of succeeding generations, then its spectral code is written into the fabric of their being, yet only ambiguously legible to those who carry it. Vang describes, in a 2011 interview, the contingent transmission of such stories from parent to child, often triggered by encounters with material remnants she dubs 'objects of exile'. Once she stumbled across a suitcase inside a closet, which turned out to contain the fraying embroidered jacket her mother was wearing as a girl the night they escaped their village in Laos: 'You might find these relics in a suitcase, and that's how the stories happen . . . Parents don't sit down and say, "Let me tell you …".'[22] In serving as receptacles for their parents' memories, such children become alienated from their own minds: 'Storage in my / mind is not my own but those // who save before me' (p. 80).

Burdened by this overwhelming legacy, how is a poet to reclaim agency for herself? *Afterland* finds a resolution to this quandary by submitting to it. Alongside the lyrics that speak from a subject-position broadly aligned with the poet's autobiographical self, the book's expanded first person shifts fluidly across different voices dredged from the bank of collective memory: 'I am but atoms / Of old passengers' (p. 3) announce its opening lines. Some poems speak in the halting tones, reminiscent of a poeticised oral history, of anonymous Hmong caught in the violence of decades past: 'With baby, I ran to the forest. . . . Then he cries, and I pushed / Opium in his mouth. // Now nothing, no sound' (p. 16). Others reach beyond the terrain we normally associate with the 'poetry of witness' into the spectral archives of shamanic and spiritual tradition.[23] 'Water Grave' opens with a 'we' struggling to make a river-crossing under gunfire, whose voices eerily blur into those of the 'crowded dead':

'We drift near banks, / creatures of the Mekong, / heads bobbing like // ghosts without bodies' (p. 13). A poem like 'Light from a Burning Citadel' firmly crosses the threshold into the afterlife, its composite voice animating now a ghostly ancestral chorus, now the devastated Laotian landscape itself:

> Now I am a Siamese rosewood on fire.
> I am a skin of sagging curtain.
> I am a bone of bullet hole.
> I am locked in the ash oven of a forest.
>
> > *Peb yog and we will be.*
> > (p. 10)

The Hmong words in the italicised refrain, a note explains, mean 'we are'. *We are and we will be*: the voice of a communal unconscious spanning Hmong past and present. Switching seamlessly between Hmong and the English of exile, the refrain's bilingual form enacts its assertion about the future of a diasporic people: that despite transformations in language and customs they, and their store of cultural memory, will survive.

Damage, carve and braid: Bhanu Kapil

In a blogpost from February 2012 entitled 'Archive Fever', prompted by teaching Derrida's text, Bhanu Kapil recounts some of her own interactions with archives in London and India. These encounters are marked less by 'archival desire', however, than by the emotional labour familiar to researchers of colour confronting the archives of painful histories that have affected their communities.[24] The writing that comes out of her spell in the archive has the quality of displacement activity – its own form of resistance, perhaps, against the potentially traumatic records of colonialism and migration:

> In an archive, I lean my head against the window at the end of the corridor. That is what I end up putting in the book, rather than the details of the research I have travelled so far, to the East End: to accrue. The rooves are reddish: a crenallate. I write that down. I describe the carpet, the walls of the corridor.[25]

Kapil directs her attention to the sensations and affects ('an almost paralyzing fear') provoked by the archive rather than the actual materials consulted, which are pushed out of frame.[26] This gesture is also characteristic of the way *Ban en Banlieue* materialises, or fails to: the text is composed of notes towards an intended work that never finally appears. The detritus of an abandoned novel, its fragments end up telling the story of the struggle to tell the story: 'On September 4th, 2010, at 7 p.m., I began to write – but did not write – [wrote]: Notes for a novel never written: a novel of the race riot: (Ban.)' (p. 20). One of the many functions of *Ban*'s square brackets is to capture the restless energy of the book's own drafts, as if advancing frame by frame through the revision process. The different orders of pause and parenthesis scored by Kapil's punctuation here convey the doublings-back and sub-vocalisations of a text kept in perpetual motion.

Kapil's blogpost proceeds to reflect on her own writing's relationship to the archive: 'The book flows outwards, from the archive, then accretes. Something crystalline about a book that it is always. My instinct. To damage. Damage, carve and braid: the book.'[27] The post dates from the years when Kapil used her blog as a 'public notebook', the print acknowledgements of *Ban en Banlieue* explain, where she 'incubated Ban under your gaze' (p. 95). These thoughts on flow and accretion come around to Kapil's work in progress: 'Yesterday, I kept thinking that Ban should be a comic book: a sequence of charcoal smudges, annotated with black ink.'[28] Liable to be smeared or rubbed away, these 'charcoal smudges' epitomise Ban's resistance to the 'crystalline' ideal of the fixed and finished book. 'Dirty. A way to predict writing but not writing itself' (p. 50), they recur in the printed text, where the body of Ban threatens to vanish into 'a warp of smoke' (p. 30) or 'a puff of diesel. Something like a smudge, already dispersing' (p. 50). The hue of these smudges is complexly racialised in a world that customarily reduces race to black and white: 'she is the parts of something re-mixed as air: integral, rigid air, circa 1972–1979. She's a girl. A black girl in an era when, in solidarity, Caribbean and Asian Brits self-defined as black' (p. 30). 'How do you caption smoke?' Kapil asks the poet Lyn Hejinian after a talk she gives on captioning. Hejinian replies, 'You'd have to trap it first' (p. 23).

In its iconoclastic physicality – 'Damage, carve and braid' – the archival poetics Kapil sketches recalls the ruined notebook that lent its shape to *Schizophrene* (2011), her exploration of migration and mental illness which first introduced readers to Ban. On its opening page, Kapil flings the notebook containing the work's final draft into her Colorado garden. The rejected manuscript interacts with a winter of snows and thaws, before she retrieves it and 'begins to write again, from the *fragments, the phrases and lines* still legible on the warped, decayed but curiously rigid pages'.[29] Her performance of rewriting out of the notebook's wreck – undoing her earlier work while feverishly retracing what has faded – places its remains between rubbish and relic: 'I transcribe what I can, then throw the dirty book into the bin'; 'I tore a page from the notebook then sealed it in a *Ziploc* bag.'[30] Running through Kapil's oeuvre is this tension between incarnation and erasure, between a visceral embodiment and the performance of disappearance. With its grainy photographs and documented rituals, *Ban* aspires to encompass something beyond mere text, to conjure a bodily presence in the vein of performance art: 'I wanted to write a novel but instead I wrote this. [Hold up charcoal in fist]' (p. 19). *Ban* catalogues performances and installations enacted by Kapil from 2011 to 2014 in Middlesex, New Delhi, Boulder, Los Angeles and elsewhere. Many take the form of healing body-art or memorial rituals: in South Delhi, she performs a 'public offering' for another Ban-figure, 'Nirbhaya' ('The Fearless One'), pouring red powder onto the spot where the girl lay bleeding to death, 'her entrails black on the pink-grey street' (p. 18), after her gang rape on a bus in 2012. At the same time, Ban's efforts at textual documentation testify to the impossibility of creating a complete archive of any performance. Faced with the loss inherent in recording any ephemeral artwork, are melancholy and mourning inevitable responses? How do you archive smoke?

Ban presents itself as an archive of remnants. The printed book opens onto a list of contents with a difference: unconfined to a table, each of the book's eight numbered parts gets a new page and prose description. These descriptions shade into poems in their own right, some running to several pages, to the point where the boundary between paratext and text begins to break down. Ban gives unusual weight to what would normally be a book's peripheral – its banlieue – components, to the point where its contents, prefaces, errata, notes, appendices and acknowledgements edge out the actual text. Still more eccentrically, Kapil's contents list points to sections of the work that appear only there. The section headed '3. Stories', for example, announces its own omission on the grounds it offered mere 'disclosure' rather than 'discharge': 'when it was time to publish them, here (in section 3), I pressed the delete button and stored them in another file' (p. 9). Likewise, '6a. Epigraphs' places under erasure a pair of '[d]eleted epigraphs' from Dolores Dorantes and Theresa Hak Kyung Cha. Just below them, the untitled subsection '6b.' consists of a single, stranded line: 'One thing next to another doesn't mean they touch' (p. 13). Spectral presences within the text, these cancelled components have their own weight; they highlight the author's 'failed' attempts and second thoughts, but also her editorial principles of omission and inclusion.

Ban's list of contents gestures towards the archive as a system of cataloguing and classification, even as it disorders and transgresses those protocols. Unsettling the relationship between container and contained, advertising its own lacunae and dead ends, *Ban*'s contents list points to the structural discrepancies recent scholars have argued are inherent to the archive, whose 'dream of perfect order is disturbed by the nightmare of its random, heterogenous, and often unruly contents'.[31] Most nightmarish of all are those 'secret or disconcerting elements ("errors", "garbage") located at its outermost edges' that defy codification.[32] An exercise in misclassification, generic and otherwise, *Ban* makes these errors its subject.[33] Is this what a decolonised poetics – a decolonised archive – might look like? The book's opening section, '[13 Errors for Ban]', reworks the conventional errata page to list all 'the errors [Kapil] made as a poet engaging a novel-shaped space' (p. 20). A central theme of this self-excoriation is Kapil's relocation from the UK to the US at the age of thirty: 'My mistake is that I perform works intended for a European audience – in California – and that I do not have the courage or the means to go home' (p. 24). Trapped in a riddle of immigrant identity, Kapil might call England 'home', but is clear she is not English: 'What, for example, is born in England, but is never, not even on a cloudy day, English?' (p. 30). Writing towards the wrong readership in the US, she cannot rely on a shared archive of cultural memory to connect with them: 'The error here is that I chose to write my book in a place where these colors and memories are not readily available. There is no bank' (p. 23). Kapil threads the word 'bank' through the book as a figure for memory – 'This is a bank for sentences' (p. 61) – partly because it is an imperfect echo of 'Ban'.

The questions of power and archival exclusion with which we began are thrown up in the air by the 'Butcher's Block Appendix' that concludes *Ban*'s printed text. The appendix's listing in the contents explains its genesis:

> 97.5% of the work of Ban happened in notebooks, public or otherwise. One day, my neighbour put her butcher's block on the curb. I got it and washed it down, stacking the notebooks in the three wire cages beneath the chopping board. I printed out the pages from my blog, where I had written Ban in a frenzy, and tucked those in as well. (p. 11)

To create the appendix, Kapil opens the notebooks on the sacrificial slab at random and allows her fingertip to settle on passages she copies out: 'This was bibliomancy. A way to make visible something that was "no longer possible to say"' (p. 11). This last phrase comes from Theresa Hak Kyung Cha's *Dictee* (1980), whose '"dead tongue"' is ritually resurrected on *Ban*'s opening page to 'lick the work' (p. 7) and whose augury presides over the book's exit. Kapil uses the aleatory as a way to keep her text in flux. Alongside the private notebooks off-stage, her blog is key to this sense of open-endedness, its accretion of years of public writing around *Ban* constituting a kind of expanded field: 'I wish I had the courage to let the blog be my book instead' (p. 95). Kapil traces her fascination with blogging, its 'archive of sensations', to the erasability of electronic 'mediums that can disappear with a simple click or whirr . . . an art form that does not decay, and at the same time, digital works do decay'.[34] That we should see *Ban*'s 2015 print publication as a momentary stilling of an ever-shifting and dispersing text is reinforced by Kapil's subsequent publication of further material, adding to the work's bibliographical complexity. This includes a 2017 chapbook, *entre-BAN*, whose 'succession of mutations and deletions' culled from her unpublished notebooks she describes as part of a longer-term 'rewriting [emptying out] of "Ban"'.[35] Prioritising the 'flow' of process over the finished book as a 'crystalline' product, *Ban* is its own archive, its own preservation and ruin.

My sense of what connects these works by Som, Vang and Kapil in their negotiations with the archive is not simply a matter of poetics, but an underlying ethics. Saidiya Hartman's 2008 essay 'Venus in Two Acts' scans the silences of the archive for the disappeared subjectivity of black women slaves. Hartman draws attention to the problem facing historians that the very desire to narrate these women's experiences – which the archive has failed to record except in disfiguring traces – risks reinforcing the same order of violence that 'transformed them into commodities and corpses'.[36] Her dilemma resonates with the efforts of these three books to tell, in Hartman's words, 'an impossible story and to amplify the impossibility of its telling'.[37] As poets rather than historians, their authors take advantage of their medium's potential to absorb historical testimony without mending its gaps and fragments, to memorialise loss without seeking to recuperate it. Swimming up from beneath their erasure, the Angel Island poems embody a dynamic of simultaneous burial and retrieval. This double movement is reflected in the spectral archives that continue to haunt Asian American poets writing today, for whom 'memory' is so often an 'opaque library'.

Notes

1. Him Mark Lai, Genny Lim and Judy Yung co-edited a volume of 135 of the poems in 1980, followed by a 2014 expanded edition: *Island: Poetry*

and History of Chinese Immigrants on Angel Island, 1910–1940, 2nd edn (Seattle: University of Washington Press, 2014).

2. Harrington, Joseph, 'Docupoetry and Archive Desire', *Jacket2*, 2011, <http://jacket2.org/article/docupoetry-and-archive-desire> (accessed 8 October 2018).

3. Cook, Terry and Joan Schwartz, 'Archives, Records, and Power: The Making of Modern Memory', *Archival Science*, 2 (2002), 1–19 (p. 1).

4. Derrida, Jacques, *Archive Fever: A Freudian Impression*, trans. Eric Pernowitz (Chicago and London: University of Chicago Press, 1996), p. 2.

5. Voss, Paul J., and Marta L. Werner, 'Towards a Poetics of the Archive: Introduction', *Studies in the Literary Imagination*, 32 (1999), i–viii (p. i).

6. See Fleming, Juliet, *Graffiti and the Writing Arts of Early Modern England* (London: Reaktion, 2001), pp. 73–5.

7. For a discussion of changing paradigms since the East Asian-focused 'cultural nationalism' of early Asian-American literary criticism, see Yu, Timothy, *Race and the Avant-Garde*: *Experimental and Asian American Poetry Since 1965* (Stanford: Stanford University Press, 2009), pp. 119–20.

8. Som, Brandon, *The Tribute Horse* (Brooklyn and Callicoon: Nightboat Books, 2014), p. 79; Vang, Mai Der, *Afterland* (Minneapolis: Graywolf, 2017), p. 70; Kapil, Bhanu, *Ban en Banlieue* (New York: Nightboat Books, 2015), p. 48. Further references in the text.

9. Derrida, *Archive Fever*, p. 91.

10. Steedman, Carolyn, *Dust* (Manchester: Manchester University Press, 2001), p. 77

11. Lai et al., *Island*, p. 17.

12. 'Andy Fitch with Brandon Som', *The Conversant*, n.d., <http://theconversant.org/?p=10009> (accessed 25 May 2018; no longer available online).

13. Ibid.

14. Ibid.

15. Ibid.

16. Lai et al., *Island*, p. x.

17. 'Andy Fitch with Brandon Som'.

18. Lee, Chiang, *Chinese Calligraphy: An Introduction to its Aesthetic and Technique*, 3rd edn (Cambridge, MA: Harvard University Press, 1974).

19. Yang's story is a rare recorded example of an individual from a pre-literate society single-handedly inventing a writing system; another is Sequoyah, the Cherokee silversmith invoked by Som, who completed his Cherokee syllabary in 1821. See Gnanadesikan, Amalia E., *The Writing Revolution: Cuneiform to the Internet* (Chichester: John Wiley & Sons, 2011), p. 133.

20. Buley-Meissner, Mary Louise, 'Stitching the Fabric of Hmong Lives: The Value of Studying Paj Ntaub and Story Cloth in Multicultural Education', in *Hmong and American: From Refugees to Citizens*, ed. Vincent K. Her and Mary Louise Buley-Meissner (St. Paul: Minnesota Historical Society Press, 2012), p. 234.

21. Vang, Mai Der, 'Heirs of the "Secret War" in Laos', *New York Times*, 27 May 2015 <https://www.nytimes.com/2015/05/28/opinion/heirs-of-the-secret-war-in-laos.html> (accessed 8 October 2018).

22. Brown, Patricia Leigh, 'A Hmong Generation Finds Its Voice in Writing', *New York Times*, 31 December 2011 <https://www.nytimes.

com/2012/01/01/us/a-hmong-Generation-finds-its-voice-in-writing.html> (accessed 8 October 2018).

23. See Forché, Carolyn, 'Twentieth Century Poetry of Witness', *American Poetry Review*, 22 (1993), 9–16.

24. See Disha Jani's roundtable discussion, 'Traces of Destruction: The Emotional Work of Studying Painful History', *The Toast* (2015) <http://the-toast.net/2015/09/21/traces-of-destruction-the-emotional-work-of-studying-painful-history/> (accessed 8 October 2018).

25. Kapil, Bhanu, 'Archive Fever' in 'The Vortex of Formidable Sparkles', 1 February 2012, archiving a post from her now defunct blog 'Was Jack Kerouac a Punjabi?' <https://thesparklyblogofbhanukapil.blogspot.com/2012/02/archive-fever.html> (accessed 8 October 2018).

26. Ibid.

27. Ibid.

28. Ibid.

29. Kapil, Bhanu, *Schizophrene* (Callicoon: Nightboat Books, 2011), p. 1 (emphasis original).

30. Ibid., pp. 59, 61.

31. Voss and Werner, 'Poetics of the Archive', p. ii. See also Greetham, David. '"Who's In, Who's Out": The Cultural Poetics of Archival Exclusion', *Studies in the Literary Imagination*, 32/1 (1999), 1–28.

32. Ibid.

33. For Kapil's long-term exploration of the immigrant's 'monstrous' undermining of categories, see especially *Incubation: A Space For Monsters* (New York: Leon Works, 2006).

34. Kapil, 'It's Like', in 'Vortex', 13 November 2017 <https://thesparklyblogofbhanukapil.blogspot.com/2017/11/its-like.html> (accessed 8 October 2018).

35. Kapil, Bhanu, *entre-BAN* (Vendome, Montreal: Vallum, 2017), p. 27.

36. Hartman, Saidiya, 'Venus in Two Acts', *Small Axe*, 12 (2008), 1–14 (p. 2).

37. Ibid., p. 11.

Chapter 9

Opening the Box:
Exploring the Bloodaxe Archive

Linda Anderson

Background

In 2013, Newcastle University purchased the archive of the independent poetry book publisher Bloodaxe Books. In the period from 1978, when Neil Astley established the press, Bloodaxe has published almost 1,500 volumes, by over 300 writers, and done much to expand and diversify the audience for poetry and the cohort of published poets in the UK and beyond. The archive consists of editorial and financial papers and correspondence and provides a unique insight into the world of contemporary poetry writing and publishing since the late 1970s.[1] The original acquisition of the archive was closely followed by the award of a preliminary, and then a major, grant from the Arts and Humanities Research Council, under a scheme which brought together three components: the cataloguing of the original acquisition, the digital exploration of the archive, and collaboration with a group of writers and artists who were tasked with visiting the archive and producing a creative response to it.[2] Unusually, therefore, the archivists' activities of receiving, sifting and classifying the papers happened in parallel with other kinds of exploration associated with the research award. The project became an opportunity for different perspectives on both the resources and the archiving process to come into play, not least because, by bringing a group of people together from different disciplinary backgrounds, it was impossible to contain the affective and physical dimensions of what we were doing within a strict designation of roles and tasks. Collaboration, one might argue, always has this aspect of disruption, exceeding the theoretical template of a single point of view, and operating in an unfinished or 'messy' intermediate space between materiality and discourse. Bringing the researchers – and not just their ideas – into proximity with each other, both disconcertingly, and productively, creates room for what is excessive, discontinuous, affective. Our research process involved physically as well as intellectually encountering each other, a dialogue where the personalities of the people involved mattered, and where unpredictable traces carried across disciplinary boundaries.

In this context Jacques Derrida's influential work *Archive Fever* seems at first frustratingly abstract and magisterial. However, the gap Derrida identified between archives as object or place and archives as imaginative vehicle remains central to thinking about archives and was crucial for our project. Famously, Derrida began *Archive Fever* by citing the notion of the law in relation to the archive. Looking at the derivation of the word from Greek, meaning a dwelling, a domicile, he also connected it with the authority of those who live there – the archons – and the power invested in them. The archive, for Derrida, has 'the force of law', yet, he could not allow it simply to rest there – rest as it were on its classical laurels – since he was also re-reading the archive through Freud and the paradox of the death drive which allied the creative and the destructive impulses.[3] The archive therefore as a public institution covers over for him contradictory aspects that have to do with private idiom, with erasure and with forgetfulness. Indeed, there is no archive, for Derrida, without an established idea of what an archive is, without a system and preconception about the kinds of meaning that can be archived, and without a location. Form and content are closely intertwined: 'The archivization produces as much as it records the event.'[4]

The present-day orthodoxies and obligatory protocols of archival practice can easily be read in terms of Derrida's analysis: the key twin tenets, often cited, of 'provenance' and 'original order' both emphasise the preservation of documents and give priority to a previously existing arrangement or sequence which enforces stability. In current handbooks for archivists, archives become associated primarily with history and with a sense of historical responsibility: 'Archives are collections of documents or "records" which have been selected for permanent preservation because of their value as evidence or as a source for historical or other research.'[5] After Derrida, the recognition of assumptions underpinning this about what constitutes 'value' cannot help but leap off the page. Yet it's also fair to say preservation, if an archive is to exist, is also a pragmatic necessity, and bears on the important issue of the materiality of archives, and the need to respect both the physical nature of the documents that constitute them and the quotidian labour of archivists themselves, overlooked by Derrida, and perhaps, as J. Matthew Huculak argues, generally 'unnoticed and unsung' in archival theory and scholarship.[6]

For Derrida, however, there is also something else at work in relation to archives, something beyond the law, something that can be neither codified nor satisfied, and which obeys another temporality. 'Archive fever' is the name he gives to the individual desire – 'compulsive, repetitive and nostalgic' – that propels us to search archives for something in the very place where it is lost or slips away. The appeal of archives may be that they offer a return to what existed before, to an original, archaic place of meaning. However, they can do so only through a repetitive gesture of mediation, by transposing meaning to a different place and time. By definition, as Derrida says, there can be no archive of what is being sought, since the secret 'remains unfindable'.[7] This 'fever' – at once paradoxical and compelling – has animated many archival researchers, who have talked about their 'intense, private search' and the 'dreams' that drive them.[8] Gail Crowther, for example, has described how her research meant overcoming physical hardship for the intense pleasure of touching Plath's letters and manuscripts, and thus experiencing the 'uncanny revivification' of the poet.[9] Susan Howe, merging her own poetry with that of others, evokes the scene of asking 'the librarian behind the desk for a cardboard box of labelled file folders containing whispering skeletons'. For Howe, manuscripts once 'shut carefully away' become occasions for creative encounter, to be 're-animated, re-collected (recollected)'. 'Each collected object or manuscript is a pre-articulate empty theatre where a thought may surprise itself at the instant of seeing.'[10] The emphasis shifts from the documents that remain to their restaging in the live encounter with a reader/researcher, who, as performer, uses their own presence and body to bring the object or text to life.

Entering the archive

Howe has also talked about how gaining access to the stacks in a library is like 'an adventure verging on trespass ...What I love . . . is that they always seem slightly off-limits, therefore forbidden.'[11] For us, from the start, there was a whiff of something illicit happening, as the two poets on a preliminary project, Tara Bergin and Anna Woodford – not trained or experienced in archival work – were allowed into the locked, private spaces of the archival storeroom, to help to open the boxes which arrived from Bloodaxe and witness the papers in a raw state, still contained in their original envelopes. Tara Bergin's poem, 'What We Found in the Archive', explores the rule-breaking nature of the process, with suitable poetic licence, ending mischievously:

> We asked the archivist to make us copies.
> We promised not to tell.
>
> We signed his orange form in pencil –
> and pocketed everything.[12]

In this transaction, the poet has made the archivist complicit in an 'unlawful' activity, as the poet, metaphorically at least, carries off her discoveries into her own domain.

Afterwards, when our poet-participants, who, as part of the main project, were set the task of responding to the archive, inspected the archival boxes – now hand-listed but not yet fully catalogued – they experienced a similar sense of entering a place bounded by prohibition, made manifest in the 'rules' handed to all users, and the strictly enforced silence.[13] Coincidentally – though, as it turned out, also significantly – the Reading Room of the Robinson Library Special Collections occupies an underground location in the library, which one participant likened to a prison visiting room. One of the rules of the Reading Room is that all users can only use pencil to make notes, common practice, of course, to protect precious manuscripts and rare books from being permanently marked or damaged. However, as with the topography of the reading room itself, the use of pencil was not neutral for the participants. For one participant it recalled childhood and the experience of learning to write; another talked about not liking writing in pencil because of the fear of the writing being lost; another mused about the sensual pleasure of the propelling pencil, which they had not recognised until now. Yet another saw it as 'underlining' the general injunction to enter the space but leave no marks yourself: 'Whereas everything else is quite permanent around you, it's like you are a ghost.'

Yet, if the size and significance of the archive – and what it represented – were widely felt, giving it a solidity not necessarily experienced in relation to their own writing, many of the participants were also surprised by the quality of their encounter, and how it fuelled their creativity. Whereas the abstract idea of the archive might be off-putting, the experience of being in the archive left traces or after-effects, a tenuous thread that might lead to a poem. One participant talked about the importance of searching and the tension created by the sense of things hidden or concealed. Always, it might be the next box that held the 'amazing' thing. This version of 'archive fever', the desire of the subject for the chimerical something created by desire itself, was also likened to the process of writing a poem, 'that looking for something, yet not knowing what it is'. For some there was a playfulness created by entering a particular space or being free from other pressures. For one participant the very presence of 'big figures' in the archive released an anarchic spirit – a freedom to innovate, to do something different.

Material and materiality

The possibilities and constraints of physical space and its internal mapping were part of our poets' experience of the archive, and the archive as place became for some, almost like Bachelard's 'oneiric house', a place for dreams.[14] Yet the resistances of the real were also very much in evidence, and the major discovery for many, accentuated by the unprocessed state of the papers they encountered, was the impact on them of the actual torn-open envelopes, paper that was ripped or folded in particular ways, old postage stamps and the appearance of scribbled marginalia. 'There's so many visual things that are interesting, and so many textures that are interesting.' One participant found the fact that the manuscripts were still enclosed in their original 'tatty' wrappings added to their precious status as 'relics'. This interest in the visual and tactile dimension of the archive extended to the curatorial paraphernalia too: 'Even just undoing documents with that cream ribbon round them is beautiful; it's like undoing a present.' As Maryanne Dever has argued, archival research practices in literary and historical studies have commonly privileged the text found on documents over the material supports of paper and ink, 'as though papers and pages can be understood as neutral containers or platforms for the transmission of such texts'.[15] Though this may be less apt in relation to poetic texts, where readers may be trained to be aware of the 'visual surfaces' of the written page as signifiers of meaning, even here, it has been argued, insufficient attention has been given to textual properties that lie outside or refuse discursive cognition.[16] Our project seems to have operated as the kind of provocation that Dever has described, an instance of heightened materiality, where attention is focused on the physicality of paper itself. In our case this was partly because our participants were offered the opportunity, when not everything had been sifted and separated into a more traditional form of archive, to delve into envelopes, undo folders, open boxes: to experience 'tattiness'. However, there was also undoubtedly an element of nostalgia. One of the features of the Bloodaxe Archive is the way it unwittingly stores in its very materials, in its paper and its forms of writing and type, a historical record of the rapidly changing means of production of poetry from the 1970s onwards. Word processing and digitisation become an ever-present horizon or vanishing point, seeming to make paper and other materials ever more precious.

Derrida has written eloquently about the sensuous appeal of paper, as a complex resource that 'echoes' with a material and symbolic history, that is bound up with originating notions of the subject and subjectivity:

> Beneath the appearance of a surface, it holds in reserve a volume, folds, a labyrinth whose walls return the echoes of the voice or song that it carries itself . . . Paper is utilized in an experience involving the body, beginning with hands, eyes, voice, ears; so it mobilizes both time and space.[17]

We enter a space; we handle paper; we engage our body in the interaction with words as sonorous and tactile. As Susan Howe has written: 'There's a level at which words are spirit and paper is skin. That's the fascination of archives. There's still a bodily trace.'[18] Archives make the numinous word flesh: as we hold the paper, so it takes 'bodily hold of us', a hold that is both real and imaginary.[19] Yet, despite the eloquence of his response to paper, Derrida is far from simply decrying the digital; rather he perceives lines of continuity between them, with paper and word processor both presenting 'screens' or surfaces of inscription. Paper, he writes, is, in current terminology, 'a multimedia resource', by which he means that it communicates with us on several different levels and through different senses – even straining towards the capabilities of the digital. He also sees paper as surviving in different forms, as technology harks back to 'the order of the page' or keeps the memory of the page alive through names such as 'notebook'. Perhaps most interesting of all, Derrida argues that technology can function as a means of telling us something about paper we did not know or recognise. While the constraints of the written or printed page – 'its hardness, its limits, its resistance' – might make working against it all the more desirable, and propel typographical experiment simply because it cannot offer the kind of interactivity we have come to expect from computers, he also believes that, 'on the other hand',

> by carrying us beyond paper, the adventures of technology grant us a sort of future anterior; they liberate our reading for a retrospective exploration of the past resources of paper, for its *previously* multimedia vectors.[20]

Perhaps paper has always been more than we thought it was, if only we had the (technological) means of seeing it.

Intrigued by the strong visual and tactile response we had to the materials of the archive, and in an attempt to memorialise the archive at the early stage of its unpacking, we asked photographer Phyllis Christopher to record her impressions. She elected to take 'macro-photographs' of envelopes and paper that in many ways proved illuminating, discovering not only textures of paper but also traces and erasures that would not have been apparent to the naked eye. In the delicate pores and tendrils of its materiality, paper seems almost to become skin, as Susan Howe observed, breaking down the border between body and page. Similarly, the camera followed the evocative meetings and separations of edges, folds and tears, and the indentations of text, almost invisible, sunk into the paper as if into the mystic writing pad described by Freud and used by him as an analogy of the unconscious. The photographs perfectly illustrate the overlapping of the present and the past as Derrida describes, and the way an archive can contain ghosts or phantoms, if those ghosts are also figures for the gaps in our knowledge, something that cannot be brought to mind or made visible until an event, a reading or recognition happens in the future (Plates 2 and 3).[21]

The suggestiveness of experiencing the material archive and having a sense of physical connection with it – of entering its time and space and feeling – quite literally – its life in our hands – raises questions about what a literary archive is, where the boundaries are and what should be kept and what discarded. The Bloodaxe Archive, now that the first accessions have been fully curated, is housed in uniform grey archival boxes, and has a very different appearance to that raggedness when it was originally received: it now appears, at least immediately, less diverse, perhaps even less interesting. The materiality of documents has as its correlative, of course, their vulnerability, and, whatever the fascination of the evidence of a human 'trace' in the archive, the work of conservation must also deal with things that might damage its longevity – in the case of the Bloodaxe Archive this included the discovery of a banana squashed between the pages, as well as safety pins and rubber bands. The case of Post-it notes is particularly interesting and helped to open up another research strand in the work of film-maker Kate Sweeney. As a publisher's archive, Bloodaxe includes business and financial records, and the Post-it notes directed attention to the 'casual' work, not of the editor, but of the other administrators who help with the associated tasks of publishing (Plate 4). They seemed to provide evidence of submerged stories and other voices, regularly excised from the archive, a surrounding discourse that enables the 'work' of poetry to exist. Our discussions have helped to draw attention to an occluded dimension that might be uncovered by looking at administrative records and their place in the overall archive. As one of our participants said, experiencing what they referred to as the 'backstage documents', 'I had no experience of publishing . . . I had no idea there was so much admin, and so much paper involved in everything.' This is an antidote to the preciousness of stored, written-upon paper where rarity is seen as an aspect of its value; on the other hand, it also allows us to ask questions about the way hierarchies exist, and about what a publisher's archive does and should contain, in relation to evidence about administrative work.[22]

Translation

One of the areas that our participants were aware of was Bloodaxe's particular commitment to translation and its contribution to bringing important European and Russian poets in translation to UK audiences through the 1980s and 1990s, as well as its wider programme of translation publication both then and since. 'It seemed like a bit of a mission', as one participant remarked. The mission, of course, had begun earlier, perhaps most notably through the inception in 1965 of a magazine, *Modern Poetry in Translation*, by Ted Hughes and his collaborator Daniel Weissport which perceived its aim to be, in retrospect at least, 'almost political',[23] giving a platform to poets suffering censorship and repression in their own countries, whose work spoke with an urgency which was transformative for many UK poets, including Hughes himself. In 2015 Bloodaxe published the fiftieth-anniversary anthology of *Modern Poetry in Translation* entitled *Centres of Cataclysm*, a phrase that Hughes and Weissport had used to characterise Eastern Europe in their first editorial: 'While we had material coming from many other areas, it was that which came from Eastern Europe, which was somehow the most insistent. It is this region which is the centre of cataclysm.'[24] Bloodaxe in the Cold War decades published translations of the Romanian poet Marin Sorescu by Michael Hamburger, as *Selected Poems* (1983), and by Ewald Osers of the Czech poet Miroslav Holub, as *On the Contrary* (1984). Though Holub had been published before in the UK, in 1967 in the influential Penguin Modern European Poets series, this book included a more substantial selection, gathering new translations and translations that had previously only been published in UK and USA poetry magazines. These publications become all the more exceptional when set in the context of Bloodaxe's own financially tenuous hold on its future at the time, and the far from established readership for translated poetry.

Perhaps most significantly in terms of its political impact, Bloodaxe in 1986 published *No – I Am Not Afraid* by the young Russian poet Irina Ratushinskaya, who was at the time imprisoned in 'the small zone', the special unit for women prisoners of conscience in Mordovia, for the 'crime' of writing and distributing her poems. The poems in the collection were smuggled out by visitors and friends, either having been memorised or, using the thin marginal papers from a Bible, rolled up and concealed in ballpoint pens. The international campaign for her release, fuelled by this publication, succeeded a few months later, and Ratushinskaya came to the UK to receive medical treatment that same year and to give her first reading of the poems, appropriately, in Newcastle, the home of her publisher.

Many of the participants mentioned Ratushinskaya, and the history that paper itself enacted in relation to her poems, in this case in its journey from Russia to the West and from prison to the outside world, with the kind of paper used – thin, flimsy strips – being an intrinsic part of the poems' survival. With Ratushinskaya the publishing history becomes part of the meaning of the poems, but for all the earlier collections our participants mentioned the increased sense of history they felt in reading the poems in the context of the archive. In many cases the proofs of collections are stored with schedules and reviews which surround them with a detailed historical context, but the slightly used or dog-eared papers also carry a sense of the past, especially when typewritten rather than word-processed, and marked up for the typesetter in a detailed and laborious way now obviated by modern technology. The indications of labour seem to reside in the creases of paper and in the irregular marks of the typewriter, those aleatory traces that seem resonant of their original history, of something having happened in the past, that involved the particularity of touch and contact – that was an intimate transaction between the body and the page.

The one work created by our participants that directly owes its inspiration to Ratushinskaya was a music-and-video piece by Helen Collard, inspired by the poetry, but which takes the title of Ratushinskaya's memoir, *Grey is the Colour of Hope*, and 'translates' the idea of tones in relation to colour into musical notation. The result is a very moving interpretation of the poems, using a fragile melody and notes, picked out against silence, in relation to a continuous grey screen, and only at one point rising to a more hectic – and desperate – crescendo.[25] This is perhaps the most radical attempt to provide a version of poems by shifting to another medium entirely and finding musical equivalents. Another participant, Anne Ryland, looking at the papers relating to an anthology of modern Polish poetry, *The Burning Forest* edited by Adam Czerniawski (1987), and focusing on the actual language, lamented the lack of material in Polish, since she wished to make her own translations. She ended up obtaining a literal translation from a native speaker and translating, Sdzislaw Stroinski's poem 'Warsaw'. It is interesting that this is a poem which itself reflects on imprints or traces which are difficult to translate or interpret:

The reflection of Warsaw's face too difficult to interpret, has left an imprint
on the ruins' twisted features,
just as in the story of St Veronica's veil.

And people who'll come here one day, some day, pledging to decipher the
city's strained expression
brushing their blue-grey fingers over her, prodding the people who dried up
between cobblestone
and in crevices –
            will burst into prayer or curse.[26]

The differences of the translation from Adam Czerniawski's version
in the anthology are not huge – in this passage at least – but the act of
translation here was 'personal', an entering into the text, leaving an
imprint, not unlike the experience referred to in the poem itself, to bring
it to life, to revoice it.

For others, however, the fact the poems were already translated seemed
to mimic or release their own acts of creative mediation. Critic and poet
Susan Stewart has written about 'an unfolding series of asymmetries' as
being part of the special character of art: the asymmetry between the
intentions of the maker and its reception by reader or viewer, who will
inevitably bring their own assumptions and experience to bear; or a
'belatedness', a gap in time, that must exist before the work is received
or read. Being 'face to face' with a work of art also involves being
open to the non-coincidence of meaning, to a non-presence, a space for
interpretation that is renewed for every receiver or reader.[27] For one
participant, going into the archive, looking at translations, operated
almost like a 'contract of co-authorship', entering into a relationship,
with a sense of occasion made obvious by being actually *in* the archive
and by the encounter being defined in terms of time and space. Another
participant, Katharine Towers, found the textual layout of the translations of Stéphane Mallarmé's 'Brise Marine' in a parallel-text anthology
of French love poems to be an analogy for that 'face to face' of reader
and text.[28] Because the poems are love poems, translation itself became
a form of intimate address:

For years we've been engrossed
In this colloque sentimental.
I suppose we must be soulmates.

Centuries ago – hearing the voices of sailors
singing far from land –
I brought them to you on a salt breeze …

Mon cœur! There's so much more I want to tell you.
Come close: we'll do this seul à seule
and whisper in a language no-one understands.[29]

Here languages mingle on the page, mimicking the closeness and merging of the lovers.

Langdon Hammer, in his review of Susan Howe's *Debths* and citing the poet and critic Allen Grossman, describes the 'prototypical lyric poem' as 'a translation and interpretation of some other "poem", some elemental music or foreign speech'.[30] Our poets, asked to engage with pre-existing writing, often figured the dilemma in their poems, turning to translation as both genre and trope, and using prosopopoeia as a symbolic equivalent of an encounter where language intervenes, adding complexity and distance – 'far from land' – and creating a space, as Stewart suggests, where a new creativity comes into play. What may be at issue in this creative turn is an exchange of positions whereby not only does the written become mobile, fluid, in process, but the poet/participant can realise themselves, non-biographically, refigured and stabilised in the form of a poem. One of our participants, Sarah Howe, became interested in a box containing the proofs of the translation by Brian Holton of Yang Lian's *Where the Sea Stands Still*, and particularly a misprint she found in the spreadsheet listing what the box contained: '1999 Yang Lian Where the Proofs Stand Still'. For her, because Yang Lian's book already embodied the motif of water running in both directions and achieving momentarily, through the contrary flow of river and sea, a point of stasis, this seemed to suggest – coincidentally – the themes of 'fixity and influx' in the archive itself. The poem that Howe went on to write, 'Where the Proofs Stand Still', which she conceived of as 'an act of atomizing untranslation' , takes all its words from one page of the penultimate proofs of Yang Lian's poetry collection – all, as Howe, says, but one, presumably the word 'proof' itself, which then inserts itself into Howe's poem, both destabilising and fixing the words:

> the lying touch of no ocean utterly
> footprints   proof the throttled tombstone years
> command you see here a fantasy museum proof forever
> greener   fragile as the trees   simply as glass
> the same madness proof of your own fingerprints[31]

Fragmentation

One of the ways in which our participants found that the archive prompted their creativity was through enjoying the 'serendipity' of what was assembled in each of the boxes, a collage effect intensified by the light-touch sorting and cataloguing at this stage of the archival acquisition. One of our participants talked about waiting for the paper bit by bit to throw up something which would catch their attention. Another talked about liking 'the fractured sense of it all'. All seem to have enjoyed reading in a non-linear way, not pursuing answers, but being open to what the material itself might present.

The idea of the fragment and fragmentation has been integral to modernist poetry, with the idea of an archive often figuring as the scattered remnants of a past that the contemporary reader and writer must infer or reassemble. The poet and critic Joan Retallack, rejecting the nostalgia implicit in the idea of 'an idealized, irrecoverable past', has talked instead about the present as 'the residue of the past': 'What, after all, is there materially but all that is after?' For her the act of composition is crucial, a making of something in the present that is – indeed must be – situated in what has been: 'The contemporary doesn't leave history behind; it further complicates it. We're still embedded in the detritus of all your centuries, better and worse.'[32] Walter Benjamin has been the key modern figure for thinking about both fragments and archives. His famous description of 'the angel of history' also invokes the idea of detritus, or 'a pile of debris', to characterise the past in material terms; nevertheless, it is within these fragments – which can also appear as 'sparks' or 'flashes' – rather than any idea of 'making whole', that an unrealised potential can be understood, the 'presence of now' within history.[33] Benjamin, who carefully catalogued and collected his own writing as well of that of others, never aimed at comprehensiveness. Instead the archives he made were a form of 'scrappy paperwork', unofficial, concerned with the incidental, the overlooked or the marginal. Less important than storage and security for him was that his collections be used productively in the present, by himself first of all: 'To renew the old – in such a way that I myself, the newcomer, would make what was old my own – was the task of the collection that filled my drawer.'[34]

The notion of knowledge as fragmentary is perhaps hard to think without reference to the loss of some previous unity or wholeness, to the partially complete or unfinished, to a melancholy severing or insufficiency. Yet the effort of postmodernism has been to reverse this hierarchy of whole to fragment, with wholeness being seen as a willed, perhaps illusory, state, never finally achieved, and never stable. Philosopher and theorist Maurice Blanchot thought of the fragment as 'a piece of meteor detached from an unknown sky', a kind of 'shattering' and 'dislocation' that nevertheless does not carry a negative value since the totality it references cannot be envisaged. In imagining how his exemplary poet René Char arranges the seemingly separate phrases in his poetry, Blanchot describes it as 'a new kind of arrangement not entailing harmony, concordance or reconciliation, but [one] that accepts disjunction or divergence as the infinite center from out of which [*sic*], through speech, relation is to be created'.[35] As Leslie Hill has commented, for Blanchot there is a close correspondence between the idea of the fragment and writing itself. The fragment for him exists as the 'un-reconciled tension between artwork and its unravelling, between its gathering and dispersion, between time past and time still to come'.[36]

Containing lightly or heavily edited versions of poems, produced on their way to publication, the Bloodaxe Archive displays its own version of 'gathering and dispersion' as part of the process of writing, as it does the paradox of time – the relation between 'time past and time still to come' – that an archive seems to figure. Not only is 'process' – the anticipated future – past in the archive, having already become object or text, it is also the case that the archive is always creating something else, something new, through different juxtapositions of materials, through different interpretations of its meanings, and by using and reusing knowledge of itself in different ways. According to Derrida, 'one will never be able to objectivize it [the archive] with no remainder. The archivist produces more archive, and that is why the archive is never closed. It opens out of the future.'[37] This has its echo in Hal Foster's speculation, at the end of his essay 'An Archival Impulse', about the desire of archival art to 'turn belatedness into becomingness' and his welcoming of a vision of archives not as established symbolic structures which enshrine 'totalities', but as places for the questioning of relations: 'construction sites' rather than 'excavation sites'.[38]

In her book on the idea of fragmentation in modernist literature, Rebecca Varley-Winter has written about the importance of the body in relation to fragments, not just in the sense of the metaphorical body – in the way we might talk about 'a body of writing' – but literally, in terms of the physical bodies of authors and readers. When we think phenomenologically, she argues, we can see how a text fragments as it is held closer to the body and, correspondingly, how our notion of completeness relies on distance. She then offers this description of a reading process that challenges 'mind–body dualism':

> Fragmentation tends to return to the particular. When I am drawn into the marks of a handwritten draft, cry or laugh in reading, read a text aloud and mispronounce it, or learn to read a new language, the gap between body and text is closed through moments of inarticulate comprehension, poised between what the text is doing to my body and what the text says or means.[39]

To have followed the journey of our participants into the Bloodaxe archive has been to follow how the materiality of the archive – the paper and its inscription – has touched and been touched by a particular group of readers and poets in ways which challenge the static nature of what the archive contains. Recently Giulia Palladini and Marco Pustianaz have offered a lyrical definition of what they call the 'affective archive', created by renewed and overlapping encounters:

> *affective archive* names for us a horizon, a limit, a possibility always ready to be enacted and released in every archive. Seen as a process of memory-making in which everybody is involved – producing the scene of our common, yet also divided, dwelling space – the affective archive wavers between materiality and immateriality, between conservation and transformation. Ultimately, the hybrid term *affective archive* is intended to acknowledge the impulse that both creates and mobilizes the archive as an endless process.[40]

Though this description of the 'affective archive' could well be applied to the project we embarked on, this is not to say that the Bloodaxe archive is not *also* a scholarly resource and an important historical record of contemporary poetry publishing, which informs us both about particular poets and about a poetry publisher over an important period in the development of contemporary poetry. However, thinking about it in the terms above, as a process of 'memory-making' and a 'dwelling space', offers a way of using and renewing the creativity it contains, opening the archive to different insights – indeed, holding it open to unanticipated encounters which will go on adding to its meaning in the future. The last word goes to one of our poets, Pippa Little, and her address to the archive:

> Another
> ordinary day, and I strum envelopes rows
> as if you're an Indian harmonium.
> I'm happy, I love the heft, the promise of you.
>   You open me
> As much as I open you.[41]

Notes

With thanks to our archivists Ian Johnson and Rebecca Bradley and digital assistant Kimberley Gaiger; poets Colette Bryce and Ahren Warner, who worked as Research Associates on the project; Tom Schofield, who researched and designed the innovative digital interfaces with the archives; and Phyllis Christopher and Kate Sweeney, who produced photographs and films for the project.

1. The Bloodaxe Archive is held in Special Collections, the Robinson Library, Newcastle University. It is catalogued on the Archives Hub <http://archive-shub.jisc.ac.uk> (accessed 23 July 2018). It also has its own innovative website, designed as part of the project, which includes a record of the

project, and digitised pages from the archive <http://bloodaxe.ncl.ac.uk> (accessed 23 July 2018).

2. 'The Poetics of the Archive: Creative and Community Engagement with the Bloodaxe Archive', under the Arts and Humanities Research Council scheme, 'Capital Funding for Digital Transformations in Community Research Co-Production' <http://gtr.ukri.org/projects?ref=AH%2FL007746%2F1> (accessed 23 July 2018).

3. Derrida, Jacques, *Archive Fever: A Freudian Impression* trans. Eric Prenowitz (Chicago and London: University of Chicago Press, 1996), p. 7.

4. Ibid., p. 17.

5. Bettington, Jackie, Kim Eberhard, Rowena Loo and Clive Smith, *Keeping Archives* (Dickson: Australian Society of Archivists, 2008), p. 15. This book was lent to me as an important textbook by an archivist at the Robinson Library Special Collections.

6. <https://modernismmodernity.org/forums/posts/what-modernist-archive> (accessed 18 August 2018).

7. Derrida, *Archive Fever*, p. 100.

8. Kaplan, Ann Yaeger, 'Working in the Archives', in *Reading the Archive: On Texts and Institutions*, ed. E. S. Burt and Janie Vanpée (New Haven: Yale University Press, 1990), p. 103; Steedman, Carolyn, *Dust* (Manchester: Manchester University Press, 2001), p. 69.

9. Crowther, Gail and Peter K. Steinberg, *These Ghostly Archives: The Unearthing of Sylvia Plath* (Fonthill Media, 2017), p. 20.

10. Howe, Susan, *Spontaneous Particulars: The Telepathy of Archives* (New Directions, New York, 2014), pp. 41, 24.

11. Howe, Susan, 'The Art of Poetry No 97', *Paris Review*, 203 (2012), 144–69 (p. 155).

12. Bergin, Tara, in outline of paper given at GLAM conference, 2013 <http://glam-archives.org.uk/?page_id=1555> (accessed 18 August 2018).

13. 'Poetics of the Archive' invited thirty-five creative participants to respond to the Bloodaxe Archive. Quotations from the participants are taken from the transcripts of recordings of the workshops held during the project. Where possible I have named the speaker, but the participants are not always named in the recordings. All the artists and poets whose creative encounters with the archive have inspired this chapter are showcased here: <http://bloodaxe.ncl.ac.uk/explore/index.html#/gallery> (accessed 23 July 2018).

14. Bachelard, Gaston, *On Poetic Imagination and Reverie*, trans. Colette Gaudin (Dallas: Spring Publications, 1987), p. 98.

15. Dever, Maryanne, 'Provocations on the Pleasures of Archived Paper', *Archives and Manuscripts*, 41/3 (2013), 171–82 (p. 177).

16. Bloomfield, Mandy, *Archaeopoetics: Word, Image, History* (Tuscaloosa: University of Alabama Press, 2016), p. 5.

17. Derrida, Jacques, *Paper Machine*, trans. Rachel Bowlby (Stanford: Stanford University Press, 2005), p. 44.

18. Howe, 'Art of Poetry', p. 158.

19. Derrida, *Paper Machine*, p. 42.

20. Ibid., pp. 46–7.

21. Christopher, Phyllis, 'Into the Archive', <http://bloodaxe.ncl.ac.uk/explore/index.html#/research/POA1PC4> (accessed 23 July 2018).

22. Produced as ongoing work for a PhD at Newcastle University.

23. Hughes, Ted, 'Preface', in *Modern Poetry in Translation* (1983), reprinted in *Centres of Cataclysm: Celebrating Fifty Years of Modern Poetry in Translation*, ed. Sasha Dugdale and David and Helen Constantine (Hexham: Bloodaxe, 2016), p. 271

24. Hughes, Ted and Daniel Weissport, 'From the Editorial to the First Issue', in *Centres of Catalclysm*, p. 23

25. See <http://bloodaxe.ncl.ac.uk/explore/index.html#/research/POA1HC1> (accessed 23 July 2018).

26. Ryland, Anne, 'Warsaw', <http://bloodaxe.ncl.ac.uk/explore/index.html#/research/POA1AR2> (accessed 23 July 2018).

27. Stewart, Susan, 'On the Art of the Future', in *The Open Studio: Essays on Art and Aesthetics* (Chicago: University of Chicago Press, 2005), pp. 23–4.

28. Eliot, Alistair, ed., *French Love Poems* (Tarset: Bloodaxe, 1991).

29. Towers, Katharine, 'Brise Marine', in *The Remedies* (London: Picador, 2015), pp. 44–5; the earlier version is at <http://bloodaxe.ncl.ac.uk/explore/index.html#/research/POA1KT1> (accessed 23 July 2018).

30. Hammer, Langdon, 'Inside & Underneath Words', *The New York Review of Books*, 28 September 2017, 31–3 (p. 31).

31. Howe, Sarah, 'Where the Proofs Stand Still', <http://bloodaxe.ncl.ac.uk/explore/index.html#/research/POA1SH1> (accessed 23 July 2018); also in *The Poetics of the Archive*, catalogue produced for Newcastle Poetry Festival, 2015, p. 27.

32. Retallack, Joan, *The Poethical Wager* (Berkeley and Los Angeles: University of California Press, 2003), pp. 10–11.

33. Benjamin, Walter, 'Theses on the Philosophy of History', in *Illuminations*, ed. Hannah Arendt, trans. Harry Zohn (London: Fontana, 1973), pp. 259–60, 257, 263.

34. Marx, Ursula, Gudrun Schwarz, Michael Schwarz and Erdmut Wizisla, eds, *Walter Benjamin's Archive: Images, Texts Signs*, trans. Esther Leslie (London: Verso, 2007), pp. 10, 7.

35. Blanchot, Maurice, 'The Fragment Word', in *The Infinite Conversation*, trans Susan Hanson (Minneapolis and London: University of Minnesota Press, 1993), p. 308.

36. Hill, Leslie, *Maurice Blanchot and Fragmentary Writing; A Change of Epoch* (London: Continuum, 2012), p. 2.

37. Derrida, *Archive Fever*, p. 68.

38. Foster, Hal, 'An Archival Impulse', *October*, 110 (Autumn 2004), 3–22 (pp. 21–2).

39. Varley-Winter, Rebecca, *Reading Fragments and Fragmentation in Modernist Literature* (Brighton: Sussex Academic Press, 2018), p. 4.

40. Palladini, Giulia and Marco Pustianaz, *Lexicon for an Affective Archive* (Chicago and Bristol: Intellect Books, 2017), pp. 12–13.

41. Little, Pippa, 'The Song of the Boxes' <http://bloodaxe.ncl.ac.uk/explore/index.html#/research/POA1PL1> (accessed 23 July 2018).

Chapter 10

'I am Already Historical': In the Archive

Sean O'Brien

I'll begin with a poem of an allegedly comic kind, whose relevance will I hope become clear as I go on.

Continuous Assessment

'Life is first bedroom then fire'
Has not in fact come on as we
Originally hoped. Has tended
To stagnate. Has failed to see
Where his best interests lie.
Has left his errors unamended.
Has been increasingly inclined
Despite the mounting evidence
To claim an independent mind.
Devoid of ounce of common sense.
And will persist in seeing things
Not as they were meant to be –
But otherwise, 'by time
And slow accretion tending
To return upon themselves' without
Completing projects as required:
Has 'other things to think about'.
Irrelevantly claims he too
Was once adored, desired,
Made much of, begged for his embrace.
Too easy now to take the piss.
Believes might still be happy ending.
Seems not to fear the loss of face
Entailed by crapping on like this.
Entirely fails to grasp that time
Does not, cannot, will not afford
The luxury of lingering where once
As was originally hoped
He should have taken one good look
And left, not vegetated.

The past is dead. It would have coped.
Love and doorways, sex and death,
Grim remorse and badger's breath.
From the outset all that stuff
Was manifestly overrated,
Like our subject, who persists
In claiming that it still exists.
Keeps revisiting the scene
Of (so-called) triumph and (in fact) decline
And stands there asking, asking
Why – as if it matters – having been
There once, he cannot go again.
Fact is, alas, fact is, this one
Is all too representative
Of those who tried, and failed, to live,
And too expensive to ret[r]ain.

In July 2017 I had been writing for fifty years. The starting point was coincidence when a stirring of interest was encouraged by an inspiring English teacher. I had never come across anything like 'Prufrock', the 'Preludes' or the half a dozen early Ted Hughes poems, such as 'Wind' and 'To Paint a Water-Lily', that we read and talked about in class. These poems made the world more real, more substantial. I remember 1967 as the summer when I discovered poetry and began to make use of the excellent poetry stock at Hull Central Library. Looking back, I think I had been slightly adrift, uncertain what to do besides trying to pass O levels, with no confidence that I would secure enough of them to get into the sixth form and from there, somehow, into the world. Poetry seemed to provide a purpose independent of other requirements. It was what I had to do. I seem to have been very certain about this. I was already a sort of rentier, living off the sense of imaginative possibility, determined never to have a proper job. Ah, well.

Most of the very early work has vanished, I'm relieved to say, although a different English teacher of mine contacted me some years ago in order to return a couple of poems I'd written for homework. I remembered having been slightly offended by the fact that he'd *marked* them, as if they were mere homework, something other than poems. He obviously found them interesting enough at the time to take them back and hang on to them. Now he was in his eighties. I was pleased to hear from him; rather less so by the poems themselves, which provided no basis whatever for the decision I had already taken that writing poems would be my life. The marks he awarded now seemed a bit on the generous side, actually.

Although I intended to keep everything, at one point I lost an entire manuscript. For some reason I had folded and stuffed it in the back pocket of my jeans, thus courting disaster. After the shock, I forgot every detail of the poems. I wrote others. It wasn't until some point in my early twenties that I began more or less deliberately to preserve drafts of poems and other writing. Some of these remained at my parents', but in time the accumulating papers began to accompany me on my travels through university and beyond, into a variety of grim bedsits and flats in unrecommended locations, in any one of which it would have been reasonable to abandon the project and seek sensible employment, though this was always impossible to contemplate. This activity – this writing on paper – was what I did, or, more to the point, *was going to do* when the tumblers fell into place and I found out how to do it properly. It was not yet.

Meanwhile, in Liverpool, next to an undertaker's, I overlooked a graveyard and the blocked-up gateway from the hospital from which those dead of fever were once taken for burial. I seem not to have been grateful for this suggestive view. In another place I was shown, briefly, the awful solitude endured by those unattached in middle age or older. Back in Hull I negotiated with a demented old Irishwoman who seemed to assume that anyone entering the building was bent on murdering her and making off with her stacks of mouldering newspapers. I felt unable to explain to her that I had my own paper-based obsession to be getting on with. Many people will recognise this temporary world, the 'before' when nothing is settled but when the first serious, chilly intimations of time passing surface in the blank grey afternoons at the desk or in the unsleeping dead of night. Other accommodation followed – a filthy, freezing bedsit in south Leeds towards the end of the Yorkshire Ripper's reign of terror; another on top of a mansion in Tunbridge Wells where the landlady forbade visitors and used the bath to prepare decaying meat for her many dogs. And so on. Eventually, somehow, there was a mortgage, a permanent address in Brighton, and then a move back north to the house on the edge of Newcastle where we've lived for nearly thirty years. The constant in all this was the boxes of manuscript, steadily growing in number. So the papers came with me, first in a battered black tin trunk and then in supplementary containers. I say 'papers' and I mean it literally: I almost always write on white A4 paper rather than in notebooks. As to notebooks, I have tended to toy with their affections, abandoning them at the drop of a hat for the white siren voice of A4 paper.

I have mentioned what I was 'going to do': the pages of poems, very nearly all unpublished and not worth publishing, were a wager of sorts, though I seem to have assumed that I had already won. After all, there was nothing else I was meant to be doing. Study and teaching were simply the meantime. The actually existing O'Brien was in a sense nowhere to be found at any stage of this early accumulation. He was a creature *in potentia*, a figment of (largely unexamined) ambition. With the handover of the manuscripts to the archive he has ceased to exist even as phantom. Take away intention, and with it the future, and he vanishes like dandruff on a white sheet. People involved in the archive project at the Newcastle Centre for Literary Arts, examining the Bloodaxe Archive which includes material from and about my first two collections, have asked me about some of the early poems. There is a poem called 'Papers', as though its name must offer to reveal something. The poem doesn't work at all and I have not reprinted it. But there it sits, as if it belongs to me, or I to it. It seems to imagine a point beyond which I have gone on adding to the stack of paper. There is something presumptuous about this teleology, as though the author had tried to leap from start to finish – a notion, if it can be called that, which I suspect is wrapped up with whatever I was reading at the time. It should not have come as a surprise that researchers looking at my material in the Bloodaxe Archive (which Newcastle acquired in 2013) found this poem particularly intriguing. I think, sourly, it might have been written as an application for an Arts and Humanities Research Council (AHRC) research grant, since it implied the same omniscience about the outcome as applicants are required to guarantee. A more interesting poem (to me) from the same period is 'The Snowfield'. When I wrote that out of the blue one wintry afternoon after walking in Pearson Park, it seemed as if the tumblers had finally fallen into alignment: this, I felt, was the real thing, which seemed to be confirmed when it was published in *The New Review*, the most prestigious and widely hated magazine of the time. It seemed like an arrival, despite the misprint (my fault, as has usually been the case). It might have been easier to call it a day there and then.

When interviewed about the archive I've felt as if I'm failing to give the researchers value for their expenditure of time and preparatory effort. What was I doing back then in the late 1970s? Generally speaking, it's hard to say. Listening to cadences with almost more attention than I gave the meaning of the poems I read or wrote? Trying to find a space in which to work – something perhaps akin to what Jeffrey Wainwright refers to as ' a particular space'?[1] And if this was going on I was also looking for a way to connect direct personal experience, a personal sense of the world, to the larger context of history and politics, and at the same time to make something out of a very powerful sense of place and atmosphere which seems to have been the governing element of my imagination.

I suppose I was trying to learn to listen, to think, and to discover the coherence of what might have sounded like rather dispersed preoccupations. Yet even this tentative description imposes too much clarity and conscious purpose on a very halting and inarticulate process of divination. When in those days I exchanged work with my friend Peter Didsbury, whose poetry has in many ways been very different from mine, the thing that excited us was the dramatically evocative phrase or turn of thought or shift of tone that could throw experience and reverie into relief while somehow keeping faith with them. But none of this can be seen as I saw it then, supposing that word doesn't – again – overstate the clarity of what took place. We lived, as it were, on the inside of an art form while trying to understand it. In an eponymous poem, Didsbury quotes Bob Seger's song 'Night Moves': 'Working on night moves / without any clues'.[2] The song is about the discovery of sex, but it applies equally well to poetry. The thing I was after was always just beyond reach and the reading I did tended to prepare me for new phases of uncertainty.

I was driven by a fumbling sense that if the perceptions, instincts and suspicions were to amount to something they must be seen, and written, in relation to, and as part of, something larger. This seems entirely obvious now, but reading Auden and then the work of Douglas Dunn, who became my friend and mentor, had the force of revelation. Here was an escape from self, from mere subjectivity, into a larger dispensation where fears, desires and unarticulated (and in some sense apparently prohibited) intimations of how things really were – such as class, money, violence, the frustration and denial of ordinary hopes – might be seen to have a shape, an order, to which the poem might, however pessimistically, be a kind of resistance, or against which it might at any rate represent a mode of wakefulness. Everything that was merely the case appeared as though transfigured: this city where I'd grown up, these people, these rules and routines and assumptions, were as real as anything else. Poetry made them so.

Whether anyone else would, or could, glean any of this from the sheaves of paper produced in the process seems to me at best uncertain: I'm talking about authorial intention, which the articles of literary-critical faith (the ones I inherited, anyway) suggest is unavailable to the reader and in any case not of legitimate interest, since the written work has its own life to live in the reader's imagination, a place just as bewilderingly over-determined as we would suppose the author's to be (were it possible or permissible to discuss that, which of course it isn't).

As to my papers, until recently there was simply an accretion of documents with only the vaguest chronological ordering principle. After a time, it became the kind of possession that occupies significant amounts of room and has to be taken account of when moving house. I don't throw anything away, so there is a great deal of it. In 2015 I was invited to sell the material to the Robinson Library at Newcastle University by the Newcastle Centre for Literary Arts, as part of its AHRC-funded archive project (Plate 5). This was a welcome solution to the problem of space, and to the cost of preventing our house from falling down under the accumulated weight of paper. In due course eighty-odd boxes were carted off to the library. But making even rather rudimentary preparations to hand the material over – such as forcing myself, with great difficulty, to dispose of pieces of paper with only the word 'the' written on them – made me read some of the work again. I found that I both recognised and did not know the work and its author. My earlier remarks about what I thought I was trying to do arise not so much from the physical material as from memory, which may not be unimpeachable evidence. The stuff itself – the files of papers – seems to be another matter, the work – I was about to say – of someone I no longer am, but it might be more accurate to say someone who never was, except in this paper incarnation; or someone who has never existed and yet is somehow present in those A4 pages.

The condition of 'not knowing' was particularly strange when I came across poems which had been worked on intensively for some time, using up a good many of those A4 sheets, and which were then abandoned, forgotten – completely forgotten by me, at any rate. One archive interviewer noted that one poem had identifiably mutated from a poem about music into an elegy for a friend in which music had a role. I had forgotten this, and the manuscript betrayed no sense – why would it? – that this was a radical shift in the direction of the poem. It was as though there was another author, the 'other' author, who seems to leave traces in this mass of material. This figment would, I infer, have a clearer sense of what he was about, or is even now about.

I imagine this other author, my exact contemporary and double, one who has read Rimbaud and Borges, as gifted with the panoptic view of time which I do not possess. Thus, he is able to inhabit the present as it erases itself heartbeat by heartbeat, as well as the entirety of what I imagine he thinks of as 'the project', past, present and future, that is a life's work. How easily he moves from the conditional into the present, as though merely to think of him sets him to work. Soon he seems to be running the show and, I suspect, writing its secret history. He is the one with the archival talent. Perhaps he could, for example, account for the fact that the immediate circumstances of 'our' joint life seem to have figured rather infrequently in the work. The climate of experience is there, but the details are omitted. What is it that reaches after a larger or different or remote context? I could hazard a guess that the reason is that authority, like life, is elsewhere, but you would have to ask him to confirm it.

I see now, and it offers me some consolation, what he reminds me of: one of those mythical 'authors' with the same names and faces as people whose work we have actually read, who are sometimes profiled in the arts and magazine pages. There is usually a view of the room they work in – charmingly untidy, chaotic, severe or serene according to taste, with a Sickertian view of north London rooftops or a shy garden sown with amaranth. This is a field of journalism which (though this cannot be the case) seems to have been created in the essay in Roland Barthes's *Mythologies* called 'The Writer on Holiday'.[3] In this kind of journalism we are shown a Platonic sphere of bourgeois authorship where all the mess and inconsequence of actual life have been refined and transformed into a seductive, modest, unaffected competence which can be summarised as 'success'. Oddly enough, it is those profiles which affirm the humility and disinterested gravity of implacably 'serious' authors which are for some reason the most provocative in this respect – because, like ourselves, such creatures cannot really be there. Fed on mere cake instead of the bread of literary heaven, if we readers had any sense such material would produce immediate and widespread homicidal feelings and the overthrow of the established order.

I can't prove it, but I suspect that in a sense the other O'Brien has already done all the work, including whatever I have still to write. I'm reminded of the experience I had about fifteen years ago, when I set out to translate the *Inferno*. I developed an eerie feeling about that perfectly conceived and executed poem. It seemed to me that Dante must somehow have already written the *Inferno* before he actually wrote it. How could he have done otherwise? The same seems to be true of *Ulysses*. But that way, perhaps, a Borgesian madhouse looms – or, in the less grandiose terms that might apply in my case and that of my invisible omniscient companion, a cell, like the cell in Thom Gunn's poem 'In the Tank', where

> The jail contained a tank, the tank contained
> A box, a mere suspension at the centre,
> Where there was nothing left to understand,
> And where he must re-enter and re-enter.[4]

Dante had a theology and a cosmology. All I have is the recurrence of obsessions – the streets and gardens and back lanes and parks where I grew up, haunted by the sound of the railway at evening, and something less like a conviction about the collective meaning of these things than a need for them to embody a meaning which survives me and all the other citizens, underwriting us even as it does not require any of us specifically. The cluster of sensations associated with this is strongest in autumn, when parts of the long, slightly foggy avenues are ankle-deep in yellow leaves. Soon it will be Hull Fair. Then Guy Fawkes Night, and the enveloping black of winter. It has meaning; it doesn't: it makes no odds either way. I remember this or I invent it; only my patient unseen doppelganger sees the matter in its entirety.

In the case of my archive (which sounds as if it doesn't actually belong to me, and technically it no longer does) it would be possible for my unseen companion to publish a substantial collection of hitherto unseen or fugitive material. This is the kind of thing that in popular music appears under the heading 'B-Sides and Rarities', for completists only, part of that sphere of lost recordings and legendary rumoured projects from which bribes are issued to mortality. I think that to release the B-sides and rarities from 'my' archive would be a very bad idea, but I sense that my opinion on the matter counts for little in the thinking of my doppelganger. For all I know he already has in mind a title, a publisher, a promotional tour and a major poetry prize sponsored by a leading manufacturer of pork scratchings. I begin to wonder if the double ever actually thinks of me, except, perhaps, as a kind of residuary opportunity, a resource in evident need of exploitation, like an old-style building society awaiting demutualisation. He is practical, venturesome, entrepreneurial.

The matter is out of my control. And, perhaps, the double also has something in him of the critic, the scholar, the biographer. Philip Larkin, whose work has suffered a great deal of posthumous scrutiny and variously competent judgement, culminating (for the time being) in the vast *Complete Poems*, where the actual poems are dwarfed by the immense apparatus of commentary, foresaw his own imagined biographer as though already in motion. This was of course Jake Balokowsky, a literary academic driven by professional necessity but without – Larkin manages to imply – an iota of actual literary sensibility.

Balokowsky is, I now see, an avatar of Larkin's own silent double, an intruder from the sphere of scholarship, with priorities of his own. He is a descendant of the scholar who figures in an anecdote recorded by Brendan Behan in one of his last books, which were tape-recorded rather than written – but the gist of the tale is this. Behan was once in the company of an American academic. Behan mentioned that his mother used to serve at table at Maud Gonne's house in Dublin where W. B. Yeats was sometimes among the dinner guests. The scholar became urgent. What did Yeats like to eat? he asked. All I know, said Behan, is that Yeats didn't like parsnips. Parsnips? said the scholar. Are you sure? Might it not have been carrots?

Was Yeats really implacably opposed to a vegetable? Was his distaste something he rehearsed at leisure, or merely the preference of a moment, deserving merely a decent forgetting? Perhaps we shall never know, but it seems as if our ignorance is really an opportunity in disguise, a new chance for invention and speculation in the realm of the root vegetable. Biography is insatiable. Already today while innocently minding my own business, I have read – against principle and inclination, but in line with a lifetime's habit – an essay which announces that X 'must have', 'may well', 'no doubt', 'probably', 'almost certainly' thought, felt, visited, met, disliked, slept with, sued, killed and ate, abolished, forgave, transcribed for the medium of contemporary dance, et cetera. Well, if you say so. And as it happens I myself had as a child a dislike of parsnips, which my mother would disguise as potatoes and which in time, as perhaps – who knows? – did Yeats, I grew to love. The intentional fallacy raises its ugly head once more, and opens its insatiable mouth.

Pardon my delirium. The present point, when my work has gone into the archive, seems to me a confirmation that our sense, in Derek Mahon's phrase, of 'our lives in infinite preparation' is revealed as a necessary fiction.[5] We think we're going somewhere. But we've already been there. The preliminaries have turned into the facts of the matter, and these in turn raise the question of what precisely these are, why they are so, and what they appear to mean or have meant.

So, what have I written? More poems than I've had chance to count; over five hundred reviews and articles; critical books; essays; public lectures; twenty or so plays; two novels; two collections of short stories; translations of poetry and drama; radio scripts; song lyrics; libretti; letters. About fifty books and other works have been published under my name. I find it impossible to account for this quantity of material. It cannot really exist, since, as I say at the slightest excuse, there is never any time to write, while at the same time I always feel criminally idle. But there they are, the covers gazing blankly back from the shelves over my desk like wallflowers at a masked ball where the electricity meter has run out. I mix too much with others of my kind, the wordy *beguines* in the almshouse of the academy. When no one else is present we seem to vanish, like Mrs Hogg in Muriel Spark's *The Comforters*, who 'had no private life whatever. God knows where she went in her privacy.'[6]

It looks like a life's work, but little of it has to do with the author's actual life. Rather it takes place in that terrain of the imagination where the actual and the possible meet. It looks as if it makes sense, but does it make sense to me? In Douglas Dunn's poem 'Dominies' a Scottish schoolmaster declares: 'I am already historical.'[7] I understand that haunted, half-absent sense of things. It seems I have preceded myself; now I have to follow in my own footsteps. Meanwhile my double has sent me a poem, a reminder, something forgotten that he claims I wrote; and I would prefer him to have written it.

Notes

1. Wainwright, Jeffrey, *Poetry: The Basics* (London: Routledge, 2011), p. 10.
2. *Night Moves* (1976) [CD-ROM], Bob Seger & The Silver Bullet Band. Capitol Records.
3. Barthes, Roland, 'The Writer on Holiday', in *Mythologies*, trans. Annette Lavers (London: Vintage, 2000), pp. 29–32.
4. Gunn, Thom, *Collected Poems* (London: Faber and Faber, 1993), p. 173.
5. Mahon, Derek, 'April on Toronto Island', in *Night Crossing* (London: Oxford University Press, 1968), p. 30.
6. Spark, Muriel, *The Comforters* (1957) (London: Virago, 2009), p. 170.
7. Dunn, Douglas, 'Dominies', in *New Selected Poems* (London: Faber and Faber, 2003), p. 75.

Chapter 11

The Archive and the Mirror

George Szirtes

The letter in the envelope, the postcard in the door, the recognition of the handwriting, the waiting for the post in the morning: such key moments, mostly lost.

I can't remember this or that thing. Who was the first to write a letter that was addressed to me? When did I begin to live an independent enough life? I can't remember. I do remember, at the age of nineteen in 1968, spending a few days by Lake Balaton, Hungary's equivalent of the sea. It was our first visit back to Hungary since leaving it as refugees in 1956 – so it was special.

It was August, some time before the 20th, and very hot. My younger brother and I had been adopted by a group of three or four young people of our own age. We kicked a football around. We lay on the beach. We walked along the railway line, picked berries, and talked. One of the girls asked me what I was going to do. Plucking up my courage I replied I was going to be a poet. Do you have any poems with you, she asked. I never went anywhere without my pocket notebook so I did have one. Read me one, she said so I read her a short piece, some nine or ten lines long. We chatted in English because my Hungarian had been dormant for over ten years. I can't remember what she next said but I knew she liked me. At one point we kissed. We returned to Budapest having exchanged addresses. A few days after that Hungary, along with the rest of the Warsaw Pact countries, bar Romania, invaded Czechoslovakia and removed Alexander Dubček from power; Jan Palach set fire to himself in Prague and Hungary closed all but one of its western borders. This was only half way through our intended three-week stay. Having driven there by car we quickly drove out again, my parents fearing that I might be called up into the army. We had our British citizenship by then but had not officially relinquished Hungarian citizenship. It was only a remote possibility but they had seen enough trouble in their lives so decided to play it safe.

A few weeks later I received a letter from the Hungarian girl. The envelope was decorated and the letter itself was in beautiful handwriting. The contents were affectionate and asked me questions that I don't remember now. I cherished the letter but didn't know how to reply. My Hungarian was nowhere near adequate. I didn't even know quite what to say so time slipped ever further by and I lost the letter. The fact that I lost it and never replied still fills me with guilt. It was a betrayal of trust. I liked her. I was glad to have met her. I remembered – and do still remember – exactly what she looked like. Besides, I had a couple of photographs of her in the group with the other Hungarians and my brother. I still have them. It is only the letter that was lost. It was, to that date – and this is something I do remember – the only time I had received an affectionate letter from a girl. Maybe that was why I never quite knew what to do with it.

Life tends to produce an inordinate number of lost, neglected and unanswered letters. I carried on writing poems and eventually publishing some, got married in 1970, finished art school in 1973 and took a job teaching in Hertfordshire. By 1976 we had two children. Sometimes, on Saturdays, I would walk past the second-hand stalls in the small town we had moved to and see boxes full of old photographs and postcards. I would sort through them in vague fashion, noting faces and locations, and reading brief messages on cards before returning them to the box with a faint inward sigh. Lives, being ephemeral, become ephemera, I reflected, recalling how *a crowd flowed over London Bridge, so many, / I had not thought death had undone so many.* I was deep in the sea of T. S. Eliot, with Dante behind him, and the phrase rose naturally enough without any straining after literary effect. The postcards did not signify the collapse of civilisation, they were only the faint sigh of all that is ephemeral as each slipped back among others like it. Easy come, easy go.

I was not a particularly organised sort of person. I could keep things roughly in order, and indeed had to in my job, but I had no natural gift for it. I did, however, keep track of my poetry notebooks. I had numbered them from the start and was soon obliged to because there were so many of them. I was enormously productive. Ever since I first started writing poems at school, aged seventeen, I had written something every day so that, after just three years, I had over a thousand poems; almost all were very poor apprentice pieces that stumbled from earnest sentimentality to an instinctive Surrealism. There was nothing really worth keeping there but it was all I had so I kept them, the notebooks numbered yet untidy, the pages not consecutive but scribbled here and there. I also kept track of the poems I sent out – mostly unsuccessfully – in other notebooks: when sent out, where, when accepted or rejected.

The poems themselves started as handwritten drafts that were later typed up, sometimes with carbon paper, and kept in ring binders, the text often altered and redrafted with many, mostly illegible, corrections. Keeping track could be a haphazard process. Poems became detached from files, sheets got torn or were lost. Typewriters did not retain the text, of course, they simply mechanised it, and gave the work a usefully objective look that, occasionally, clarified that which had got blurred. I had a succession of typewriters from heavy old Gothic and rococo monsters in black, to orange and green portable, eventually electric Olympias and Olivettis.

I had a toy typewriter in Budapest, in early childhood. I carried its case over the border when we walked into Austria that night in 1956. By then it contained only photographs and not the typewriter itself. Of the typewriter I retain only the faintest memory but it had to be left behind together with its Hungarian keyboard. We would not need that where we were going. We needed only minimal belongings. By the time we reached Austria we didn't even have those. I still have the case though. It is sitting under my desk as I write this.

By the time I was – somewhat regretfully – through with typewriters I was an independent writer and receiver of letters and postcards, still mostly by hand. I wrote to my parents – not as often as they wrote to me – and to a couple of school friends who had moved on to universities, and later, jobs. Some of those letters were newsy, some jokey, others 'philosophical'. I don't know what my friends did with mine. I never asked. It wasn't important. I also had official rejection cards and brief letters from editors as well as some more encouraging letters, from the poet Martin Bell, the first real poet to champion my work at art school and, after art school, a few more from Peter Porter to whom Martin passed me as a possibly interesting protégé.

I had already begun to keep correspondence. I started in my last year of college. I bought a box file and deposited all letters and notes there, roughly in the order in which they arrived.

Why did I do that?

It certainly wasn't because I thought my correspondence was likely to become an important literary resource. Coming to poetry as I did, having dropped English Literature at O level and without any directly relevant academic background, the idea of publishing poems in magazines, let alone producing books of poems, seemed a very distant hope through most of the 1970s, and even if, by some miracle, I did succeed in publishing a book, who would notice it? I was not an important person. I was a refugee to whom English was a second language. I was teaching art in a provincial girls' school. We had children that needed support. I was still trying, without any success, to be a painter too. Success seemed unlikely. It was distinctly not an expectation. Hope was something else, of course. The poems, rather than their public success, were the true objects of hope. They had to be as good as I could make them. They had to tell some kind of truth in a way as real as the Eliot lines about people flowing over London Bridge. Still, I kept the letters and wrote some myself, trying to make them good enough to read.

There were two main reasons for keeping letters in box files. More than anything it was the fear of chaos, a matter of keeping chaos at bay by holding fragments of life together. Having to be organised at work, and soon enough having to run a small department, entailed a certain acquired orderliness in that I had to order time and lessons and money. That meant filing which made things easier to find. It was the same at home. Box files looked controllable. I could find things there in much the same way as I could find a particular book among the growing number of books on the shelves. I had, after all, to educate myself through everything I had missed at school and university. My wife, Clarissa, herself a visual artist but very much caught up with motherhood at that stage, had actually done English A level and still had the notes. We would read texts together, sometimes in bed. I tried to read what Eliot had read. Together we looked to read through English literature, at least the poetry and drama part, mostly through second-hand books that seemed to multiply without any conscious effort on my part.

The second, possibly deeper, reason was related to the letter from the Hungarian girl and the junk market with its photographs and cards. It was a form of piety. Throwing out a letter was, in effect, throwing out a person. One throws away rubbish. People are not rubbish. If I threw them away, the discarded and forgotten would continue to sit at the back of my mind: muttering, turning their eyes directly on me.

Box files continued to mount but the system was beginning to break down. In 1976 Clarissa and I founded the Starwheel Press with two machines, one for text and one for etchings. We invited artists and poets to collaborate and made portfolios of their mutual work that went to subscribers and collectors. In 1979 the first of my books, *The Slant Door*, appeared and shared the Faber Memorial Prize. With that the amount and diversity of correspondence grew. Some of it was formal – official letters, notifications of this or that event or publication – others parts were personal. There were contracts and invitations, notes from friends, descriptions of projects, even bills and tabs from taxis. I was invited to write reviews and miscellaneous articles. The content of the box files was growing too miscellaneous for its own good. And, of course, I was still school-teaching full time.

Life was to grow more complicated yet. In 1984, after my third book, *Short Wave*, I returned to Hungary as a visiting writer and British Council scholar, and a life of translation began. This entailed more drafts, more books, more magazines and more correspondence. I couldn't do it all and still paint so gave up practising visual art just as Clarissa was beginning to pick it up again with haunting large drawings of Budapest. One stalled artistic career was over, one was starting up again, and a third one, translation, started on its long course.

Still, everything was more or less under control. There were box files and sheets of paper still fitted them.

The real problems began with a solution. In 1986, following the advice of my brother-in-law, I bought an Amstrad. Now my drafts could be kept in a machine. I could draft more, and more quickly, which suited me. I needed – and still do need – momentum to write and to make fast, instinctive decisions. On the Amstrad I could rewrite the same text immediately without crossing out and retyping everything. One draft immediately cancelled the previous one, unless saved, but I had no thought of turning my drafts into a museum. I did not imagine anyone would be interested in them as such. What mattered was the poem.

I could keep the letters too. My letters, that is. I wasn't using email as yet so they were still printed out, albeit on a broad, perforated roll of thin paper that was the wrong size for standard A4 folders, but suddenly an incentive to write longer, better letters. Meanwhile, my teaching work was kept on Amstrad disks in plastic disk boxes, the labels written on by hand. It was all very compact. Though not quite paperless, the computer was almost an office. The disks had low capacity, of course, but I was only interested in text.

By 1989 I had reduced my working time to 0.5 and Clarissa was teaching at the same school, in the same art department. I had twice had grants from the British Council, in 1985 and 1987, for two-month scholarships in Budapest, and in 1989 I was given the opportunity of five more months that, under the political conditions of the time, extended itself to close on nine months. I wrote a good part of *Bridge Passages* (1991) there, a sequence that was more or less a diary of events during the collapse of the whole political system. I also wrote a couple of radio reports in the form of Letters from Budapest.

I call the poems a form of diary because I have only occasionally kept a real diary. Diary-writing was serious business and took time. It had to be proper writing, not just notes. My handwriting was becoming illegible anyway since my habit of writing and thinking fast meant the beginning of a new word would often run into the end of the previous one. There were constant crossings through that I couldn't read. Besides, I argued to myself, possibly wrongly, the essential matter of the diary might find its way more valuably into poems. That was convenient enough as far as the diary went but it also meant there would be fewer records of the drafts. Nevertheless, the idea of some sort of diary equivalent did not go away.

Over the years I progressed from Amstrad to various shades of Mac while changing jobs and moving house. Our children grew up and went to university, I was offered a post at the art school in Norwich, not to teach art or art history (nor did I ever teach those subjects again or write much for the art press as I had been doing) but poetry, on a course I myself was asked to devise as part of a Cultural Studies degree. In 1994 we moved close to Norwich. Clarissa took a job teaching art at the cathedral school and I was appointed Senior Lecturer on a 0.5 contract. My time with Oxford University Press came to a close when they closed their poetry list and I moved to Bloodaxe. It was a couple of years after that – after *The Budapest File* (2000) and *An English Apocalypse* (2001) – that I started a blog.

The earliest blogpost I still have dates back to 2003. I kept it daily and it served for a diary in most respects until the advent of Facebook. I should explain that far from being knowledgeable about technology I am still somewhat awkward with it and, just as I was nudged into the computer age with the 1986 Amstrad, so I was nudged into blogging, then into Facebook, then, later still, into Twitter. But this new episode is worth exploring.

It is difficult to remember exactly when things happen unless you write them down and do not lose the reminder. I have lost a good deal through carelessness so I cannot quite remember when I asked my son, Tom, to set up a website for me. It isn't the Blogger website you see now. Its lease ran out. It expired and has vanished as if it had never existed. Part of it was supposed to be a diary, part just notes. There was a section for the CV too and a space for poems. This might have been about the turn of the millennium.

I soon found the diary and notes merging, the notes representing ideas, the diary events. But ideas come with events, arise out of them and can become events themselves, and the process works the other way too. But that is not what is essential about a website. The point is that, however restricted the readership, it is a public space. It is a diary that is read, that is to say published, and a set of ideas or meditations that are open to comment. I had included a facility for comments and soon people were commenting.

One needn't maintain a constant presence on one's website but as soon as I started I was aware of some obligation to continue. If this was a diary, then, for the first time, it was one with a conscience. Not only conscience of course, but self-consciousness. This was no longer a private diary. I was no longer addressing simply myself but others. That may be the case with notable people who expect their diaries to be published at some stage. Some might expect their letters to be published too. I was not expecting either but this was going public; in other words, it would be not be just a diary and notebook but *writing*.

I suppose that is what attracted me. I had always written to work out what I think but the extra demand of semi-public readability might, I thought, exert a useful pressure. I was teaching at the same time – creative writing by now – where articulacy is particularly important. One should be able to home in on specifics while keeping a sense of the general when addressing a small group of people, every one of whom is present before you as an individual face.

This was a relatively new medium. In 1997 only some ten million people worldwide were using email regularly and in 2000 or so I was just getting used to the way it was replacing regular mail. Email proposed a different range of formalities and informalities. We became less likely to address people as 'Dear Sir' or 'Dear Madam' and to sign off with a 'Yours faithfully' or even 'Yours sincerely'. The immediacy of delivery lent itself to various options, mostly adapted from earlier models of letter writing, or postcard writing, or telegram writing, or note-leaving. To some degree it went along with the more relaxed dress and conversation of the mid-1960s: it embodied and developed it while leaving correspondents uncertain about the nature of their relationship.

That was one of the first subjects that interested me in writing on the blog. What is the distance between a *me* and the unknown yet vaguely intimate readers who might respond to it? The answer to that seems so natural now it is hardly worth mentioning, but there were points at which the issue presented itself quite keenly. How to respond to an intimate-style note from someone I have never met? To someone signing only with a first name? To an unknown but perfectly genuine woman who signs off with an x?

I was, of course, used to writing occasional reviews and articles for the literary and daily press. There is an accepted range of registers for that kind of writing so it quickly sounds natural. But readers of such articles stand at a greater distance from the writer unless the writer develops a style that invites closeness. A professional journalist, for instance, may look to develop a 'personality' that is not so much a byline as a familiar presence. Philip Larkin's famous answer as to why he didn't do more readings – 'I couldn't go round pretending to be myself' – is relevant to the idea of such familiarity, though it is worth remarking that despite not doing a lot of public readings, Larkin's persona was not unfamiliar from both his poems and his interviews. Poems too are characterised, for most readers, by a particular voice range and it is a common enough literary game to identify authors from quotations. People used to talk about 'finding a voice'. But that was easier said than done. Some poets found a voice all right but it was Philip Larkin's voice, or Sylvia Plath's voice or some shade of another. But say you found a voice that was not too much like someone else's. Would that be too limiting, too much of an act, too much something in the way, too much pretending to be yourself? Isn't that what Eliot partly meant when he said that poetry was not an expression of personality but an escape from it?

Those questions are always worth asking and may become more usefully vexatious with time – and indeed with the 'times' we live in – but they were not of major importance to me when the blog started. The part that remains from 2003 begins with a visit to India. It behaves like a letter to an acquaintance, not to a close friend, but relaxes at points into something more intimate, more personal.

Following further visits of various duration, when we were resident in Budapest for nine months during the dramatic changes of 1989 that were to reshape Europe and the rest of the world in due course, I wrote the two letters I mentioned earlier from Budapest for Radio 4 to broadcast. They tried to tie up groups of observations and events into a coherent yet personal sense of the place at what was clearly an important historical moment. The poems I was writing at the same time as I was observing for the broadcast letters formed a parallel narrative that did not have to be held together in quite the same way. In one way they are simply different genres, but different genres produce different voices and personae.

I don't want to make heavy weather of this at the moment. The point is, I had a readily identifiable public persona. It would only be identifiable to a few, but rather more than you usually find in a class or seminar.

The blog developed from there. I wrote something most days and I tried to write it well. I would of course have tried to write letters or a journal just as well but without expecting quite the same responses. It wasn't that there was a vast readership for the blog but whoever did read it was able to respond as soon as they read it, which might be almost as soon as I had posted it. I tended to write the blogs straight off, but with more complicated material I would draft and redraft. Each post was a performance of sorts, the performance entailing a certain register of voice that was finding itself as it went along. It was not quite like a letter in that respect. In letters one writes to specific people and hones one's voice to their specificity. However direct the feeling or thought in the letter, it was the feeling and thought as performed to the specific recipient. Writers correspond with each other addressing each other's concerns in terms of lesser or greater familiarity, and some of my commenters turned out to be writers, but I wasn't addressing them personally.

The blog continued to gather readers in their hundreds, though the readership came and went. I was not looking to monetise it or to carry advertisements so I turned down the odd request to do so. The blog was doing exactly what I wanted, functioning somewhere between a diary, a notebook and a commonplace book. It could have turned into a book blog or an online reviews site but that felt like too much commitment among all my other work. I made friends and acquaintances this way. There were a few I got to meet in real life, but there was no lack of reality in the online acquaintanceship. In that sense, it was like having penfriends.

Somewhat later – in 2007 according to my Timeline – I started on Facebook, which I immediately conceived of as a shorter version of the blog with more readers. Like the blog it was, for me, a literary space composed of diary and notes rather than a social medium. I was not desperate to make new friends but I quickly made the acquaintance of others with similar interests in visual art, photography, film, translation, politics and literature, of course.

Facebook is far less private than a blog. A blog is a commitment to a person: Facebook is something people can flick through. It is, by its nature, brief. It is not the best place for essays of even 500 words, preferring concision. Although there is a privacy setting whereby only selected people can see what you post, I didn't choose it and went openly public while continuing to think along personal lines and increasingly engaging with the commenters. It was, and remains (mostly), a brisk exercise but one briefly accompanied by people with whom I formed an informal but regular relationship There were other writers there, of course, but chiefly I met readers, lovers of music, people with a capacity for retaining vast amounts of literature, and young beginner writers, some with remarkable minds and great erudition. They would appear, enter into conversation, then get on with their own lives. I met some of them in real life in due course, some in Britain, some abroad, some far abroad.

That would seem to take too much time but I did not become too involved in chatter or in the personal affairs of people I had never met. I could skip in and out. I had the odd troll, the odd invitation to hook up with people who were (with various degrees of subtlety) offering sex or goods, and the odd argument, including a few 'unfriendings' and – very few – blockings. The Friend notifications grew. I soon had the maximum 5,000 with a thousand and more waiting. I could put up links to newspapers and journals. I could write serial posts on politics here and in Hungary. I could even gather signatures in an attempt to save the Central European University (I gathered well over 700 people in the arts, starting with Colm Tóibín, whose name would have attracted others). Journalists began to read me and, occasionally, ask me to write articles.

Occasionally I posted poems there in draft. It was like hanging washing on a line and letting it dry. People responded one way or the other. Sometimes they would make suggestions. Being aware that the drafts were public was an encouragement to ensure that the draft was decent enough to be seen. Magazines would write to ask if they could have this or that poem. People who saw poems there translated them into various languages. It was almost an alternative literary life. I couldn't take it entirely seriously as such because, surely, real life was books and occasional print magazines. But this too was readership.

Eventually I was nudged into Twitter too. I had resisted it partly because of its silly name, but a well-known fellow poet suggested it would be useful for all kinds of things. It wasn't social in the same way as Facebook: there was not enough space for chat, but it carried a very wide range of links to fascinating articles in magazines I wouldn't regularly see, or rouse interest in events of this or that kind.

But it was not so much that that fascinated me. It was the 140-character limit. This too was a potential literary space. I should explain that after the publication of my 540-page *New and Collected Poems* in 2008, I very much wanted to explore new ground and new ways of working. The poems in *Burning of the Books* (2009) and *Bad Machine* (2013) represent that desire. Having always been attracted to given or self-manufactured constraints in verse – each form working some variation in the voice – I wanted more marked differences. It was not that I didn't want to be myself, more that I did not want to be restricted to the self in the collected poems, writing poems in the ways I had already learned to write them. What, after all, did it matter if I made the occasional mess or took a wrong turn. I was over sixty. The evidence of my labours was readily available. Let's move on.

This isn't a chapter about my poetry, it is about the notion of the archive, something that gathers correspondence and notes, then edits and stores them in an orderly way. A *New and Collected Poems* is an archive of poems. Twitter became a laboratory between poetry and correspondence. I first sought brief poetic forms: the epigram, the gnome, the limerick, the proverb, the haiku and, later, the cinquain, as well as fragmentary prose narratives. I began to write series of such fragments, inventing characters including Langoustine, a lobster, and her companion, a crab who had once been a doctor; Child Helga, who was in constant conversation with her father; Uncle Zoltán, a kind of ageless Baron Münchausen; Germania, which consisted of a mass of invented Gothic-style comic Germans; two nameless children who moved through terrifying worlds; an entirely new version of my father as a talking ghost; over a hundred 'proverbs' and, besides these, a series of haikus (many of which appeared in *Mapping the Delta* (2016)). All the series were published in one or other small press.

A good deal was written on insomniac nights, when one haiku would kick off nine others. I would lie in bed wide awake with the phone on, sending haiku after haiku into the dark, fast-flowing river of Twitter in which something appears once and once only before vanishing far downstream (unless someone else likes or quotes it). It was oddly stimulating to write in this manner. I could rescue my own children or leave them to drown. The process could lead anywhere. My followers grew. (They are currently about thirteen and a half thousand. These are nominal figures, of course, comprising occasional people willing to dip into my own stream who would not be there all the time.) Usually I would gather Twitter fragments and hang them out on the Facebook line to dry. The two would be linked.

How does this hectic activity relate to any notion of the archive or the identification of a voice or persona in the context of some historical scale, however limited? Scanning tiny parts of it I am surprised, not always pleasantly, by the figure that seems every so often to emerge, a self constructed in its own present but refigured in my current retrospect. I can't afford to think too much about that self. I would prefer to keep it arm's length but I can't reject or distance it too much, if only because other people are involved. It is not all about *you*, as people rightly say, and yet there is a *you* there and it won't be as interesting to the world as it is to yourself and, perhaps, to those who were close to you.

We live in the era of the selfie, the constant photographic location of the self as public presence, however minor, however ephemeral that self might be. At any one point in time we can become the centre of a minute universe, the briefest of brief suns in a world of invisible planets.

A few years ago now, perhaps five or six years ago, maybe a little longer, maybe several years ago – see how vague I am with dates? – John Wells of the Cambridge University Library asked if I would be willing to let the Library have my archives. I thought of all those box files and couldn't remember what, of interest, was in them. I had grown careless with them ever since email came along. Despite a vast increase in correspondence, fewer hard-copy letters arrived in the post and the sense of chronology was confused. I lost things, especially cards. I had a lovely congratulatory postcard from Seamus Heaney when I won the Eliot Prize in 2004. Heaven knows where it is now. Did I even reply? I might have been too dazed, incapable of knowing how to respond. Praise is hard. To simply say 'thank you' might sound as though I thought I deserved it. I am never sure about the concept of deserving in literature. There is too much sheer luck involved. Sometimes I think it is all luck.

John Wells had started with a poet friend, Peter Scupham. Peter, who, like Clarissa and I, had run a press – his longer and more substantial than ours – is more orderly. He kept his drafts in ledger books, carefully in order. His archive would certainly be worth having. Was mine? I never thought it worth my while trying to sell it. Who would pay for it? It was very flattering that Cambridge wanted it at all. I'd give, not sell.

I hesitated a long time, perhaps for years (I suspect it was years), then finally, after one of my regular cleanups, I told John he could take things when he was ready. He sent a van, we piled up the box files, and off they went. Once he found time to sort through and catalogue, he organised an exhibition based on it. I did a talk and a reading. Later he organised an exhibition of Clarissa's art, especially the parts most associated with Budapest and my books.

I did not give John my poetry notebooks or any form of brief diary. I think I was ashamed of my earliest efforts, but I kept them because of that sense of piety. I had burned a lot of my artwork when we moved house. It hadn't really come to anything substantial, much of it was no good, but it was different with the notebooks, including the one labelled number one, the very first. The piety was personal. Or so it seemed. A few years later I decided to give everything I could find to Cambridge, including the notebooks and the diary fragments. I have found more notebooks and diary fragments since but now think they must have quite enough of me. There were two critical books about my work. One was Michael Murphy's *Poetry in Exile*, where I was one-third of the book with (grossly flattering!) Auden and Brodsky, and the other was the full-length study by John Sears, *Reading George Szirtes*, published by Bloodaxe to coincide with the *New and Collected Poems* of 2008. These were huge privileges. Surely that would be enough.

Later still the University of East Anglia, the university where I finished my teaching career, also asked for my archive. I told them Cambridge had it all. It was then the question of the digital archive arose. The emails, the blog, possibly more, such as extracts from the Facebook posts. The trouble with the older digital archive is that it was in Amstrad format on Amstrad disks I still had somewhere, possibly in the attic with all the daily press of 1989 Budapest. But what of this is archive material? It is not only my own writing that matters, it is the writing of those – and this may matter far more – who have written to me. Those letters were in the box files. In digital form they remain in my email box. The endless correspondence one develops in emails and on social media does offer a picture of the times. The blogs had mini-essays on form, on the idea of subject matter, on working with music and much else.

It may well be that the archive is a kind of mirror. The task of art, according to Hamlet's well-known injunction, is to hold a mirror up to nature. There are mirrors everywhere, nature's own selfies of which we are a part. If we stand in front of it, it is ourselves we see and, beyond us, all that is in the background. Of course, we prefer a decent mirror, a decent selfie. We prefer this or that lighting, this or that expression. We pull the faces we like. We show those faces in forms of writing. The background changes. So does the light.

Chapter 12

AA(A), or Affect, Archives and Anecdotes

Ahren Warner

Part One

1 I am sitting in a red-brick coffin. I know it was once de rigueur to be buried with a convoluted system of strings and pulleys leading from your own coffin to a small bell hung above the head of a poorly paid manservant. I do not have such a bell.

I have an open file of Xeroxed manuscript papers pertaining to a book called *The Vigil*. I look down at them and notice that a line of poetry that now reads: 'the true history I inhabit, its sea of suffering, its wave to which I am froth, scum', once read 'spume, froth, scum'.

2 I am sitting on floor thirty-something of a rather tall, red-brick coffin. The man in front of me has so little time left that vultures are already circling overhead.

'Did you see it? It's a vulture', one Charles Kenneth Williams exclaims to me.

'So it is', I reply. 'But, I need to ask you about this line in your poem 'The Hovel' from your book *The Vigil*. 'I have seen an earlier draft in which you deleted the word "spume"', I say, 'I'd like to talk about *why*.'

'I've no idea.' He eyes me sadly: 'are you *sure* I deleted "spume"'?

'Yes, I've checked', I reply, incredulously.

'I don't know', he replies, disinterestedly. And then: 'I probably did it for the sound.'

How inconvenient, I think. Why couldn't he have spontaneously mentioned his aversion to the hendiatris, the rule of three, as rhetorically outmoded and avowed his compulsion towards a rougher, disruptive prosody rooted in his own neo-modernist inheritance?

3 In either *The Tain of the Mirror* or *Inventions of Difference* – I can't remember which – Rodolphe Gasché directs the reader to Hegel's *Wissenschaft der Logik* as a prerequisite for more fully understanding the philosophical lineage of Jacques Derrida and his construction of *différance*.

In the chapters of the *Wissenschaft* to which Gasché directs us, or somewhere near those chapters, or in the vicinity of those pages – by which I mean within the pages of the *Science of Logic* – Hegel writes:

> the infinite is; in this immediacy it is at the same time the negation of an other, of the finite. As thus in the form of simple being and at the same time as the non-being of an other, it has fallen back into the category of something as a determinate being in general.[1]

Thus, for Hegel, the infinite, defined as other of the finite, becomes finite itself by virtue of being defined by the limits of the finite as other. In this instance, the concept becomes little but a finitised or *spurious* form of infinity.[2] Hegel's antidote to this particular and rather prickly paradox is to argue the *real* infinite is supplied by the transcendence of the infinite–finite dialectic in which 'each moment actually shows that it contains its opposite within itself . . . the relation to self which is not immediate but infinite'.[3]

4 I am sitting in a red-brick coffin. The sign on the door says 'Special Collections Reading Room', but I'm almost certain it is a red-brick coffin. Somewhere down a corridor in an airtight, triple-locked, steel-lined antechamber so many books, so many poems have died and have been buried in tiny cardboard coffins, coldly categorised and ordered. So many coffins within a larger red-brick coffin like Russian dolls, if Russian dolls were Chinese boxes, and if the boxes in question were acid-free, archive-quality coffins. I have seen it with my own eyes – not so far from here – and thought of Eliot, who in turn, of course, was thinking of Dante, '*I had not thought death had undone so many.*'

5 Don Paterson likes to say, or at least he has said on more than one occasion, that a poem is not complete until it is published, until it is birthed into the world as dialogue. What then is an unpublished draft, if not 'stillborn'? At the desk at the front of the 'Special Collections Reading Room', an archivist keeps watch. I think I can hear her muttering 'Come, you spirits, that tend on mortal thoughts . . . '. She is sighing.

6 The English word 'anecdote' derives from the Greek *anekdota*, meaning unpublished, and invoking *ekdotos* (published), *ek* (out) and *didonai* (to give). The 'anecdote' might therefore be as much the 'ungiven', that is, the 'taken', as, in its current meaning, the 'brief, amusing story'. One might feel drawn to ask if the writer's draft, the archival paper more broadly, can really only exist *as draft*, can only sustain itself as *becoming*, as long as it remains *anekdota,* as unpublished and ungiven.

If the living or live writer sitting in a red-brick coffin is thus placed in the position of thief, of one who 'takes', how might such an act be thought against the archival draft as a crystallised moment of progress, of movement towards the finished literary document, as becoming, as a form of *negativity* defined, as it is by Hegel, as 'the middle term of the syllogism'?[4]

More pressingly, as reader, perhaps as a writer looking for influence, source, for what is known in the business as inspiration, what would the literary draft as a frozen moment of becoming make *me*?

A kind of microwave, perhaps, set to defrost, slowly reheating the moist ekstasis in which Williams struck out the word 'spume' as both an infinite improvement and testament to his own will.

7 It seems, here, in my red-brick coffin, that the extent to which the archival document, the draft in process, might constitute the *arche*, or at least the trace of the genesis of an eventual *ekdotos* – and might thus offer a crystallisation of what Hegel would call *negativity* ('the middle term of the syllogism') – is radically compromised by its own innate relationship to the published text and to itself as immediately published, as given, in the moment the reader confronts it.

To what extent does the unpublished draft maintain itself as live, as becoming, as a trace of the event in process, only to the extent it is *anekdotos, not* read and thus unpublished? To what extent does the liveness of the archival trace die the moment it becomes the object of our attention, the moment it is published as artefact? In a slightly sketchy analogue of Hegel's critique of the spurious infinite, isn't the taking of the ungiven, the reading of the draft, a deadening that mirrors the finitisation of the infinite by a finite other?

8 'I have forgotten my umbrella', writes Nietzsche, or so Derrida reports to us in his *Eperons: Les Styles de Nietzsche*. Words, as Derrida informs us, 'found, isolated in quotation marks, among Nietzsche's unpublished manuscripts'.

As Derrida continues, maybe this phrase is

a citation. It might have been a sample picked up somewhere, or overheard here or there. Perhaps it was the note for some phrase to be written . . . There is no infallible way of knowing the occasion of this sample or what it could have been later grafted onto. We never will know *for sure* what Nietzsche wanted to say or do when he noted these words, nor even that he actually *wanted* anything.[5]

And yet, Derrida is also right to caution us against the designation of these words as a 'fragment'. For, as he writes, 'the concept of fragment . . . since its fracturedness is itself an appeal to some totalizing complement, is no longer sufficient'.[6] The fractured fragment can never offer a clean conceptual break, complete insularity, because it always already invokes the totality from which it is unhinged. In this sense, the fragment is a spurious concept, in the Hegelian sense of the word.

9 And yet, one should perhaps mention Peter Osborne – himself a good Hegelian, or at least Schlegelian – and his *Anywhere or Not At All: Philosophy of Contemporary Art*. In that book, Osborne offers an instructive exploration of the notion of the 'fragment' as exemplary of the spatial modality of contemporary art, which he sees as analogous to a temporal notion of artistic practice as project. One way to understand contemporary art practice, Osborne suggests, is as an art that '*lives* only in its incompletion, as project'.[7]

Is it too neat to suggest that Nietzsche's 'I have forgotten my umbrella', Derrida's myriad unpicking of its philosophical implications, Williams's striking through of the word 'spume', 'live only in their incompletion'? Perhaps. And yet Derrida continues to needle us with the possibility that Nietzsche may not have *intended* anything with his words. Derrida asks us: 'what if Nietzsche himself meant to say nothing, or at least not much of anything, or anything whatever'?[8]

10 If we return to Williams's too-cute response, that he 'probably did it for the sound', that – in the moment – he 'meant to say nothing, or at least not much of anything', might not such a disavowal of the very horizon of meaning allow us also to fold back what Osborne designates as the vitality of the fragment onto the archival trace stripped of the quasi-imperialism of the published, the *ekdotos*, as the straitjacket of a given future perfect?

If the fracture or the fragment could be crowbarred into a full breakage, a full disarticulation from the totality of the published document to come – broken off not by a breach of logic, but by a slight tonal shift, the blasé renunciation of intent – might we not (if only via a necessarily erroneous perspectival shift, to offer a polite inversion of Žižek's notion of the parallax) come near what Derrida suggests as an account of the trace that 'would withdraw it from any assured horizon of a hermeneutic question',[9] leaving the spur *as intensity and instantaneity, as illogic or affect?*

11 Here, Derrida's metaphor is helpful. At least to the extent it allows a certain figurative consistency as one moves seamlessly from the seamed sail of Derrida's spur, via the metaphor of the 'hermeneutic horizon', backwards, beyond Hegel, to Kant's first of his far *too many* critiques. In that book – the *Critique of Pure Reason* – one reads that

> Objects of perception . . . also contain . . . the real of sensation . . . by which we can only be conscious that the subject is affected . . . But the real, which corresponds to sensations in general . . . only represents something whose concept in itself contains a being, and does not signify anything except the synthesis in an empirical consciousness in general.[10]

That is, as is well known – and perhaps well worn, not least by Deleuze in his two volumes on cinema or his book on Francis Bacon – Kant's epistemology, the Kantian schematisation of logic, which is pretty much the same as saying our own Occidental horizon of conscious thought – is fundamentally spatio-temporal. Occurring in time and space, thought – for Kant, as for Hegel, and indeed for Derrida, even if Derrida kicks against it – must occur within certain horizons, within spatial and temporal expanses. To withdraw from the horizon is to withdraw from the hermeneutic register.

12 I am sitting in what has become my own, *oh-so-homely*, red-brick coffin. I am sitting with the proofs, the last corrected typescripts of C. K. Williams's *The Vigil*. On the page in front of me I can see that Williams has struck out the word 'spume' in favour of the line 'the true history I inhabit, its sea of suffering, its wave to which I am froth, scum'.

I want to ask *why*, and yet, by now, I am convinced that such a question is both fundamentally eschatological, and a little dull.

13 Williams is dead. Somewhere between the day I entered this Special Collections Reading Room and now, he died. And thus, my insistent, involuntary question ('why?') is forever met with the echo of that non-committal phrase, 'I probably did it for the sound.'

On one level, I think, Williams probably 'did it for the sound'.

But I can't help the excitement that rises as I hear Williams's response as a homologue for Derrida's ventriloquisation of Nietzsche, as another way of saying he 'meant to say nothing, or at least not much of anything'.

There is a way, it seems to me, in which the boredom implied in Williams's response, the disinterestedness, the refusal to offer more than the slightest of his attention to the issue, far from invalidating the other's gaze, far from diminishing the interest, the fascination, of that striking through of 'spume', actually reanimates it, invokes a certain kind of galvanism memorialised in *Frankenstein* by one Mary Shelley.

Such writerly disavowal offers the prospect of liberating the archival moment, offers an authoritative 'who cares?', a 'wotevs' that is simultaneously the call to which one might respond that, in fact, I 'care', with all the Heideggarian overtones that this implies.

14 And, here, all of a sudden, the prospect of incompletion threatens to return in a sincere, completely un-spurious form. The incompletion, indeed, of a kind of readerly attention, that is also writerly care, that is a moment of affect without horizon, if only because it exists fundamentally as a spur, as the hard kick towards further work, a spur that can and must 'mean almost nothing at all'.

It is a *spur* because it must exist as devoid of totality, it must echo as project, as practice, as without totality in the sense that such totality is always already subverted by its own future, the futurity of work to come. It is a spur towards a kind of futurity that must be felt as, to cite Alain Badiou reading over Mallarmé's shoulder, a 'mystery in letters', that must be felt as a 'genuine imperative' towards poetry as a form of thought without, in a solidly Kantian sense, horizon. A spur towards a form of thought 'enslaved to the . . . sensible', *sure*, but one that 'cannot [therefore] be discerned or separated' as thought at all.[11]

Part Two

1 All that appears above was presented verbally, and verbatim, during a constituent panel of an academic conference. It was presented in front of a lecture hall brimming with almost nineteen whole and wholly attentive human beings. At the end of this panel, a scholar of Robert Graves asked: 'Isn't it possible that Williams just made that change because it sounded better?' A polite, nasal chuckle spread throughout the other seventeen and a half members of the audience. The eminent presence to my immediate left smiled. I winced.

2 Why would one wince at such a polite witticism? Why would one begrudge the mirth of a scholarly comrade? One might return, here, to Don Paterson's rather churlish 2004 T. S. Eliot lecture, in which he declares to an audience no less solipsistic than my own (or myself), that 'our defining heresy as poets is that we know that sound and sense are the same thing'.[1].

That sounds good, doesn't it?

And yet: 'we know that sound and sense are the same thing'. One suspects that if this were the defining heresy of the lyric art, then we would – rather unfortunately – have to admit Joseph Goebbels and Donald Draper to our particular party.

Beyond the obvious weaknesses of this position, one finds an infinitely more sophisticated, if not altogether unconnected, argument for the illogic of lyric sensation in Alain Badiou's *Handbook of Inaesthetics*:

> Even presuming the existence of a thinking of the poem, or that the poem is itself a form of thought, this thought is inseparable from the sensible. It is a thought *that cannot be discerned or separated as a thought*. We could say that the poem is an unthinkable thought.[13]

3 For Badiou, the original, Platonic, heresy of poetry is also related to the dichotomy of sound and sense – or, more accurately, of sense as meaning and the sensible – based on the fact that 'what poetry forbids is discursive thought', that 'the poem is not a rule-bound crossing, but rather an offering, a lawless proposition'.[14]

From the Platonic perspective, the poem is 'enslaved to the ... immediate singularity of experience', in opposition to logic, for which Badiou substitutes the matheme, and which he describes as 'begin[ning] instead from the pure idea and afterward depend[ing] on deduction alone'.[1].

Yet, moving beyond the Platonic exile of the poem, Badiou turns explicitly within the same essay to 'modern' poetry, by which he means poetry after Mallarmé:

> Through the visibility of artifice, which is also the thinking of poetic thought, the poem surpasses in power what the sensible is capable of itself. The modern poem is the opposite of a mimesis. In its operation, it exhibits an Idea of which both the object and objectivity represent nothing but pale copies ... Within the poem, syntax is the latent power in which the contrast between presence and disappearance (being as nothingness) can present itself to the intelligible. But syntax cannot be poeticized, however far I may push its distortion. It operates without presenting itself.[16]

Here, the movement of Badiou's thinking is astonishing in its logical transformation of the Platonic rejection of poetry into a defence of the poem that maintains a certain fidelity to philosophical rigour:

> Plato banished the poem because he suspected that poetic thought cannot be the thought of thought ... we will welcome the poem because it permits us to forgo the claim that the singularity of a thought can be replaced by the thinking of this thought.[17]

4 Of course, it is tempting here to return to the Kantian opposition of sensation and logic, and to note the philosophical space that Badiou opens up for poetic form, for syntax or lyric sensation to transcend this dualism.

And yet, whilst I'm making connections, one might also recall a short essay by the late American poet Michael Donaghy, in which he argues for the poem on the page as a form of pediscript, the map of a dance, writing that 'in order to interpret [it]' you must 'get up and move'.[18]

Or, and perhaps even better still, one might point to a not entirely dissimilar, and perhaps more developed, logic at work in a late essay by Yves Bonnefoy, *Poésie et photographie*:

> poetry rattles the scaffolds of conceptual thought, which is based on empirical data from which it deduces laws, and not from the totality, the compact, that we perceive, however spontaneously, in things when we confront them in the living moment. This kind of conceptual approach that proceeds by choice, by the selection of aspects, and thus which simultaneously simplifies *and* generalises, deprives the mind of recognising the unity of that which it perceives, the breathing together of diverse facets, or, in other words, that which makes it a particular thing, finite, even at the moment where it opens out into reality as such. It is a blindness that affects the self-awareness of the person that can no longer fully think their belonging as a being in the world. Poetry is the memory of this loss, an effort to re-establish this lost contact.[19]

5 Perhaps, though, it is better to stick with Badiou. To stick to poetry as that which 'cannot be the thought of thought'. For, of course – and to return to the archival space – this is precisely what is at stake when confronted, as one might be, by the typescript of a poem by one C. K. Williams.

And here, because good academic practice is totally built on the empirical agglomeration of data or, as we might also say, examples, I'm moved to turn to another of Williams's poems, 'Storm', and to another, seemingly minor amendment that Williams has marked within the publisher's proofs. In the pre-published version of 'Storm', one would have found that, with a flurry of biro, Williams intervenes again to dictate that the original 'million years' in the last line is changed to 'epoch'. The final published form of the poem is:

> Imagine the emergence: oh, this way, the sky streaked, oh, that way, with miraculous brightness;
> imagine us, starting over, timid and tender, with an epoch more this time to evolve;
> an epoch more on all fours, stricken with silence and shame, before we fire our forges.

6 It has been a rare occurrence over the past few years that I have not used this particular example when teaching a workshop or class on poetic practice. Despite all the warnings given above – from Badiou's definition of poetic discourse as that which 'cannot be the thought of thought' to Hegel's location of negativity as middle, rather than *telos* – I still find myself so often, sitting cross-legged and clad in scholarly corduroy, in front of a dozen or so students of the 'poetic arts', invoking a specific, solitary question, declaimed in a tone that I hope conveys profundity (but which I know is just a little *smug*):

'What is the difference between an epoch, and a million?'

At this point, I cross my fingers under the table and hope that I have no astronomers in the room (for whom the answer, incidentally, derives from the definition of an epoch as a 'moment in time used as a reference for the orbital elements of a celestial body').[20]

Occasionally, there is an astronomer in the room. This is unfortunate.

Mostly, however, the discussion putters along until the fundamental ambiguity, the essential lack of finite signification is ascribed to the word 'epoch', in contradistinction to the specificity of a 'million years'.

And then I ask (*oh-so-profoundly*):

'If you had to choose, would you rather be "on all fours, stricken with silence and shame" for an epoch, or a million years'?

and, then:

'If you're "on all fours, stricken with silence and shame" for an epoch, when exactly do you get to the *good bit*, when specifically can you "fire your forges"?'

And we agree, as we always do – because I am the 'big Other' – that it would be, *like*, so much more preferable to be 'stricken with silence and shame' for a specific, even if particularly lengthy, period of time, rather than committed to the infinite deferral of 'firing our forges'.

7 It strikes me that the archive is – at its best, and beyond the protestations of archivists and what Nietzsche might have called 'antiquarian' man[21] – a site of *active, felicitous betrayal*.

We do not need to recall the now almost unrecollectable Harold Bloom to suggest that the act of situating oneself within the literary archive, within the archive of literature, as creative practitioner is also to inhabit, to perform, a myriad betrayal.

To return to my jocular Gravesian friend, this is precisely what is so profoundly *sad* about his interrogative witticism: 'Isn't it possible that Williams just made that change because it sounded better?'

Well, yes, *of course*.

Of course, but only (and absolutely) if one also extends the concept of

'sounding better' to mean 'thinking better', to producing a more char-
ismatic event of thought, that in its very being as sensible event cannot
be thought *as* thought, and which thus renders such questions the most
epistemologically pure betrayal of the poem.

A betrayal, incidentally, an *infidelity* not unlike that which I enact
every time I sit with students and enquire into the performative difference between an 'epoch' and 'a million years'. Yet, here (I plead in
mitigation), it is also meant as a spur to the practice of learning to write
as *necessary* betrayal, to the inhabitation of writing as the inevitably
failed attempt at fidelity to the poetic instant.

To force the didactic out of the properly sensible is fundamentally,
aesthetically incongruent. Yet it is also the necessary performance of –
philosophically speaking – epistemological infidelity. To ask students to
think, schematically, the profound *affective* difference between epoch
and finite time is to ask them to think something they should have
already felt at the very moment of their performance of the poem *as
event* (and, as Monsieur Lacan might argue, it is here that one has
already fallen into antinomy).

8 Yet, and as a form of solace, we might decide to recall, here, to intone,
Michael Donaghy's wonderful poem 'Machines':

Dearest, note how these two are alike:
This harpsichord pavane by Purcell
And the racer's twelve-speed bike . . .

. . . So this talk, or touch if I were there,
Should work its effortless gadgetry of love,
Like Dante's heaven, and melt into the air.[22]

9 I would observe that Donaghy's parallelism of the poem, of love (as
sensation) and of 'the racer's twelve-speed bike' might also provide the
rationale for the kind of necessary betrayal I have suggested is inherent
in the didactic moment, a moment which includes the archival autodi-
dact. As Donaghy goes on to write: 'So much is chance / So much agility,
desire and feverish care, / as bicyclists and harpsichordists prove', and
though – as Donaghy's final couplet tells us – it may be true that 'only by
moving can [one] balance, / Only by balancing move', it is equally true
that it is only by falling repeatedly that one learns a sense of balance.

And here one might also recall – because, *why not?* – Jacques Rancière's
wonderful meditation on the *ignorant pedagogue* as he takes it up once
again at the beginning of *The Emancipated Spectator*. If, for Rancière,
the stultification of education is the presumption of fixed positions, of
difference and distance between the intelligences of teacher and student,

so the stultification of spectatorship is paradoxically found in radical theatre's attempt to activate the spectator, an attempt to liberate the viewer from a passivity that is defined as such in the attempt to negate it.

As Rancière asks:

> What make it possible to pronounce the spectator seated in her place inactive, if not the previously posited radical opposition between the active and the passive? Why identify gaze and passivity, unless on the presupposition that to view means to take pleasure in image and appearances while ignoring the truth behind the image and the reality outside the theatre? Why assimilate listening to passivity, unless through the prejudice that speech is the opposite of action?[23]

And, as Rancière goes on to argue, 'emancipation begins when we challenge the opposition between viewing and acting ... when we understand that viewing is also an action that confirms or transforms the distribution of positions'.[24] So too, I would suggest, one must understand a critique of thinking poetry as unthinkable thought not just as amounting to a profound betrayal, but as a kind of betrayal that is also fidelity when it is felt as a form of *trauma*.

10 I am sitting in a red-brick coffin. I am sitting in a Special Collections Reading Room musing on the difference between an almost impossibly great temporal duration (a 'million years') and the infinity of time that the word 'epoch' implies. Two things occur to me.

One: a red-brick coffin is not an ideal place to consider temporal infinity.

Two: Sigmund Freud's discourse on his son Ernst's repetition of *fort/ da* as he stages the disappearance and reappearance of an object seems entirely pertinent.[25]

For Lacan, the repetition of the symbolic filling of absence occurs as the reaction to one's own confrontation with the trauma of the Real, which is also, and always, absence or lack. Partly, the Real is always an absence because the symbolic world, language, can never signify the Real, and partly it can never signify the Real because the Real is both unconscious and outside of language. As Lacan once stated,

> la pensée ... barre, dit Freud, l'accès à un savoir ... Le *Selbstbewußtsein* de Hegel, c'est le Je sais que je pense, tandis que le trauma freudien, c'est un Je ne sais pas lui-meme impensable, puisqu'il suppose un Je pense démantelé de toute pensée.[26]

Against this, the ultimate statement of epistemological ruin, one might attempt to shore certain fragments: Julia Kristeva, for example, once seemed certain that there was still a place for an 'unbounded generating process . . . [an] unceasing operation of the drives toward, in, and through language; toward, in, and through the exchange system'.[27] Yet – as with Badiou's valorisation of the poetic – Kristeva's position tends towards a certain regression into philosophical Romanticism.

11 I would suggest, rather, that – sitting in a Special Collections Reading Room, or reading the facsimile of Eliot's *Waste Land*, or having got one's own grubby hands on the early draft of a poet's work by other, more nefarious means – one should reconceptualise this confrontation as simultaneously a kind of necessary betrayal, the repetition of an inevitable trauma, and as an *emancipated* event in the sense that Rancière deploys the term.

Sitting with, or teaching, the negative moment of – for example – Williams's writing, his draft-in-process, which can never be the 'middle term of a syllogism' that it always already terminates in its existence as read text, the event of the poem as *being written* and *being read* is betrayed to the didactic or reflective moment, no longer as sensation but interpreted as signification, as craft, as model.

And yet this betrayal, the inability to access the draft as process, the inevitability of experiencing the draft as product, the trauma of being denied access to the text as sensation, or the trauma of betraying the text as sensation by treating it as schematisable example, might also be an affirmation of the 'lack' of this particular kind of 'viewing', not as the opposite of 'acting', of 'writing', but as the kind of trauma, the kind of studied inhabitation of uncomfortable passivity (of the epigone – again, to conjure Nietzsche), that, when felt as pain, is also a part of writing, and perhaps *why* we write.

12

> Every morning of my life I sit at my desk getting whacked by some great
> poet or other.
> Some Yeats, some Auden, some Herbert or Larkin, and lately a whole tribe
> of others –
> oi! – younger than me. *Whack!* Wiped out, every day . . . I mean since
> becoming a poet.[28]

These lines are from one of Williams's last poems, 'Whacked'.

And, in the guise of a dusty, Leavisite scholar, I want to conclude this 'chapter' by drawing your attention to three phrases: 'Every morning of my life', 'getting whacked by some great poet or other', 'since becoming a poet'.

In the guise of a dusty, Leavisite scholar, I want to conclude by drawing your attention to the insistence of the present continuous tense, the poet is *getting* whacked, every morning, whilst *becoming* a poet. And – in case one worries that I am labouring the continuity of Williams's present solely in order to transcend the dowdy corduroy of a Leavisite scholar and pave the way for a sparkly final allusion to Gilles Deleuze's eternal return – one might note that Williams tells us that he is '*trying* to write' (my italics), that 'one never *is*, really, a poet' (my italics), that by 'becoming a poet', Williams means simply 'wanting to'.

13   Why am I still sitting in a red-brick coffin?

Why am I still sitting with the drafts of a now-dead poet? Why do I insist on the scrutiny, the interminable dissection of my own failed relation to these drafts? Why do I repeat this trauma, over and again?

It is not, I promise, I *insist*, because – as our friendly Gravesian once implied – Williams's ear for the mellifluous has enchanted me into a kind of antiquarian stupor of appreciation, a desire to appreciate and enumerate the 'effortless gadgetry' of Williams's craft, to elucidate what Michael Donaghy might have called the 'machinery of grace' by which, as Don Paterson suggests, 'sound and sense [become] the same thing'.

No – and perhaps it is time to say this rather simply – such acts are rather the active inhabitation, the performance, of the position of 'not-poet', and of 'not-poet' as an ineluctable aspect of the position 'poet'.

Because, precisely as Williams tells us, one never really *is* a poet, one is only ever *becoming* one, one is only every *trying* to write, and writing itself occurs, restages, performs, projects or exists as the event of this becoming. Understood like this, the trauma of the draft as lifeless relic of poetic liveness becomes the necessarily painful, the necessary betrayal, of writing that also constitutes writing itself; that is both the spur to, and the event of, writing as always already not-writing. It is the eternal return, the repetition of the same as different, of writing as process, as project, and as lived event.

It is in this sense, fellow poets, that we're all, and always, in a red-brick coffin.

Take a seat.

Notes

1. Hegel, G. W. F., *Science of Logic*, trans. A. V. Miller (London: George Allen, 1969), p. 138.
2. Ibid., p. 145.

3. Ibid., p. 152.
4. Ibid., p. 747.
5. Derrida, Jacques, *Spurs: Nietzsche's Styles*, trans. Barbara Harlow (Chicago: University of Chicago Press, 1979), p. 123.
6. Ibid., p.125.
7. Osborne, Peter, *Anywhere or Not At All: Philosophy of Contemporary Art* (London: Verso, 2013), p. 169.
8. Derrida, *Spurs*, p. 127.
9. Ibid., p. 127.
10. Kant, Immanuel, *The Critique of Pure Reason*, trans. Paul Guyer and Allen M. Wood (Cambridge: Cambridge University Press, 2000), pp. 290–5.
11. Badiou, Alain, *Handbook of Inaesthetics*, trans. Alberto Toscado (Stanford University Press, 2005), p. 18.
12. Paterson, Don, 'T. S. Eliot Lecture 2004: The Dark Art of Poetry', <http://www.poetrylibrary.org.uk/news/poetryscene/?id=20> (accessed 20 March 2018).
13. Badiou, *Handbook*, p. 19.
14. Ibid., p. 17.
15. Ibid., p. 18.
16. Ibid., pp. 21–5.
17. Ibid., p. 27.
18. Donaghy, Michael, *Wallflowers* (London: Poetry Society, 1999), p. 6.
19. Bonnefoy, Yves, *Poésie et photographie* (Paris: Galilée, 2014), pp. 10–11. Note: the English translation of Bonnefoy's *Poésie et photographie* is my own. It is taken from a forthcoming contribution to Romer, Stephen, et al. *Yves Bonnefoy: Collected Works*, vol. II (Manchester: Carcanet).
20. Here, I wish to convey my gratitude to Wikipedia.
21. Cf. Nietzsche, Friedrich, 'On The Uses and Disadvantages of History for Life', in *Untimely Meditations*, ed. Daniel Breazeale (Cambridge: Cambridge University Press, 1997), pp. 57–124.
22. Donaghy, Michael, 'Machines', in *Collected Poems* (London: Picador, 2014).
23. Rancière, Jacques, *The Emancipated Spectator*, trans. Gregory Elliott (London: Verso, 2009), p. 12.
24. Ibid., p. 13.
25. Freud, Sigmund, 'Beyond the Pleasure Principle', in *The Standard Edition of the Complete Psychological Works of Sigmund Freud*, Vol. 18, ed. James Strachey (London: Verso, 2001), pp. 7–66.
26. 'thought ... bars access to knowledge, Freud tells us. Hegel's *Selbstbewußtsein* is an I know that I think, whilst the Freudian trauma is an I do not know that is itself unthinkable, since it supposes an I think devoid of thought'. Lacan, Jacques, *Le Séminaire de Jacques Lacan, livre XVI: D'un Autre à l'autre*, text established by Jacques-Alain Miller, trans. Ahren Warner (Paris: Seuil, 2006), p. 273.
27. Kristeva, Julia, *Revolution in Poetic Language*, trans. Leon S. Roudiez (New York: Columbia University Press, 1984), p. 17.
28. Williams, C. K., 'Whacked', in *Writers Writing Dying* (Newcastle: Bloodaxe, 2013), pp. 11–12.

Chapter 13

Musée des Fragments: The Secret Memories of Ordinary Things

Carolyn Forché

As a poet, I have long kept notebooks, not of poems-in-progress, but rather of random notes and images, legible and illegible, that constitute, over time, a repository of attentions. On the shelves of my study, there are at least one hundred and fifty notebooks from the past fifty or so years. Most of them are small, some no larger than a pack of cards, a good number abandoned rather than finished. These contain what I have called 'gleanings of world', images captured in nets of attention, pencilled lightly for safekeeping, later to seed a passage or stanza, to be joined with others separated in time, to form early drafts or to remain orphaned in the silence of the pages. These notebooks are part of a larger museum now that includes written records and pressings of attention, but also objects amassed by chance and preserved as specimens of world. I began prior to beginning this collection – that is, items arrived at the museum before it was established, markers from a journey towards many changes of sky. From childhood, there are rock and butterfly collections, fossils of trilobite in limestone, ferns and wildflowers pressed between dictionary pages. From later travels, I have matchboxes, cancelled tickets, currency no longer in circulation. In recent years, I began to assemble and curate my own 'Museum of Fragments', inspired by that of my friend Ashley Ashford-Brown, a British painter who now lives in Normandy. Mine includes such specimens as a small paving stone from the courtyard of the Louvre ('it was loose, anyone could have made off with it'), a pressed bluet from the possible unmarked grave of poet Federico García Lorca, and a scrap of the Berlin Wall the size of my palm. It also includes a matchbook from a hotel in Zagreb that arrived on my desk on its own, as I have never been to Zagreb. Ashford-Brown calls such objects 'volunteers' in the horticultural sense.

Ashford-Brown modelled his 'Museum of Fragments' after the original one created by his ancestor, Edwin Ashford of Moorlands, 1838–93.

All we know about Edwin was that he had wanted to practise medicine but was prevented from doing so by a wife who wished him to live as a country gentleman. He spent his life travelling, filling a steamer trunk with an array of items that constituted his 'specimens of world' (Plates 6 and 7).

The steamer trunk was lost for a century after Edwin's death. The neatly labelled items later found in it by his descendent, Ashford-Brown, are curiously and significantly *unimportant* – for example, the lump of coal wrapped in brown paper and tied up with string, for which he was, apparently, over-charged. Also: fossilised wood which he labelled as 'a bit of an old stump found near the house'. He notes that it was: 'picked up by Dr. Ashford in Englishcombe Lane near the Lodge on Sunday April 28th'.

There is also a bit of black clay 'found in a fig orchard', and 'a cannonball supposed to be from the field near Sedgemoor' from 'the last battle fought in England'. The frustrated man of science notes precisely that the contents of one of his ancient, cloudy bottles 'represents the amount of slime deposited from 4 gallons of water taken at full spring tide. – E. C. Ashford, April 18??'

As if commenting on his own predilection, there is a scrap of paper from the novel *Marriage*

> by Miss Ferrier, 3 volume, page 150 -You will find these words: '*Well, said Lady Maclaughlin, there are two things God grant I may never become, an amateur in charity and a collector of curiosities, no Christian can be either – both are pickpockets. I would not keep company with my own mother, were she either one or the other.*' E.C.A. 5 Dec. 1878.

Perhaps the disparagement of curiosity collectors was a source of amusement to him? We are not to know the answer to this or other questions, as all that remains of the world and thought of Edwin of Moorlands are the things contained in the steamer trunk.

It should be noted that such items as are preserved in the trunk and assembled in later 'museums of the fragment' would have been discarded as without value in any other context. These collections resolutely set themselves against 'the poetics of archival exclusion', preserving not the best and most culturally significant things, items that might be included in a time capsule delivered to the future, but those that may not seem so worthy of being bequeathed to posterity, those that, by virtue of their destiny in the landfills, will become rarest of all. This status is strangely mirrored by the consignment of digitised literary texts, letters and notes to 'clouds' in the cyber-sphere. The material culture of paper, vellum, ink, bindings and boards will conserve for the future the 'matter' of literary creation and will determine its archival afterlife, despite the onslaught of damage from fires, floods, mould and thoughtlessness that are perhaps its true curators.

For years, Ashford-Brown lived as an artist in Paris, supporting himself editing film strips, and when Christmas or birthdays came around, he made gifts out of things he'd scavenged from the city's environs. That was probably the beginning of his own museum, he now thinks, owing 'its name to an initial aspiration: to be a museum whose elements, once gathered, are again dispersed': the rescue of the ordinary, and common-place, to be preserved as gifts, and given new importance through the meticulous documentation of their provenance and context – the more precisely detailed, the better.

In 1982, he noticed that certain objects 'refused to play the game of dispersal', opposing 'all efforts at delocalisation by forming an inde-structible hub of resistance', and so began the assembly of his Musée des Fragments: apothecary bottles filled with river water; battered tea-spoon 'without a story'; scrap of metal from the wreckage of Pearl Harbour; pebble from the Great Wall of China. There are now almost four hundred catalogued items (Plates 8–19).

'It is now', he admits,

> a museum of fragments rather than a fragmented museum. But it is agreed that it should remain centred on the idea that the fragment is the representa-tion of the whole – that it holds within itself all that is missing from its total-ity. Accordingly, absence is the cornerstone of the museum, there being no other choice when undertaking a task as gigantic and as futile as an inventory of the world.

To display his collection, he uses old typesetting trays and cardboard boxes that once held nails, and writes labels in cursive, providing name, date and, when known, the place where the thing was found, and most importantly, its context and provenance. The objects arrived, sometimes by his own discovery, sometimes as donations, and then there were those that appeared mysteriously, placed there perhaps by visitors or friends, his aptly named 'volunteers'. The Musée des Fragments took on a life and mind of its own:

> Absence took control and the museum became a repository, not to say a refuge, where neglected fragments of the world came knocking on the door in pursuit of recognition. In the realm of objects, word got around that there existed a sanctuary where ordinary things were not only honoured for what they are, but also for what they represent when given the opportunity to reveal hidden aspects of their secret nature. . . . Even the most ordinary object has a story to tell. . . . Once perceived as having a unique and singular identity, it can henceforth be measured unabashed against the rarest of relics

. . . my museum has become a gathering place for objects of all kinds, where are revealed the known histories and secret memories of ordinary things.

The only rule, in fact, was that each item *be* ordinary and of no inherent value.

Ashford-Brown's studio had always brimmed with specimens, but they were not arranged into a proper museum until he came into possession of Edwin's trunk, discovered by an elderly aunt in the attic of her house as it was about to be sold. She had intended to toss it out, but noticed something familiar about the contents, and telephoned Ashford-Brown's mother, who also saw the uncanny resemblance the trunk's contents bore to her son's own collections: odd, unimportant things, wrapped, mounted and meticulously labelled. When Ashford-Brown opened the trunk and unpacked it, he felt his hair stand on end: not only was this collection like his, but his handwriting was almost indistinguishable from Edwin's.

I met Ashley Ashford-Brown when my husband and I moved into an atelier in Ivry-sur-Seine in the summer of 1992. Our son, Sean, had been born in Paris, and we often tried to spend time there during his childhood years. Ashley lived two floors above us, behind a door marked 'Atelier de repos pour l'artiste fatigué'.

For our son, Ashley's loft was a magical world – spacious and tall-windowed, its rafters filled with marionettes, rolls of canvas, provisional paintings, brushes, and raw materials of all kinds. A backroom held a trove of obsolete machines, dead telephones and radios, clockworks, salvaged lumber, jars of screws, hinges and, in the empty jars, air, smoke and light. On the shelves, there were books he had further transformed into works of art: papyrus scrolls roped together, a padlocked volume about a prison with nails barring a small window cut into its front board.

The *musée* then occupied a vestibule, lined with display shelves and showcases. He had built his own mounting blocks, with metal prongs for holding his exhibits:

shovel from the Battle of Verdun
Saharan desert sand
fragment of the Hôtel Lutecia
brick from the wall of the harem of Emir de Boukhara
fragments from the Imperial city of Hue
iron from the Eiffel Tower obtained during its restoration
gloves used in renovating the Louvre and for painting the Eiffel Tower
pebble from the Great Wall of China
bottled rainwater with an apple leaf
fountain water from St. Ediltrude in Brittany
Roman sword dug from an English garden

As a boy, he was drawn to the mysteries of Britain. He walked the chalk roads by moonlight through ellipses of ancient circles and dolmens and made studies of runes – the earliest Teutonic alphabet, thought to have magical powers. Lowering himself into burial chambers, vaults, tombs and caves, he copied the ancient scripts. He later studied *gematria*, the science of Kabbalists, wherein each letter of the alphabet has a corresponding number in the cosmos, forming a link between mathematics and literature. In his later years in Paris, he began painting on unprimed linen with pigmented concrete: cobalt, burnt sienna, raw umber and red oxide, creating a stone surface for his images of rocks, mounds and languages.

We often visited him in the afternoons and were given tea and biscuits or glasses of Bordeaux. Our son raced about this magic world, finding coins, shells, hardware, and lengths of celluloid that had landed on Ashley's cutting floor during his work hours. When biscuit crumbs scattered across the table, I showed Sean how to scoop them up and carry them to the wastebasket. Of course, he didn't want to do this.

'Never mind, then', Ashley said, 'no one likes to clean up a mess. We should have a little machine to do it for us!'

He brought the child to his work table, and for the next hour they assembled such a machine, out of wood block and wheel, heavy rubber band and paintbrush, a little crank imbedded in a wine cork, and the whole of it, within the hour, capable of brushing up crumbs.

'Just the thing to do the job', Ashley said. 'One can always invent something.'

'Would you mind if I created my own *musée*?'

'Why not? It wasn't my idea after all, it was Edwin's, and he would love to know that his museums were spreading across the world. Here, for your start, a little bit of the Louvre.' He put a small stone in my hand. 'Don't worry. I simply gathered the pieces. All the buildings are falling apart.'

To this bit of the Louvre, I have added sleigh bells rung in Prague during the Velvet Revolution; a corked test tube of water from the Dead Sea; a rose tossed through my window, mistaken for Simone de Beauvoir's who lived next door. My husband donated the bullet that shattered his camera lens in El Salvador, its casing peeled back like husked corn, and a Salvadoran campesino's bullet-riddled supper plate, retrieved from an abandoned hut after the massacre of Mozote in 1981.

Unlike Ashley, I have not – or not yet – catalogued these things. They are on the shelves amidst letters, notebooks, manuscripts, recordings and photographs. Over the years, they have joined an earlier collection of tiny clay folk-art figures called *miniaturas*: market women selling mangoes, men and women making love under small clay domes. There are also Mexican 'Day of the Dead' skeletons shooting pool and sewing clothes, skeleton mariachi bands, and wedding tableaus.

Some artefacts are from elsewhere: a matchbox replica of a synagogue from the Jewish quarter in Prague, clay Japanese scholars sculpted to study and converse in groves of bonsai, and Russian lacquer boxes, where sleighs glide through snow and St George slays his dragon. As with Ashley's collection, there are also common, ordinary things and specimens of the natural world: a sun-bleached rat's skull, a robin's egg filled with the dust of a bird's remains, a sack of random stones from sacred and special places across the world.

I have some *miniaturas* from El Salvador that are now broken into many pieces, and I had always planned to repair them, but for that I would need patience and time, tiny tools, and whatever glue would hold unfired clay. The project of restoration would require days of sorting: a pile of limbs, hats, water jugs, market baskets, another of shoes, heads and roofless huts. I have saved the pieces, so this wouldn't be impossible, just as certain thoughts have kept their broken moments in my forgetfulness: the abandoned road, the still smoking crib of blackened corn, the blue smoke rising from the ruined fields. But if it *were* possible to assemble a single broken figure, say, that of a campesina returning her bright lemons to their shattered basket, it might also be possible to restore her village: palm fronds glued back to their trunks, bells to their mission steeple, just as the Argentinian forensic specialist in El Salvador had, in my presence, pieced together the skeletons of infants small enough to fit in a shoe box: the greater and lesser wings, the twenty-two bones of the skull. 'You brush the bone, you blow the dust away, you note / the beak marks of vultures and the deeper marks of machete.'

My friend, the late novelist Charles Newman, wrote of a museum he visited in Russia:

> Grim History proceeds painstakingly and openly from room to room, until the last very small one (devoted to the near present) where it dribbles away into a meaningless collage of artefacts; a sword from the Russo-Japanese War, a bust of Stalin, a cosmonaut, a photo of an expedition to Antarctica, a Chinese vase inlaid with Brezhnev's visage and some Gorby [Gorbachev] buttons – all in no particular order, and without explanation. It's as if – 'here are the pieces' – you figure it out.

Although I have not been as disciplined as Ashley, my *musée* has accumulated over the years, and occupies various boxes and shelves. There is broken majolica from the Tintern de Voto Abbey in County Wexford; an assortment of prayer books in Latin and Church Slavonic; the prayer book carried at my first Communion, covered in mother-of-pearl; a porcelain Christ missing an arm, found lying face down in the Cimitière Montparnasse; a faded black swallowtail butterfly caught in 1959 in a field that was once a Potawatomi burial ground; a stone brought back from the volcano Mount Teide on Tenerife in the Canary Islands, which last erupted in 1909; a doll's house constructed entirely of pebbles by a convict in Jackson State prison, which opened in 1842, is now closed, and was once the largest walled prison in the world.

There are also many small stones taken from the ground during my travels, pebbles from:

the cenotaph at Hiroshima
the innermost chamber of the Bru na Boine passage tomb in Ireland
the ancient St Nicholas cave at Lake Ohrid, reachable by boat
the rubble after the shelling of Ras Beirut in 1984

There is a seashell from the Cape of Good Hope, a fifty-year-old pack of Soviet cigarettes, a bouquet of paper cranes folded in Nagasaki, and a pamphlet of poems written by an Irish hunger striker. In the notebooks, I have written about these acquisitions: the seashell was lifted from the beach across the water from Robben Island, where Nelson Mandela had been imprisoned for eighteen years; the pack of cigarettes was dropped from a tank during the invasion of Czechoslovakia in 1968, and retrieved by the poet Daniel Simko, who would give it to me before his death in 2004, joking that I was the only person he could think of who would not throw it away; the paper cranes were folded in the city where my father walked, days after the atomic blast; the hunger striker was Bobby Sands, and the pamphlet was given to me by his mother, Rosaleen, during a visit to their house in West Belfast, the summer after his death. Seashell, crane, cigarettes and pamphlet are silent on their own, but together with notes on their provenance (were the two ever conjoined), they resist their own ephemerality by becoming evidentiary specimens of lived world.

It may be a species of madness, this practice of gathering, but it is also part of the poetic process, as poetry, for me, always begins with notes. Ashley, too, has his collection of notebooks, where, for decades, he has faithfully documented each day of his life, writing descriptions and sketching what happened, who visited, what was accomplished in the studio. I have never been able to draw, so beyond an occasional doodle, my notebooks are filled with written images and lines that sometimes find their ways into poems, often years later. I have never thrown a notebook away, as I hold to the odd superstition that what is committed to paper will remain available to me, even without re-reading it, while what is burned or otherwise destroyed will not. These notebooks, as well as my writings in cursive on legal pads and envelopes, and those hand-typed on yellowing paper, however randomly preserved, constitute an archive of the written imagination, for which there is an established tradition in libraries, just as there is for the curation of works of art and objects from antiquity deemed important enough for museums.

For Ashley, each rescued article speaks for the lost world of which it was a part, each presence for an absence. His musée was an artistic project, and, as he tells it, 'the nature of things is such that projects become corrupted by evolution. My collection of objects was no exception, and as a result, I lost authority over my museum.'

Ashley's 'Museum of Fragments' has been moved and moved again, from Paris to Ivry-sur-Seine, before finding its present home in Le Bois de Valet, where I saw it again this past winter. Some items were broken en route and some were lost. Some travelled away in the pockets of museum-goers.

My museum has been less visited, except for the night of 27 January 2003, when a watermain burst deep under our road during a frost heave in the midst of a blizzard, and for three hours, water coursed into our house, thousands of gallons, icy and clay-coloured from having passed through the ground. For those three hours, we fought the water, pushing it with brooms through open doors, helped by our Swiss neighbours, but it was no use. The water destroyed most of the house. Still, we thought that the barricade we erected at the top of the stairs would preserve the basement study.

After three hours, the water stopped. The main valve had been shut off. It was quiet and cold.

I ventured downstairs, to have a rest in what I thought would be a dry room lined with books. The desktop computer was giving off purple sparks. Wading ankle-deep in water, I grabbed the electrical cords and yanked them from the wall, plunging the room into darkness. Later, I realised that I could very well have electrocuted myself. The water, it seemed, had not gone down the stairs, but had circled and entered the house through its garden windows. I returned with a lighted candle held to the swirl of books and papers on the water's surface. My husband came down, pulled me away, and spent the night bailing the water from that room. A librarian from the Library of Congress responded to my husband's phone call the next morning with a surprise, pro bono, visit to assess the damage and give his advice: pack everything up immediately and put it into storage. The water-soaked debris was tossed into 'black construction sacks and heaved into the snow, along with a wet kilim rug that froze stiff in a rumpled pile.

My husband had a sense of what was in the sacks, as he himself had filled them. 'You have lost a lot', he told me, 'but not everything.'

It was several years before the house was restored enough to move back in, and the study repaired and dry enough to receive its books and collections. For a few years more, I unpacked the boxes when I could bear to do so, slowly re-shelving the books that survived, and peeling papers apart that had been damp when packed. Many of the books and papers were streaked with the mud from that night. Dark blossoms of mould grew in the margins. The flood made its marks. The water had decided where to go, which was everywhere it could, and also what to choose: anything on the lowest shelves, anything in a box that touched the floor. There were ironies and regrets: a box with drafts of poems and notes towards other poems was destroyed, but on top of it, a box of blank printing paper was preserved. For a long time, I thought that a letter from Graham Greene had been lost, but one day I found it in an otherwise empty manila folder. Most of the 'Museum of Fragments' remained intact, as did many of the notebooks. I kept certain papers that had become illegible due to the bleed of ink, maybe thinking that if, one day, I looked long and hard enough, I would be able to read them again.

It is very quiet in the study now most of the time. Although it has been returned to a semblance of order, I no longer work there, preferring to take my laptop to an upper-storey window. But I do visit. The room remembers everything. The jingle bells remember Wenceslas Square in Prague on a winter night, the pebble house remembers the convict in his cell, gluing one stone to another, the cigarettes remember the soldier who must have wanted to leap from his tank to retrieve them before a local boy snatched them up, the various bottles of water remember their rivers, as the paving stone remembers Paris. Someday, no one will be able to decipher what any of this means. The fragments will not make a whole, but the whole will constitute an archive of the secret memories of ordinary things, and the writings will issue their own silence, very like the silence that reposed in the steamer trunk left by Edwin of Moorlands, and the presence that attends to each object in Ashley's *Musée*, suggesting the absence of everything else; the silence of the watermain pipe before it burst under the road; the silence of notebooks, of papers and of poetry, wherein, according to Max Picard, 'language seems to forget its despair'. I come here to remember that I gathered these things, this archive of the incomprehensible, in case one day someone would come.

Further Reading

Arvatu, Adina, 'Spectres of Freud: The Figure of the Archive in Derrida and Foucault', *Mosaic*, 44/4 (2011), 141–59.

Bachelard, Gaston, *On Poetic Imagination and Reverie*, trans. Colette Gaudin (Dallas: Spring Publications, 1987).

Benjamin, Walter, 'Theses on the Philosophy of History', in *Illuminations*, ed. Hannah Arendt, trans. Harry Zohn (London: Fontana, 1973).

—, 'Excavation and Memory', in *Selected Writings*, Vol. 2, Part 2 (1931–1934), ed. Marcus Paul Bullock, Michael Williams Jennings, Howard Eiland, Gary Smith and Rodney Livingstone (Cambridge, MA: Harvard University Press, 2005).

—, *One-Way Street and Other Writings*, trans. Edmund Jephcott and Kingsley Shorter (London: New Left Books, 2009).

Bettington, Jackie, Kim Eberhard, Rowena Loo and Clive Smith, *Keeping Archives* (Dickson: Australian Society of Archivists, 2008).

de Biasi, Pierre-Marc, 'Toward a Science of Literature: Manuscript Analysis and the Genesis of the Work', in *Genetic Criticism: Texts and Avant-Textes*, ed. Jed Deppman, Daniel Ferrer and Michael Groden (Philadelphia: University of Pennsylvania Press, 2004).

Blanchot, Maurice, 'The Fragment Word', in *The Infinite Conversation*, trans. Susan Hanson (Minneapolis and London: University of Minnesota Press, 1993).

Bloomfield, Mandy, *Archaeopoetics: Word, Image, History* (Tuscaloosa: University of Alabama Press, 2016).

Bodmer, George R., 'A. S. W. Rosenbach: Dealer and Collector', *The Lion and the Unicorn*, 22 (1998), 1–16.

Braddock, Jeremy, *Collecting as Modernist Practice* (Baltimore: Johns Hopkins University Press, 2012).

Brereton, John, 'Learning from the Archives', *College English*, 73/6 2011), 672–81.

Brinkman, Bartholomew, *Poetic Modernism in the Culture of Mass Print* (Baltimore: Johns Hopkins University Press, 2017).

Bushell, Sally, *Text as Process: Creative Composition in Wordsworth, Tennyson, Dickinson* (Charlottesville: University of Virginia Press, 2009).

Cook, Terry and Joan Schwartz, 'Archives, Records, and Power: The Making of Modern Memory', *Archival Science*, 2 (2002), 1–19.

Crowther, Gail and Peter K. Steinberg, *These Ghostly Archives: The Unearthing of Sylvia Plath* (Stroud: Fonthill Media, 2017).

Culler, Jonathan, *Theory of the Lyric* (Cambridge, MA: Harvard University Press, 2015).

DeLanda, Manuel, 'The Archive Before and After Foucault', in *Information is Alive: Art and Theory on Archiving and Retrieving Data*, ed. Joke Brouwer and Arjen Mulder (Rotterdam: NAI, 2003).

Derrida, Jacques, *Archive Fever: A Freudian Impression*, trans. Eric Prenowitz (Chicago and London: University of Chicago Press, 1996).

—, *Spurs: Nietzsche's Styles*, trans. Barbara Harlow (Chicago: University of Chicago Press, 1979).

—, *Dissemination*, trans. Barbara Johnson (London: Continuum, 2004).

Dever, Maryanne, 'Provocations on the Pleasures of Archived Paper', *Archives and Manuscripts*, 41/3 (2013), 171–82.

Dorney, Kate, 'The Ordering of Things: Allure, Access, and Archives', *Shakespeare Bulletin*, 28/1 (2010), 19–36.

Drucker, Johanna, 'Graphical Approaches to the Digital Humanities', in *A New Companion to the Digital Humanities*, ed. Susan Schreibman, Ray Siemens and John Unsworth (Chichester: John Wiley & Sons, 2016).

Eichhorn, Kate, *The Archival Turn in Feminism: Outrage in Order* (Philadelphia: Temple University Press, 2013).

—, *New Companion to the Digital Humanities* (Chichester: John Wiley & Sons, 2016).

Elsner, John and Roger Cardinal, 'The System of Collecting', in *The Cultures of Collecting*, ed. John Elsner and Roger Cardinal (London: Reaktion Books, 1994).

Ernst, Wolfgang, 'Between Real Time and Memory on Demand', in *Digital Memory and the Archive*, ed. Jussi Parrika (Minneapolis: University of Minnesota Press, 2013).

Fordham, Finn, 'The Modernist Archive', in *The Oxford Handbook of Modernisms*, ed. Peter Brooker, Andrzej Gasiorek, Deborah Longworth and Andrew Thacker (Oxford: Oxford University Press, 2010).

Foster, Hal, 'An Archival Impulse', *October*, 110 (Autumn 2004), 3–22.

Foucault, Michel, *The Archeology of Knowledge*, trans. A. M. Sheridan Smith (New York: Pantheon Books, 1972).

Freshwater, Helen, 'The Allure of the Archive', *Poetics Today*, 24/4 (2003), 729–58.

Frost, Elisabeth, *The Feminist Avant-Garde in American Poetry* (Iowa City: University of Iowa Press, 2003).

Gnanadesikan, Amalia E., *The Writing Revolution: Cuneiform to the Internet* (Chichester: John Wiley & Sons, 2011).

Greetham, David, 'Who's In, Who's Out: The Cultural Politics of Archival Exclusion', *Studies in the Literary Imagination*, 32/1 (1999), 1–28.

Halberstam, Judith, *In a Queer Time and Place: Transgender Bodies, Subcultural Lives* (New York: New York University Press, 2005).

Hamilton, Ian, *Keepers of the Flame: Literary Estates and the Rise of Biography* (London: Pimlico, 1992).

Hammer, Langdon, 'Inside & Underneath Words', *The New York Review of Books*, 28 September 2017, 31–3.

Harrington, Joseph, 'Docupoetry and Archive Desire', *Jacket2*, 2011, <http://jacket2.org/article/docupoetry-and-archive-desire> (accessed 22 January 2019).

Hay, Louis, 'Genetic Criticism: Origins and Perspectives', in *Genetic Criticism: Texts and Avant-Textes*, ed. Jed Deppman, Daniel Ferrer and Michael Groden (Philadelphia: University of Pennsylvania Press, 2004).

Helle, Anita, ed., *The Unraveling Archive: Essays on Sylvia Plath* (Ann Arbor: University of Michigan Press, 2007).

Hickman, Ben, *Crisis and the US Avant-Garde: Poetry and Real Politics* (Edinburgh: Edinburgh University Press, 2015).

Hill, Leslie, *Maurice Blanchot and Fragmentary Writing: A Change of Epoch* (London: Continuum, 2012).

Howe, Susan, 'The Art of Poetry No 97', *Paris Review*, 203 (2012), 144–69.

—, *Spontaneous Particulars: The Telepathy of Archives* (New York: New Directions, 2014).

Kapil, Bhanu, 'Archive Fever', in 'The Vortex of Formidable Sparkles', 1 February 2012, archiving a post from her now defunct blog 'Was Jack Kerouac a Punjabi?' <https://thesparklyblogofbhanukapil.blogspot.com/2012/02/archive-fever.html>(accessed 8 October 2018).

Kaplan, Ann Yaeger, 'Working in the Archives', in *Reading the Archive: On Texts and Institutions*, ed. E. S. Burt and Janie Vanpée (New Haven: Yale University Press, 1990).

Kirschenbaum, Matthew G., *Mechanisms: New Media and the Forensic Imagination* (Cambridge, MA: MIT Press, 2008).

Kristeva, Julia, *Revolution in Poetic Language,* trans. Leon S. Roudiez (New York: Columbia University Press, 1984).

Lanham, Richard, *The Economics of Attention* (Chicago: University of Chicago Press, 2006).

Laplanche, Jean, 'L'interprétation entre déterminisme et herméneutique: Une nouvelle position de la question', in *La révolution copernicienne inachevée: Travaux 1967–1992* (Paris: Aubier, 1992).

Lehman, Robert, *Impossible Modernism: T. S. Eliot, Walter Benjamin, and the Critique of Historical Reason* (Stanford: Stanford University Press, 2016).

Lord, Albert, B., *The Singer of Tales*, 2nd edn, ed. Stephen Mitchell and Gregory Nagy (Cambridge, MA: Harvard University Press, 2003).

Manoff, Marlene, 'Theories of the Archive from Across the Disciplines', *portal: Libraries and the Academy*, 4 (2004), 9–25.

Mao, Douglas and Rebecca L. Walkowitz, 'The New Modernist Studies', *PMLA*, 123/3 (2008), 737–48.

Marx, Ursula, Gudrun Schwarz, Michael Schwarz and Erdmut Wizisla, eds, *Walter Benjamin's Archive: Images, Texts, Signs*, trans. Esther Leslie (London: Verso, 2007).

Palladini, Giulia and Marco Pustianaz, *Lexicon for an Affective Archive* (Chicago and Bristol: Intellect Books, 2017).

Perloff, Marjorie, *The Poetics of Indeterminacy: Rimbaud to Cage* (Evanston: Northwestern University Press, 1999).

Poe, Edgar Allan, 'The Philosophy of Composition', in *Essays and Reviews*, ed. G. R. Thompson (New York: Library of America, 1984).

Posner, Miriam, 'What's Next: The Radical, Unrealized Potential of Digital

Humanities', in *Debates in the Digital Humanities 2016*, ed. Matthew K. Gold and Lauren F. Klein (Minneapolis and London: University of Minnesota Press, 2016).

Rainey, Lawrence, *Ezra Pound and the Monument of Culture: Text, History, and the Malatesta Cantos* (Chicago: Chicago University Press, 1991).

—, *Institutions of Modernism: Literary Elites and Public Culture* (New Haven and London: Yale University Press, 1999).

Retallack, Joan, *The Poethical Wager* (Berkeley and Los Angeles: University of California Press, 2003).

Rosenbach, A. S. W., *Books and Bidders: The Adventures of a Bibliophile* (Boston: Little, Brown, 1927).

Rota, Anthony, 'The Collecting of Twentieth-Century Literary Manuscripts', *Rare Books & Manuscripts Librarianship*, 1 (1986), 39–53.

Shaw, Lytle, *Fieldworks: From Place to Site in Postwar Poetics* (Tuscaloosa: University of Alabama Press, 2013).

Siraganian, Lisa, *Modernism's Other Work: The Art Object's Political Life* (Oxford: Oxford University Press, 2012).

Steedman, Carolyn, *Dust* (Manchester: Manchester University Press, 2001).

Stephens, Paul, *The Poetics of Information Overload: From Gertrude Stein to Conceptual Writing* (Minneapolis: University of Minnesota Press, 2015).

Stewart, Susan, 'On the Art of the Future', in *The Open Studio: Essays on Art and Aesthetics* (Chicago: University of Chicago Press, 2005).

Stilling, Robert, *Beginning at the End: Decadence, Modernism, and Postcolonial Poetry* (Cambridge, MA: Harvard University Press, 2018).

Theimer, Kate, 'A Distinction Worth Exploring: "Archives" and "Digital Historical Representations"', *Journal of Digital Humanities*, 3/2 (2014), n.p.

van Mierlo, Wim, 'The Archaeology of the Manuscript: Towards Modern Palaeography', in *The Boundaries of the Literary Archive: Reclamation and Representation*, ed. Carrie Smith and Lisa Stead (Farnham: Ashgate, 2013).

Varley-Winter, Rebecca, *Reading Fragments and Fragmentation in Modernist Literature* (Brighton: Sussex Academic Press, 2018).

Voss, Paul J. and Marta L. Werner, 'Towards a Poetics of the Archive: Introduction', *Studies in the Literary Imagination*, 32 (1999), i–viii.

Yu, Timothy, *Race and the Avant-Garde: Experimental and Asian American Poetry Since 1965* (Stanford: Stanford University Press, 2009).

Index